MM/YY _3/13_

$$ _26.99_

Vend. _Amazon_

Series #_____

#/Discs_____

J   YA   (A)   PAR

Other:

_____

Patrons Initial here
CJF

BATTLE
READY

BATTLE READY

Memoir of a SEAL Warrior Medic

MARK L. DONALD

WITH SCOTT MACTAVISH

St. Martin's Press
New York

BATTLE READY. Copyright © 2013 by Mark L. Donald. All rights reserved. Printed in the United States of America. For information, address St. Martin's Press, 175 Fifth Avenue, New York, N.Y. 10010.

www.stmartins.com

Library of Congress Cataloging-in-Publication Data

Donald, Mark L.
    Battle ready : memoir of a SEAL warrior medic / Mark L. Donald with Scott Mactavish.—1st ed.
        p. cm.
    √ ISBN 978-0-312-60075-4 (hardcover)
    ISBN 978-1-250-00976-0 (e-book)
    1. Donald, Mark L.   2. Afghan War, 2001—Personal narratives, American.
3. United States. Navy. SEALs—Officers—Biography.   4. United States.
Navy—Medical personnel—Biography.   5. Afghan War, 2001—Medical
care.   6. Afghan War, 2001—Campaigns.   7. Hispanic American
soldiers—Biography.   8. Post-traumatic stress disorder—Patients—Biography.
I. Mactavish, Scott.   II. Title.
    DS371.413.D66 2013
    359.0092—dc23
    [B]
                                                                      2012037788

St. Martin's Press books may be purchased for educational, business, or promotional use. For information on bulk purchases, please contact Macmillan Corporate and Premium Sales Department at 1-800-221-7945 extension 5442 or write specialmarkets @macmillan.com.

First Edition: March 2013

10   9   8   7   6   5   4   3   2   1

I dedicate this book to my mom, who always seems to be able to make the hard right decisions. You are my inspiration in everything I do. I also dedicate this book to my wonderful wife and kids—you are the most precious to me. I would be lost without you. I love you all!

CONTENTS

AUTHOR'S NOTE

The people in this book are real. However, to avoid any inadvertent exposure of tactics, techniques, or procedures I purposely removed details or altered events utilizing open source information. I would like to add that this narration is solely derived from my memory. I purposely did this to avoid security concerns for teammates, colleagues, and friends. Furthermore, I condensed and occasionally avoided discussing specific periods of time, utilized pseudonyms, and interchanged repeating first names and similar nicknames in order to avoid confusing the reader as I covered nearly a quarter of a century of military service. For those who were with me, I apologize for the ambiguity and alterations. I hope it does not diminish the reader's understanding of the friendship and mentoring you provided me. My intent was to deliver my story based on how I experienced it and in a manner that was both respectful and appreciative of what I have received during my lifetime. The views expressed in this book are my own and do not necessarily reflect those of special operations, military medicine, the Department of Defense, or veteran organizations mentioned within these pages. Thank you for understanding.

BATTLE
READY

1

WHO I AM

In war, there are no unwounded soldiers.

—JOSÉ NAROSKY

Those who know me understand I never intended to write a book, but over the years of learning how to cope with combat stress, I realized how cathartic writing had become. What started as an adjunct to therapy became an incredible psychological release. However, as my notes turned into journals I discovered the writing was less about me and more about the individuals and events that shaped my life. I felt compelled to tell others dealing with similar demons what I had learned, but I shunned the idea of letting anyone read what I had written—not because of a lack of writing ability but more from a reluctance to expose personal aspects of my life that I have kept hidden from even my own wife. As you will find out, I am neither the all-American boy nor a conquering warrior. I am simply a man who held many titles over his military career; some I worked very hard to attain, while others were simply assignments. The most difficult and at times haunting label that I have had to contend with is "hero."

I am not a hero, but I know many worthy of the title. I have had the distinct honor to serve among them for most of my career. I dedicated my life to preserving theirs. I trained with them for battle, bandaged them in combat, and listened to their revelations about life, everything from the birth of their first child to the burial of their closest friends. I am a man who worked hard to serve among the world's most elite warriors. I am a sailor who to the detriment of his own family placed service for his country and teammates above all else. A medical officer who struggled to maintain an oath to preserve life through medicine while taking lives in the defense of his country. A veteran who still suffers from the mental scars of war but through the grace of God, the love of my wife, and the support of the families of the fallen learned how to deal with it before it destroyed me. I am a Navy SEAL who lived by a creed and did what was expected. I am a lot of things, but a hero is not one of them.

The awards I received represent the actions of a team, not the deeds of a single man. I know how each citation reads, and I am not trivializing what is written. The line between hero and fool is razor thin, and it was the actions of the team that allowed me the opportunity to do what was required. Had the others not provided cover, coordinated air support, or maneuvered on the enemy as I moved under fire I would be buried at Arlington right now, my legacy viewed much differently. Truth be told, *they*, the team, are the reasons why I wear these medals, and I am honored to have received them on their behalf.

Until I wore the medals, I never understood their true significance. Our nation's medals represent more than the actions of any team on a single day. They embody the principles upon which our government was founded and are a tangible depiction of our military's core values: honor, courage, and commitment. The fact that the nation's top three medals for valor require a multitude of evidence only demonstrates the reverence our country has for them. However, it is my personal belief that this same standard of inviolability has also prevented many of my brethren from receiving awards commensurate with their actions. These are the heroes of whom I speak: Americans who, when asked to face danger and adversity, continually answered the call, not for notoriety or distinction but solely out of their love for their country, family, and teammates. They are the quiet and often unknown professionals of special operations and the parents, wives, and children who support them. They are both whom I served and to whom I am forever indebted.

Out of respect of their privacy, to protect those who continue to carry the sword and for reasons of national security, many names, locations, dates, and circumstances have been changed or omitted. If you are reading this in an attempt to discover information about special operations, I recommend you look elsewhere. If you're curious about the internal struggles of a combat medic, dedicated to saving lives but forced to take them, this book is for you.

2

GETTING UNDER WAY

I know well what I am fleeing from but not what I am in search of.
—MICHEL DE MONTAIGNE

I grabbed my backpack and navigated through the boxes, clothes, and household items stored strategically throughout our home and bolted out the front door into the frigid dawn air of Albuquerque. Mom was waiting patiently in the car, listening to a local news station on the radio. I jumped in next to her, careful not to slip on the ice.

"Did you remember your report, Marky?"

"Yes, Mom," I answered while rubbing the sleep from my eyes. It was five thirty in the morning; wrestling season was upon us, which meant early-morning practices. Like most teens my age, I would have preferred a warm bed until the last possible minute, but I was committed to the team and duty called. Mom was working three jobs per day back then and dropped me off on her way to the first.

As we drove in the dark, Mom passed the time by telling stories that morphed into life lessons, all with a common theme: Live for others, not for self. On that particular day, she shared a story about cleaning homes in rural Texas. She grew up in a poor but loving family, and everyone worked, including the kids. She started her first housecleaning job at age nine.

She wrapped up the anecdote just as we pulled into the diner parking lot, nearly wiping out a newspaper machine by the front entrance.

"Mom!" I gasped.

"What, mijo?" she asked, genuinely confused.

"You don't need to park so close! One of these days you're going to hit someone. I can walk the few extra steps to get inside."

"No," she quipped, "God will let them know I'm coming. Besides, I'm your mother and I can take you anywhere I want. Now, do you have enough money for your oatmeal?" She started digging in her purse.

"Yes, Mom, I have money for breakfast. I love you," I said as I jumped out of the car.

"I love you, too," she said in her motherly voice before tearing out of the parking lot, off to clean the home of a rich landowner. I smiled as she left, utterly amazed at her work ethic and love for family.

Vip's Big Boy was a popular restaurant with a friendly staff that started each day well before dawn. I walked into the bright dining area and took a seat at the counter. It would be another hour before Coach opened the gym, so I made good use of my time by doing homework.

"Marky, how's Mom?" Rosa asked from behind the counter as I plowed into an geometry book.

"She's fine," I responded while trying to focus on a particularly tricky geometric equation. Rosa always asked about Mom as she gathered up my breakfast. Everyone knew my mother, and it was impossible *not* to; she was extremely sociable and knew everyone that remotely touched our lives. Mom always had the ability to make people feel loved; she draws them to her like a magnet. Within minutes of meeting her she'd ask what she could do for you and, by the end of the conversation, offer a solution. If you were cold she'd put her jacket around you, even if you were a stranger. It didn't matter that she would go without; she simply couldn't allow others to suffer. She devoted her life to making other's lives better, even at the sacrifice of her own. Rosa's questions weren't small talk; she and the others thought of her as their mom, too, and they looked after me like family.

The diner was like a second home during wrestling season. My family was dealing with serious financial hardships due to my father's illness, and Mom worked three jobs in order to provide for my siblings and me. Mom's first job started before dawn, an hour before wrestling practice, and the only way I could attend practice was to wait outside the school for an hour until it opened. She simply would not have that, so one Saturday morning she walked me into the diner and asked to speak with the owner. He, like everyone else, was immediately charmed by her humility and willingness to solve a family dilemma. He listened for a short time, then interrupted her by putting his arm around her 4' 11" frame and offered a solution. The arrangement was simple; he'd let me in the diner each morning and provide a meal for a nominal cost as the staff prepared the restaurant for business.

It was the way she solved all her problems: Honestly explain the situation to those in the community and then ask for help. "Marky," she'd say, "don't be afraid to ask for help. People want to help. You just have to let them know how." This lesson would resonate throughout my life.

I started many school days in that diner even when the season had ended. Those drives with Mom taught me a lot about personal pride and the differences between self-esteem and arrogance, and the interaction with diner staff taught me about the inherent goodness in people.

MOM

Mom grew up during the 1930s and '40s experiencing the effects the Great Depression had on both sides of the border. She was raised in

Matamoros, Mexico, and Brownsville, Texas, the youngest of a very large Mexican family. It was a tumultuous time for a region experiencing the terrible effects of the Depression and heightened racial tensions due to the various ethnicities competing for work. Instead of becoming bitter and untrusting, Mom and her siblings were taught the value of family and religion during trying times, and it was those lessons of unity, commitment, forgiveness, and self-sacrifice that she'd later instill in each of us.

I distinctly remember one story that emphasized her point. At the time Mom was working as a maid for a large hotel chain, and one of her bosses treated the laborers with contempt, especially the cleaning crew. Instead of becoming angry with him like some of the others, she waited for the right opportunity to speak with the man in private. She explained how she and the cleaning staff took pride in the quality of their work, not in the type of work they did for the company. It took time and persistence, but eventually her message sank in. By the end of the year he was their most ardent supporter.

Mom's dedication to hard work and caring for others wasn't anything new. Since childhood she always held a job and balanced it with service in the church and community. Even in her eighties she still insists on working and taking care of those in need.

Back then, Mom would start her day as a personal maid for the wealthy, then head home for dinner with the family before leaving to clean offices until late at night. Housekeeping was her life's work.

Ironically, our home looked like a hoarder's paradise, at least to outsiders. In reality, the "junk," as Mom jokingly called it, was a meticulously inventoried collection of clothes, housewares, canned food, and anything else she felt our family or friends might need. It started with her collecting the obvious items, jackets and gloves, but over time, and as our financial situation deteriorated, she expanded her collection to include every type of necessity, taking full advantage of closeouts, garage sales, and the generosity of others. Everything from blankets to school paper was cataloged, organized, and placed in a closet or a makeshift cardboard cabinet. If something was needed I guarantee Mom would be able to pull it from the rubble, which is what the rest of us called it, in a matter of minutes.

It wasn't like she was suddenly afflicted with some pathological condition that drove her to retain useless or sentimental items. Rather, it was a reasonable reaction to our circumstances based on her experiences during her youth and my dad's health; perhaps a primitive survival instinct to provide for the family. Still, I was ashamed and embarrassed when a stranger came to our home. They must have thought we were all a bit nuts, and perhaps we were, but our house wasn't a manifestation of mental derangement. It was a means of our survival, and had been for years.

DAD

Dad was a gringo born to parents that neglected him. At age seventeen, he enlisted in the U.S. Army and never looked back. He worked hard and rose through the ranks, eventually attaining the rank of chief warrant officer. After retiring from the military, Dad placed the family savings into a small gas station he was sure it would allow him to enjoy a simpler life being his own boss. What he didn't count on was the Middle Eastern oil restrictions and governmental regulations that threw the country into an oil and gas crisis. To make matters worse, even though the shop was in a rough neighborhood, Dad insisted on living close by in order to spend as much time with the family as possible, a luxury he never had in the military. Instead of making a quick trip home for lunch, though, he spent more time away dealing with the break-ins, vandalism, and robberies that seemed to occur on a weekly basis. The economy was in a free fall, and major oil companies were shutting out independent dealers like Dad. It didn't take long before the business went under, leaving him searching for work during a time of high unemployment and financial uncertainty.

In just a few years Dad went from being an army officer to being an unemployed veteran in a recession. His decision to leave the military to become a businessman had given him little time to plan for life's contingencies, and he didn't have the coping mechanisms to adapt. I believe it was this loss in status and a return to the same impecunious life he knew during his early years that escalated psychological problems that began in his youth and intensified over his military career.

In an effort to quell his inner demons Dad reached for the bottle. Of course, no one outside the home knew anything about Dad's problem. He was a master at hiding his drinking from the outside world—so good at it, in fact, that he finally landed a job in corporate collections and began to climb the company ladder. Shortly after, he decided to move us to the Heights, an upper-middle-class neighborhood on the good side of town. I suppose buying a house on the right side of the tracks was his way of making it up to us after struggling for so long.

In his heart, he believed he was giving us the opportunity to succeed, however, Mom saw it differently. She understood that fights, teen pregnancy, and gangs were realities of Albuquerque, and our ability to reject temptations was the key to our survival. For Mom the ability to counter these entrapments wasn't based on a geographic location but on how involved she and Dad were in our daily lives. That meant spending time together as a family and not working extra hours or a second job to live in a neighborhood we couldn't afford. In hindsight I am sure Dad wished he'd listened. Instead he was committed to moving the family, so he went to work trying to convince Mom, and himself, that everything would work out fine. While Mom ended up being supportive, she definitely wasn't secure with the decision, and she was right.

Mom had a sixth sense for cause and effect in our family and could predict with shocking accuracy the consequences of our family's individual and collective actions. I believe she has a direct connection with the Almighty, and he speaks to her on such matters. In this case the Good Lord was right. Just as Mom predicted, the move would serve as a catalyst for breaking the family apart; despite her objections, Dad moved us anyway, miles away from the crime-ridden streets and underperforming schools.

Over the next couple of years, the family started to fall apart. The effects of Dad's alcohol were magnified, and, quick to anger, he might erupt into a fit of violence. At first Mom would stand in front trying to protect us, but her small frame hardly stood a chance. Then Dad wrecked the company car in a drunken stupor, the first of several DWI accidents that would eventually leave him permanently disabled and unable to work. Feelings of inadequacy continued to build inside until all he knew was hate. Refusing to abandon him with a divorce, Mom rented a small apartment for him across town so that she could care for him without continuing to put her children at risk.

Strangely, Dad's absence from the home hurt all of us, but Dad's decline was hardest on Michael.

MICHAEL

Michael was my older brother and my greatest protector. In our youth he helped Mom look after my sisters and me, but as we grew older he took a much more hands-on approach. Tall, thin, and shy, he was an easy target for schoolyard bullies and Mexican gangs, but as he matured and used the weight room to release anger, his body began to develop into a hulking figure. Unfortunately, without Mom and Dad's direct involvement in his life, his naïveté allowed others to influence his decisions, and his judgment began to slip.

As early as I can remember, Michael was enamored with Dad's military service. He and I would play soldier with his army equipment and reenact key battles with toy soldiers. But where I was concerned about the types of gear the men carried, Michael concentrated on the circumstances that caused the battle. Dad was an ardent history buff and patriot who would spend hours explaining America's history, and Michael ate it up. Dad spent every spare moment discussing American history or visiting museums with us; narrating the past had become his way of nurturing. Considering Dad had no interaction with his own parents, and therefore no parenting model, his history lessons proved remarkably effective with Michael. The themes of Dad's stories of history and life were honor and loyalty, and it was just those values that influenced Michael to put aside his dream of serving in the Ranger Battalions to support the family after Dad's decline.

Mom tried to stop him, but his mind was made up. "No, Michael, you don't need to worry about me."

"Mom, I'm not going to let you work more and more hours when I can make money at the construction yard." Michael raised his voice, as if raising his voice were going to make a difference with Mom.

"No, Michael, we'll get by. We'll ask for help, just until you get through school."

"Mom, no one should help us when we have the ability to help ourselves," he declared. His voice shifted to a softer tone. "You raised me better than that. You tell us all the time the difference between a handout and help is the effort those in need put into the solution. I can do this."

I heard Mom reluctantly agree through tears, but what else could she do? Things were falling apart, and she knew we couldn't survive this way much longer. She also knew that her role as teacher and loving parent would diminish the second Michael took a job in the adult world; others would influence his life, and that's hard for any parent.

Dad's internal pain and alcohol abuse had transformed him from a loving parent to a violent brute, and through the years, Michael and my eldest sister were often at the receiving end of his rage. I remember coming home and finding my brother's blood on the floor and walls as he stood protecting our mother or simply absorbing the anger before my sister and I arrived home. At first Michael had no ability to counter the blows, but as he grew into a streetwise young man weighing 200 pounds, he could better defend himself. Still, he couldn't raise a fist to the one man from whom he so desperately wanted approval, so each week he'd take a beating for the rest of us. Over time the effects changed him from a friendly and innocent teen to an introverted and indignant man who locked himself in his room, which he began to call "the dungeon."

The dungeon wouldn't shelter Michael from a family tragedy that would soon shake us all to the core.

SISTERS

My oldest sister, Diana, married a serviceman at a very young age and left the house when I was in my early teens. Today we're close, but as a youth maturing into a man, I only saw her sparingly and of course on holidays.

I was much closer to Cassandra, who was my older sister by four years, a sweet and intelligent girl with a promising academic future. She got top grades in high school and earned a scholarship to a small Christian school back east, thirteen hours from Albuquerque.

During the spring of my sophomore year, the chaos at home had calmed, until a fateful day when Mom received a call from Cassandra's school. "Something" had happened to Cassandra in her dorm, and she was in a serious crisis. I arrived home from wrestling practice to find Mom and Michael packing frantically for the cross-country journey to Cassandra's school. An hour later they left with little ceremony, both frightened and desperately concerned for Cassandra.

I was left alone with no money, expected to care for myself and still make it to school and wrestling practice on time. Mom was cleaning buildings at night to cover the expenses of Dad's apartment, and I was expected to assume those janitorial duties as well. All of this at age fourteen. I tell you this not to elicit sympathy but to illustrate the expectations I faced as a young man. My mother's *find a way to get it done* attitude, I firmly believe, built a foundation in my psyche that would later prove invaluable in my special operations career.

Cassandra returned home with Mom and Michael and was exhibiting symptoms of acute schizophrenia. It's impossible to say if the illness existed in her early teens or if the traumatic event at college triggered it. Regardless of the impetus, she was in desperate shape and suffered terrible hallucinations; she claimed to be Jesus on several occasions and the president of the United States of America on others. She saw biblical scriptures flowing from the stucco walls and engaged in conversations with imaginary persons that were very real to her. None of us was equipped to deal with Cassandra's illness, especially Dad, who exiled himself from the rest of us as a means to cope with his daughter's condition. This, of course, led to more anger at everyone but himself and more chaos at home. I did my best to concentrate on academics and sports, and Mom did her best to keep the family intact. Yet we knew the family was falling apart, and my chances at a decent life in Albuquerque were fading away.

COACH SPARAGO

For me, wrestling was more than an athletic endeavor. It was a lifestyle that embodied every aspect of physical and psychological conditioning, and I believe it's one of the main reasons I made it through SEAL training. Coach Sparago was a big influence and encourager and pushed me to meet my goals, both academically and on the mat. Although I never told him I had troubles at home, I think he sensed it and concentrated on teaching me how to stay focused on both school and sports. Later, when Mother Nature forced me into a weight class with one of my best friends, who just happened to be city champion, Coach was there to remind me what the sport, like life, was really about.

"Mark," he said pulling me aside, "you may have to move up in a weight class and wrestle kids bigger than you, but that doesn't make you less competitive. It's not the size of the dog in the fight, it's the size of the fight in the dog." He paused to see if his point was sinking in. He often used clichés but spoke with such sincerity that the point hit home every time.

"I want you to be competitive at everything you do. If you're on a conditioning run, try to be the first one in. If you're in the classroom, try for the best grade in the class. Heck, if you get up to sharpen your pencil, try and make it the sharpest pencil in the room. You'll never be the best at everything, but that doesn't mean you can't be the best at something. Just don't quit trying to get there!"

I absorbed his advice and tried to incorporate it in all aspects of my life, including my choices during military service.

STAFF SERGEANT SANDOVAL

I first met Staff Sergeant Sandoval in the main hallway at the high school. He stood next to a folding table covered with recruiting materials, and he looked damn sharp in his dress blues. He was smart and personable, a good combination for a recruiter. He saw me walking by and mentioned my wrestling shirt, which led to a conversation about the sport and my love for it. He didn't even mention the marines that day, although he made a big impression on me.

Not as big as the next time I saw him, though. It was two weeks later, and I was wrestling in a regional tournament at the high school. Staff Sergeant Sandoval showed up and greeted me by name. He had driven all the way out to the school to watch me wrestle, and frankly,

I was stunned. Yes, I know, it was probably a recruiting ploy, but he was *there,* and aside from Mom, who made every match, even if it was on her way to one of her three jobs, no one really cared about my wrestling career.

A week later, I found myself in the staff sergeant's office, and a week after that, I broke the news to Mom that I wanted to be a marine. It's important to understand Mom's position in all of this. She saw how the military affected my father, and she was scared witless the same thing would happen to me. On the other hand, she also knew the military would take me away from the streets of Albuquerque and the stresses at home and would present opportunities that would allow me to succeed on my own. I relayed Mom's concerns to Staff Sergeant Sandoval, so he invited Mom and me to the office for a chat. Upon arrival, we were introduced to his parents, who both happened to be deaf. He spoke sign language to his parents and fluent Spanish to Mom, which of course melted her on the spot. We visited for two hours, and Mom began to admit this might be good for her "mijo" but was still unable to let go. Staff Sergeant Sandoval listened politely, fully grasping Mom's concerns; after all, he'd heard them many times before from other concerned mothers.

He crossed the room and sat next to Mom, then patted her hand and spoke gently. "Mrs. Donald, I understand you want to keep your boy close by. It's the way of our people." He then gestured to his mother and father. "My parents are right here; family is very important to me, too. But Mark is a smart young man with tremendous potential. Maybe he'll have a better chance of reaching that in uniform. Mark seems to think so."

"I understand, Sergeant, but he is my boy, and like you say, family is everything," she said. "This is very difficult for me."

Staff Sergeant Sandoval paused for a few seconds and then smiled. "I think I have an idea."

He then proposed a reserve contract and explained that as a Marine

Corps reservist, I would be a part-time marine, which meant I could stay in Albuquerque and drill on the weekends with a specialized unit. I would attend boot camp, of course, but otherwise serve as a reservist and live at home. Mom was amenable to the idea and agreed to meet again in a couple of weeks. I, however, had a hard time with the compromise. I wanted to enlist and get far away from Albuquerque, and the thought of returning to the same hell I was currently in didn't make me happy. Still, I wasn't going to leave without Mom's approval, so I met privately with Staff Sergeant Sandoval to discuss the options.

We met after practice at Vip's Big Boy, my early-morning sanctuary and study hall. Staff Sergeant Sandoval explained how reservists were expected to attend schools just like active-duty marines; not only that, they could also apply to join one of the United States Marine Corps Reconnaissance units, commonly known as Recon. He briefly explained the missions of Recon Marines, and the thought of being part of a secretive small unit that gathered intelligence and did cool-guy missions similar to those carried out by the Navy SEALs and the army's Special Forces really intrigued me—but there was a catch. First, the closest reserve Reconnaissance command was right here in Albuquerque. Second, I would eventually have to qualify as a Reconnaissance Marine, which meant passing a grueling training program; otherwise, I might have to drill with another unit. I didn't care for the idea of coming back home, but if I made it I could be spending many months and sometimes years in schools far away from here. I was in optimum shape at the time, so I couldn't imagine not being able to make the cut. That was it. My mind was set on joining the Corps, and I knew Mom would eventually come around, too. Another week passed, and we all met to discuss details.

Mom finally agreed, but with one requirement. As tears welled up in her eyes, she looked at Staff Sergeant Sandoval and said, "Staff Sergeant, my husband served over twenty years, and I know men in dress uniforms will visit me if something were to happen to my boy. So when you come to take him away from me I deserve that same respect. Do you understand what I am telling you?"

Staff Sergeant Sandoval took her hand, looked her in the eye, and promised he did. To this day, I choke up thinking about that moment and the impact a mother feels hearing her child will be leaving her for the military.

It took a couple of months to finish school, fill out paperwork, visit MEPS (the Military Entrance Processing Station) for a medical exam, and button up the details of my enlistment, but the day finally came. We all watched as Staff Sergeant Sandoval pulled up to the house in the government sedan, exited the car, and walked to our door, in his United States Marine Corps dress blue uniform with his medals dangling. Mom opened the door, and the staff sergeant politely removed his hat and formally announced, "Mrs. Donald, I'm here for your son."

3

EMERGENCE OF
AN AMPHIBIAN

★ ★ ★

There's a fine line between courage and foolishness. Too bad it's not a fence.
—Anonymous

oot camp at Marine Corps Recruit Depot (MCRD) San Diego was challenging, but I followed Staff Sergeant Sandoval's advice and made it through by "keeping my mouth shut, ears open, and following orders to the letter." Of course, it didn't hurt that I was still in top physical condition from wrestling season and had trained in the mountains of New Mexico before arriving at sea-level San Diego, both of which helped me breeze through the PT (physical training) with relative ease. Like other kids from a blue-collar background, I was accustomed to hard work and thrived in the highly structured environment that was lacking at home. I missed my family but didn't have time to think on it.

Not everything came easy. The Marine Corps is an amphibious assault force, and all marines have to be able to survive in the water. So it only stands to reason that basic water survival training occurs at the recruit depot. I'll never forget the day our senior drill instructor, Staff Sergeant Shanhurst, marched Platoon 1097 to the pool for our first swim lesson. Up to that point I had excelled at every event and was in the running for top recruit and a meritorious promotion on graduation day, however, on pool day, humility came knocking. Many recruits already knew how to swim, but I wasn't one of them. Having almost drowned at an early age, I went to great extents to avoid water over waist deep. However, being a naive and cocky recruit, I not only ignored those memories but somehow convinced myself that sheer willpower would see me through. I must have been quite a spectacle as a seventeen-year-old Mexican American kid getting ready to embarrass the hell out of myself. Heck, I'd pay good money to watch it today if I could.

It all started when the drill instructors who worked at the training tank came out and started separating us into categories. Without any regard for my own safety I jumped in the line with the experienced swimmers. After all, that's where my competition for honor graduate was, so I had to be there, too. After a short briefing on the upcoming event, we were marched through the building and onto a cold pool deck. There the lead instructor explained that our group would be starting first so they could clear the area for the others requiring more training. Assuming things would go quickly, with no surprises (such as non-swimmers in the pool), the instructors informed us we would first swim in camouflage utilities. After a quick demonstration we were asked if anyone had any questions or doubted his ability to pass the test. Still feeling arrogant, I thought, *How hard can this be? You put on some clothes, jump into the water, and swim to the side. I can do this.*

As I approached the rack to get a pair of the wet fatigues, I saw the remedial swimmers, the group I should've been with, make their way to the shallow end of the pool. That's when I started to feel as if I had made a grave mistake. Even so, rather than swallowing my pride and accepting the countless push-ups that recruits receive for their blunders, I proceeded to learn my lesson the hard way.

As I pulled the wet clothing over my body I immediately felt every piece of my skin retract underneath. It was as if I were trying to isolate the chilly fabric to my shoulders in order to preserve my body heat by ensuring the rest of my body remained dry. I took a spot at the back of the line and watched my fellow recruits go before me and realized exactly what I was getting myself into. Still, I blindly followed the recruit in front of me. Perhaps I thought my aquatic abilities had changed over time or I had intuitively learned to swim, or maybe I felt that St. Jude, the patron saint of lost causes, would somehow see me through. Whatever the reason, I climbed the ladder leading to the platform that overlooked the 12' pool and readied myself for the exercise, which started with an "abandon ship entry."

I walked to the edge and looked down and was instantly terrified. Had we actually been at sea and had to make this jump to survive, I would have chosen to go down with the ship, that's how scared I was. Apparently that wasn't scared enough to turn around and walk toward the angry drill instructor at the end of the platform, so I decided to jump.

I landed as instructed, and the cold water collapsed around the fatigues, grabbing me and pulling me down. Miraculously, I hit bottom on my feet, and the familiarity of being upright gave me a glimmer of hope, so I looked up to the pool deck for instruction. I waited for a second or two, but when no order came down from above I started to flail as if I were trying to ascend some invisible ladder. I know the drill instructors must have thought I was some joker who was acting as if he couldn't swim, but I was about to prove them wrong. I don't remember much after that except waking up in a puddle of my own vomit, with a group of drill instructors yelling at me mercilessly. The Marine Corps had just handed me my first slice of mean green humble pie, and I ate every bite.

Never again would I let my ego convince me something easily demonstrated by an expert is actually *easy*! Lesson learned, and with my tail between my legs, I got up and joined the other recruits at the shallow end of the pool. Unfortunately, my stunt in the pool blew my chances at honor graduate—not because I minimally qualified as a swimmer but because I knowingly deceived my drill instructors and my fellow recruits. That was simply was unacceptable by Corps standards. Although my senior drill instructor gave me no written punishment in my military record (I'm sure the humor and humiliation of the event were more than enough for everyone involved), he had to do something. Staff Sergeant Shanhurst called me into his office and explained how I couldn't be expected to maintain Marine Corps standards of integrity if my first lesson in the Corps was that the standard doesn't always apply. He was right: The Marine Corps is built and survives on its values. They define the Corps, and to be a part of the Green Machine I had to live by them.

Aside from military training, boot camp is meant to be an intense life-lesson incubator. Everyone learns the basic military skills it takes to be a marine, but each individual takes away vastly different lessons. In addition to swimming, I absorbed three other extraordinary life lessons that changed the way I saw the world. First, the Marine Corps sees everyone as green. There were no rich kids, no poor kids, no black, white, or red kids. We were all Marine Corps Green, and the playing field was level for everyone, even a Mexican American kid like me. Next was what I now call the perseverance paradigm: Your success (or lack thereof) is based purely on your initiative and refusal to give up, regardless how tough the task. If you fought hard and refused to quit, if you persevered, you would succeed. Finally, I learned that smaller, aerobically fit guys had an advantage over the big muscular ones when it came to military PT. I could rip out pull-ups and clear the obstacle course in record time because my muscle mass was lean and compact. The large football players had to lift their own weight and often struggled with obtaining the maximum score for the physical fitness test. Running was second nature for smaller guys; I ran many miles as a high school athlete and enjoyed the solitude of long runs, yet most of the weight lifters struggled hauling their heavy muscle mass around the base perimeter during the three-mile timed runs. To be fair, the big guys had the advantage when carrying heavy combat gear and enjoyed cleaning up on a few of the smaller recruits during hand-to-hand combat training, especially when pitted against a wise-ass wiry guy in the pugil stick pit. Then again, I also noticed that it was much easier for two smaller recruits to drag or carry one another than it was for two of the larger ones when we simulated a wounded man. I didn't realize it then, but I was already making observations related to the physiology of a warrior and the biomechanics of warfighting.

The thirteen weeks of boot camp were rapidly coming to a close, and as crazy as it sounds I didn't want to leave. The Marine Corps brought structure to my life, taught me lessons in humility, and forever changed me for the better. Now it was my job to continue on that path, and that started with four vital lessons: Never assume expertise in anything, an individual's background doesn't matter, perseverance pays, and the battlefield can favor the lean combatant. Staff Sergeant Sandoval's advice had served me well since I arrived, but those four rules would become critical building blocks for my future career.

On a sunny September day my mother proudly watched me march across the parade deck as a marine. I caught a glimpse of her through the corner of my eye as my platoon made a facing movement in front of the stands. Even from a distance I could tell she was crying as she clapped and cheered for her "mijo." Mom may have been reluctant to send her boy off to the Corps, but when she met her grown marine, she was absolutely convinced it was the best decision he (and she) had ever made. Unfortunately, while I was away, yet another high school friend joined the ones already jailed for gang-banging or drugs, cementing her opinion that the Marine Corps was the right decision for her son.

From the second she set foot on MCRD, she was no longer a worried mother. She had become a "Marine Corps Mom" and had the stickers on her car to prove it. Conversations with friends, family, and even strangers inevitably led to her son "the marine." To her the Marine Corps had become something for her son the army never was for her husband: a savior. As a military spouse she quietly stood by as the army continually took her husband away from the home. While she was supportive of his career in every way, the family was separated, and in the Hispanic home, or even a half-Hispanic home like ours, leaving the nest borders on sacrilege. At the time of my enlistment, my brother was locked up and my sister was receiving psychiatric care, and the thought of her Marky leaving for the military must have been agonizing for her. Still, deep inside she realized the Corps gave her little one the best chance to make it, and graduation day confirmed her intuition. To this day she remains a passionate supporter of the United States Marine Corps, and woe unto you should you have a disparaging remark or disrespectful attitude toward "her marines." That includes me, too.

MOS

All marines are riflemen, but not everyone is a grunt. Marines are assigned a military occupation specialty (MOS), which is intended to serve as their primary job in the Corps. As in all the branches of service, a marine's MOS is based on three factors: the individual's score on the military's aptitude screening test, the member's personal interests, and most importantly, the needs of the Corps. At the time of my enlistment I needed a billet that allowed me to universally serve among the infantry units, so I took a job as a radio operator.

After boot camp, I spent a few days of downtime with my mom and sister Diana in San Bernardino, California, before checking into FROC, as the grunts called the Field Radio Operator Course at Twentynine Palms, California. Diana had relocated to the area a year earlier, and the idea of having family within driving distance was comforting to me. We hadn't spent much time together since our move into the

Heights; she'd married a local airman at a young age and moved away. This may have saved her from some of the chaos we experienced over the last few years, but it's my belief that feelings of guilt and an overwhelming obligation to Mom had eventually brought her back home.

"Marky, when do I have to take you to the base?" Diana asked, stirring a pot of green chili stew. Diana was always the best cook in the family, so I took full advantage while I could.

"I need to be there no later than midnight on Sunday," I replied, trying to sneak a taste.

"Can I take you Saturday?" she asked while slapping my hand as it neared the top of the pot. "It's almost two hours from here, and after Mass I need to help Julio get the shoe shop ready. It's going to be a busy week." Julio was her second husband, a much better fit for her.

"Two hours? You've got to be kidding me. Where the heck is this place?" I asked, answering her question with a question.

They both laughed and told me that I would be living in the middle of the Mojave Desert for the next three to four months. They knew more about my duty station than I did. We sat down to Diana's excellent chili and enjoyed some much-needed family time, the last for several months.

The coursework at Twentynine Palms was uninspiring, but I worked hard and made sure I'd graduate among the top of my class so I could concentrate on what I really wanted to learn: swimming. Classes were taught a couple of miles down the road at the base's training tank. Needless to say, there wasn't much for a young marine to do, especially without any personal transportation, so I devoted my off-duty time to conquering one of my greatest fears, the fear of drowning.

The outdoor pool was huge and intimidating, much larger to me than the one at MCRD, but that was a mental hurdle I had to set aside. I passed the basic swim test at boot camp, but just barely, and that wasn't good enough. I recalled a story Coach Sparago told us about a wrestling champion who won his title by continually practicing each move that had defeated him until his weaknesses became his strengths. That was exactly what I wanted to do, so I marched my nonswimming self down to the training tank and inquired about lessons. An old marine who worked there greeted me and asked how well I swam. "Like a rock, sir," I answered bluntly. After what happened the last time I wasn't about to misrepresent my abilities.

"How long are you going to be stationed here?" He was skeptical of my commitment.

"I'm just here for FROC training, sir." I could tell by his hesitancy that he didn't want to take this on, but I wasn't taking no for an answer. During the course of our conversation I told him about the pool, my desire to be a Reconnaissance Marine, and how Coach Sparago, my mother, and Michael taught me never to quit anything I started. In fact, I just kept talking until he finally agreed to give me lessons, if for no other reason than to shut me up.

"Okay, marine, we'll start tomorrow. Bring your swim trucks and a towel, and be ready to work. Hard."

Over the next three months I went to the pool as often as I could, and with his help I learned to swim well enough to turn my terrifying weakness into a personal strength. I succeeded by drawing on the wisdom of my family, encouragement of my coaches, and an old leatherneck willing to help a young man conquer his fears.

4

A HIGHER CALLING

★ ★ ★

Every calling is great when greatly pursued.
—OLIVER WENDELL HOLMES

F ollowing FROC at Twentynine Palms, I returned home and checked into Delta Company, 4th Reconnaissance Battalion. Prior to my arrival I had applied for a billet with one of the company's four-man Reconnaissance teams and was accepted, but I still had to earn my qualifications to remain on the team. The long road to becoming a Recon Marine had just begun. The next step was to pass a rigorous assessment and selection program, followed by two months of in-house training. After several weeks of classwork and constant physical testing, I was finally given the opportunity to compete against my brother marines for the best "high-speed" schools in the military, including SERE (Survival, Evasion, Resistance, and Escape), Army Airborne, Navy SCUBA, and, of course, Amphibious Reconnaissance, among others. I wasn't Recon, though; not yet.

Recon Marines worked hard and played hard and took immense pride in their training. They weren't in it for the silver SCUBA bubble or gold parachute wings pinned to their uniforms or even the public ego stroke. They thrived on being different and doing something unique and dangerous. In a service that trumpets "Every marine is a rifleman" and then practices what it preaches, it's easy to blend in with the rest of the Corps. Recon was a means to break free, and that's why they volunteered for the job. They were destined for extremely dangerous missions, sneaking among a sea of enemy, hiding in miserable conditions and gathering intelligence, and doing it with little acknowledgment that the organization even existed. *They* knew it existed, and they acknowledged it among themselves. To a Recon Marine, that's all that mattered. Recognition among their peers drives men to endure things others wouldn't, and I knew I wanted to be a part of that elite and highly selective brotherhood. During the testing, assessment, and training phases, I pushed myself as if training for the city or state wrestling tournament, determined to win a slot at Recon school.

After four months of training, I received orders to Navy SCUBA School in Panama City, Florida. Training was hard, but I was well prepared after hours and hours of swim practice at FROC and Recon Battalion. I received my SCUBA bubble on graduation day, and a day later I was issued orders to the highly coveted Amphibious Reconnaissance School (ARS).

HEART OF A LION

Arrival day, Amphibious Reconnaissance School. The icy wind ripped through the cracks in the concrete walls, creating a constant chill that lingered throughout the old building. I had checked in the previous day along with Erik Little, my close friend and teammate from Delta Company. We were busy prepping our gear for the first day of training while other marines streamed in from various overseas units. I sat on my steel-framed bunk, a rickety remnant from World War II, and worked feverishly on my H-harness, repositioning components and changing them back again, a never-ending task of indecisiveness. Like every other infantryman in the military, I had convinced myself that by moving a few pouches around I'd find a more efficient, and perhaps comfortable, way to carry my combat load.

Despite my compulsive drive to finish numerous tasks before morning PT, I set aside my gear and greeted the marines still arriving from around the globe. I figured if we were going to be living together for the next few months, I should meet them now rather than later.

As dawn broke, Gunny Russo, a rock-solid gunnery sergeant, suddenly entered the hooch and barked orders, sending the marines scrambling for the classroom next door. We had barely settled into our desks when Gunny Boyd, another broad-shouldered senior NCO, growled, "Attention on deck," causing the room to snap to attention as Captain Bradford entered the room and stalked to the podium at the front of the room. The captain was sharp, like all marines, but carried himself with a confidence earned through years of distinguished leadership. He straightened his papers on the podium, ordered us to sit, and then jumped right in with no pretense or small talk. He told us our time at ARS was going to be hard but fair, and training evolutions would be based on a mutual respect between the students and the cadre, our instructors. He knew that many of us had already received a great deal of training prior to arriving at ARS and others had been doing the job for more than a year before earning a slot at the highly coveted school, and he acknowledged our efforts.

He then engaged the class directly. "Can anyone tell me what it takes to be a Recon Marine?" asked the captain.

Erik, who had never been short on words or shy about pronouncing his opinion in a crowd (which is probably why we bonded in the first damn place), yelled out in a manner that made everyone crack up, including the captain, "Being a lunatic and PT stud . . . ssssir!"

In some ways he was right. Back then if an infantry marine was a first-class swimmer in exceptional physical shape and possessed the intestinal fortitude to gut through the screening process, he could be a Recon Marine.

"Not exactly the answer I was looking for, marine. It's having the heart of a lion, possessing the courage and bravery to accept a mission against insurmountable odds while isolated deep inside enemy forces and driving on. It's all in here." The captain pointed to his heart. "Not here," he said, pointing to his flexed bicep that stretched his uniform sleeve to its limits.

I felt a sense of pride as the captain spoke because I understood his point. With the help of many mentors and the encouragement of my brother marines, along the way, I went from using my uniform to keep me afloat and a dog-paddling breaststroke in boot camp to graduating Navy SCUBA School in a year's time. Now, I wasn't sure if tackling my fear of the water would be the type of bravery needed under fire, but I felt I met the captain's definition of a Recon Marine, and it gave me a feeling that I was at the right place.

The captain then walked over to Erik, who popped tall and stood rock still. "Now drop down, Lance Corporal, and push out a hundred. That shouldn't be too hard . . . you PT stud," the captain said with a grin. Needless to say, we all joined Erik on the floor and began knocking them out, figuring that if you're only as strong as your weakest man, then we definitely wanted to make certain all of us had equal opportunity to develop.

TURNING POINT

Once again, a small, innocuous incident led to a major turning point in my career. Several weeks into ARS, I was on a routine training patrol with my platoon, practicing land navigation at night in a thick forest. As we crept along in pitch-black darkness, I stumbled on a root and cut my arm on a sharp branch. It was a relatively shallow cut but continued to bleed through the night. I sure as hell didn't want to get med dropped for an infection, so the next morning I went to get it checked out.

I walked into the small medical office the navy corpsman had established for "sick call," an expression the navy uses for treating sailors and marines for minor injuries or ailments or evaluating them for the possibility of a serious underlying condition. The place was spotless, unlike the rest of the compound, which was flooded from the tropical storm that hit us earlier in the week. Except for the pictures on the walls you'd have a hard time differentiating it from any other medical clinic in the fleet. Instead of the typical photographs of nature scenes or health reminders, the HM1 (hospital corpsman first class) had covered the bulkheads with some of the more gung-ho Marine Corps recruiting posters and personal mementos from his time in a Force Recon company. Although his decorating style gave off an atmosphere of "suck it up—you're a marine," his attitude was anything but; he was a focused and empathetic medical provider.

HM1 had given us a medical class a couple of weeks earlier, and it was clear to everyone that he knew his stuff. He captured my attention when he started with "There's no ambulance in the bush that's going to take you to a big white hospital, so you better listen up." I had seen the gang and drug violence that plagued the streets of Albuquerque; I understood the seriousness of his curriculum. I also found unconventional medicine fascinating, and it wasn't long before fascination turned into real interest.

"What do you need, Lance Corporal?" he asked as I entered. He was wearing glasses and had a stethoscope around his neck. He looked different to me, and for a moment I thought I was in the room with someone I had never met. Strange how a few common personal items and a change of scenery can completely transform a person. Later, when I became a provider, I'd experience this same thing; I could be on the shooting range in the morning, just one of the boys with an oversized aid bag, but later in the afternoon at the medical clinic, a teammate would come in to review lab results and treat me a little differently. I suppose the lab coat threw them off.

"I got sliced by a branch," I said.

"Come on over, let's take a look," he said, signaling me to come toward his desk. After examining the wound and asking a few questions, he decided I needed a few sutures. "Doc," perhaps the most commonly used byname in the military, moved across the room gathering syringes, needles, and sutures while explaining the procedure. "The class is out of the water today and tomorrow, and with the weekend you should be fine," he said.

Like any other marine, I trusted my corpsman and did everything he asked as he patched me up. I sat mesmerized as he flushed the wound, injected Xylocaine to numb up my arm, then threw half a dozen stitches into it. No medical doctor came in to check the wound or question his decisions; there was no need to. The navy had trained him for independent duty, which gave him a great deal of latitude and responsibility. Realizing there weren't enough doctors for every ship, submarine, or expeditionary force in the fleet, the navy responded by developing an intense medical program that focused on everything a corpsman would need to know to keep warriors fighting in any environment. It was, and still remains, their job, and they are very good at it. Doc had been through the course years ago, and after watching him work it was clear he was a seasoned provider who knew his limits but also how to keep marines in the game.

Like anyone else in America, I had been to the doctor's office and the emergency room while growing up, usually for trauma related to foolish behavior or fistfights. So it goes without saying that getting sutures put in was nothing new. Watching Doc work was the first time I really paid attention to the *process,* though, and it served as my first real exposure to medicine. I greatly admired how he performed tasks normally carried out by licensed doctors in the civilian world, and did so without traditional medical school or a fancy license on the wall.

Every marine knows the magnificent deeds these sailors perform in combat. It's no secret that the corpsman rating is the most decorated in the navy for valorous acts, and the vast majority of those come from serving with the marines. Even so, the idea of providing health care beyond the battlefield was an aspect of the job I never considered until that day. From that moment on I couldn't get enough. At each school I went to I would watch the corpsman work his magic. For example, the docs at dive school were responsible for evaluating divers who didn't look or act quite right after surfacing. In some cases, the symptoms were obvious, while at other times it took a meticulous exam to make a determination, which they could execute in minutes. They had an instinct for the job and were highly valued and trusted members of the dive team.

I was excelling in my occupation as a Recon Marine and greatly enjoyed the challenges that came with the Corps. Still, something was changing internally and I couldn't stop it. The question was no longer *if* I should become a corpsman but how it would affect my mother.

THE DIE IS CAST

I always believed my mother had a direct line to the Lord. I know God loves us all equally, but her dedication and support for anyone in need had to give her priority messaging. She proved this on occasion, including the prediction that a move from the valley to the Heights would be disastrous. She didn't make a big deal about her link to the Almighty; she simply acknowledged it and was always right.

I was traveling home from a training trip in Minnesota when I made up my mind. I was leaving the Marine Corps for the navy and would tell Mom when I got home. It was something I just had to do; I couldn't deny it any longer.

I called Mom from the airport and learned the whole family would be there for a big dinner, including those she had taken in off the streets and now called her kids. I figured this would be a great opportunity. I'd have supporting forces watching my flank, and with the right coordination I might be able to establish an escape and evasion plan should things go awry. Mom took her marines very seriously.

I arrived home around noon to a warm reception, and after many handshakes and hugs I was put to work. In Mom's house everyone had to chip in; that meant everyone, including invited guests, friends, family, strangers, it didn't matter. I always loved that format. Everyone congregates in the kitchen anyway, so to quote Mom, "Might as well put them to work." It also left plenty of room for short stories that started over the stove and continued as we moved to the dinner table. In New Mexico it's customary for a couple of family members or guests to give oral dissertations while the rest add distinctive Hispanic elements to the conversation, such as "I know, huh" and "No, really?" These conversations and side comments are quite colorful and become increasingly so as some of the orators enjoy their cerveza—I know you all know what that word means.

Mom insisted I stand next to her, chopping the onions, peppers, and such. I knew I had to break the news to her then, and while I had practiced on the plane for hours, I was nervous and tongue-tied, like a little boy who had broken a window with a baseball.

The mood was festive; family and friends were laughing, and Mom seemed amenable to just about anything. When I turned to break the news, though, all I could get out was a jumble of words about the Marine Corps and my life. It must have sounded bizarre, judging by the puzzled stares on my family's faces. Marky was speaking in tongues!

Mom never missed a beat. Knowing the room was all hers, she kept staring at the masa harina she was kneading and said, "Marky, man can choose any occupation on earth except for two. One is serving others through the cloth, the other through medicine . . . those are chosen for you." She stopped and looked up at everyone, then turned to me and said, "And mijo, you'd make a lousy priest."

I knew then that whatever I had to say, she had already heard it from God. I leaned down for a kiss on the cheek and thanked her for understanding.

The rest of the family was still confused, so my sister Diana belted out, "Marky is going into the navy to be a medic." On cue, the side comments rolled in. "No, really?" "Mom will need new stickers for her car." "I know, huh."

I would soon start over, from the bottom.

5

ANCHORS AWEIGH

★ ★ ★

Twenty years from now you will be more disappointed by the things
you didn't do than by the ones you did. So throw off your bowlines. Sail away
from safe harbor. Catch the trade winds in your sails.
Explore. Dream. Discover.

—H. JACKSON BROWN JR.'S MOTHER

fter breaking the news to Mom and getting past the emotional sensationalism that seemed pervasive at home, I began the tedious process of transferring from the United States Marine Corps to the United States Navy. Finally, after mountains of paperwork and months of waiting, it all came down to one short ceremony followed by another. In a matter of minutes I was discharged from the Marine Corps and enlisted in the navy. Before I started the transfer from the Corps, First Sergeant Dickens wanted to make sure I didn't have a last-minute change of mind. "Lance Corporal, you've read the letter I wrote in support of this transfer, so you know how I feel," he said in a fatherly tone that only the top enlisted man of the company can get away with—hence the nickname Top. "But marine, you need to understand that once you do this, there's no turning back."

"I understand, First Sergeant—but I will be back," I said with a confident smile. "Just not in this uniform."

Top laughed under his breath and pointed to a document that I needed to sign. Neither Top nor any of the other marines in the battalion were bitter about my transfer; actually it was quite the opposite. I had more support than I could have imagined. Maybe it would have been different if I picked another service or perhaps a different occupation, but I was going to be a corpsman, and marines share a bond with navy corpsmen like few others on the face of this earth. Top's apprehension was based on his experiences over his decades of service. First and foremost, rules had been put in place by the Pentagon to prevent service members from surfing between branches. Second, he knew navy administration rarely got anything right when it came to the Corps, and lastly, he'd miss me. Needless to say, remaining a marine was no longer an option. I felt as if the Lord had spoken, and I was determined to answer the call.

I stepped up to the table, grabbed the pen lying atop the paper, and signed. It took thirteen weeks to become a marine but only a couple of seconds to leave the corps. I felt immediately uncomfortable, as if I'd just signed a divorce agreement. Sure, I knew it was coming, and I was responsible for the transfer, but in an instant my world had changed, and it was a surreal feeling. Well, there was no use getting sentimental; I was fully committed and had to stay the course.

Knowing I only had a few minutes to fully enjoy my civil liberties, I decided to take full advantage of the right to free speech. Turning back toward Top, I looked at him and said, "Top, there's some things you should know. Your cadence desperately needs some new material, and your coffee is really bad."

"Ummm" was all he said, with a slight hint of a smile as he looked at the rest of the room trying not to chuckle. Well, everyone except the second lieutenant. He looked at me and sighed, knowing that somehow he'd end up getting the brunt of it.

"Mr. Donald, shall we get on with the rest of this?" asked ET1 Crain, my navy recruiter.

"Sure," I replied. Suddenly a naval officer came forward to swear me in. Unfortunately, I don't remember much about him. I knew he was someone important from the local Recruiting Command but not much else. Top and the CO pulled strings to have him come to the company so I could have a personal ceremony instead of joining up with a group of strangers at the Military Entrance Processing Station, which meant a lot to me. I'm ashamed to say that I can't even remember his face. I guess I still had the Corps mentality of being the best among the services. Marines may not verbalize it, but they all feel as if the Corps is the top dog. It's a belief instilled in boot camp and maintained by having every marine, from the lowest-ranking private to the Commandant of the Corps, hold every other accountable to the Corps standards. I knew it, I loved it, and I missed it, even though I'd been out just a few short moments.

Shortly after the ceremony, I thought I was shipping out to the Naval Training Center San Diego to attend the Other Service Veterans (OS-VET) training program, a crash course in navy culture for veterans entering or returning to the navy. I remember hearing the program was akin to a college course in navy etiquette and administration requirements, with none of the yelling or other pleasantries associated with boot camp. When I went to USMC boot camp, Staff Sergeant Sandoval dropped me off at the airport; this time it was my close friend Erik, from Delta Company.

Erik drove up to the area marked DEPARTING FLIGHTS and in his typical sarcastic tone said, "I guess it's time to get out of the car, squid," using the universal derogatory term for navy sailors.

"I guess so." I started to open the door and step outside.

"Are you sure that's all they gave you?" he asked, referring to the few sheets of paper I carried in a folder.

"That's all I got," I said as I closed the door.

"Those squids are f***ed up. I don't feel good about this. Get back in the car," he said, craning his neck toward the window.

I leaned on the window. "That's the paranoid Erik I know. You never feel good about anything. There's either something wrong or something about to go wrong."

"That's 'cause there always is," he said in his naturally sinister laugh. Then he got serious for a moment. "Mark, I support what you're doing. I don't like it, but I support it. Don't worry about your mom or your sister; I got that, too." It was his brotherly way of saying "I love and will miss you," but moments like those don't last more than a few seconds with him. "Now go get your squid on and get back here to take care of my wounds."

"Aye, aye," I shouted and then watched as he drove off. I'm pretty sure he flashed a profane gesture, and I would have been disappointed if he didn't.

I scanned the meager collection of papers ET1 Crain had given me and realized I wasn't told much of anything or given specific instructions, which is odd to a former marine. In fact, I was so busy saying good-byes that I never bothered to ask. This was very different from my first experience with the Marine Corps, which was meticulously planned on my behalf by the recruiters. Paperwork was packaged into a large envelope and sealed shut, with a page of step-by-step instructions stapled on the front. We knew precisely where to go and when, and how to act when the drill instructors got there. This felt more like my recruiter was being purposefully vague, as if to say, "OK, marine, let's see how you do in my navy." Regardless, I wasn't going to let him see me sweat, so with the same arrogance that sent me to the bottom of the pool at marine boot camp, I gathered what little documentation I had and charged on.

When I arrived at the San Diego International Airport it was the same as it was two and a half years earlier, empty. Unsure of a direction, I followed the herd of the long-hair "regular" recruits arriving from across the country and boarded the bus for the Naval Training Center. Once there, I tried to speak with the staff and the CC (company commander, the navy's version of a drill instructor) about the OSVET program, but it was to no avail. No one seemed to know anything about it, so I decided to keep following the line on the floor that processed everyone into the system.

It didn't take long before I realized that I was entering basic training all over again, rather than the OSVET program, and that I was either going to have to get along or move along. Suddenly all I could think about was what Top had told me. This was a one-way trip, and the last thing I needed was to be thrown out. Nervous and confused, I did what any young marine would do and just followed orders. I guess I thought things would eventually get worked out, and since the navy's boot camp wasn't anything like the marines' I had no problem waiting. Besides, this gave me plenty of time to familiarize myself with the nuances of the navy, and there were plenty of differences. One of the biggest, barring the physical aspects, of course, was the significance the Marine Corps placed on knowing the battle history of the Corps, as well as its traditions. That may not sound like much, but I can tell you that from an infantryman's perspective it means everything. Once you hear of the deeds of your predecessors and realize how revered they are for their bravery, any thoughts of retreat are instantly erased.

However, where the Marine Corps emphasized a physical and mental toughness, I felt the navy concentrated on understanding the reason for each action. What a fundamental difference. Every bit of training I received from the Corps, from boot camp to Amphibious Reconnaissance School, had the same mantra, "Nobody ever drowned from sweat." The navy's perspective was more along the lines of "Work smarter, not harder," and I welcomed the challenges of learning the "navy way." Both services had their strengths and their reasons for doing things a particular way, but neither had a weakness in developing its force.

Toward the end of the first week, the company commander gave us a schedule of the upcoming events, which annotated any clothing, books, or equipment that was required. When I looked at the next morning's agenda it simply read "Training Tank," but there was no requirement for swim trunks, which seemed a little odd. While the company readied for lights-out, Petty Officer Dieter, one of the CCs who had served on a gator freighter (a fleet term used to describe ships that transport marines), called me into the office. He was aware of my prior service as a Recon Marine but, like the others, knew nothing of my supposed assignment to OSVET. Away from the eyes and ears of the other recruits, he addressed me by my first name.

"Mark, tomorrow the dive motivator will be speaking with the class. I know you want to return to Recon as a corpsman, but I think you should consider screening for BUD/S." He was referring, of course, to Basic Underwater Demolition/SEAL training. I had always been curious about how hard the training really could be, but this wasn't in the plan.

"Thanks, Petty Officer Dieter. I appreciate the advice, but I think I'll pass."

"Suit yourself, shipmate, but I'm going to speak to them about you anyway. You shouldn't limit options."

Walking back toward my rack, I thought about what he said about the differences between the SEAL Teams and Marine Recon. Back then the Marine Corps hadn't embraced Reconnaissance with the same fervor as the navy did its SEALs. Like everyone else in the Corps, we made do with what we had, but the SEALs had backing from the fleet, and even from a distance it showed. Marines had Quonset huts and old converted buildings; SEALs had a large compound that straddled the Coronado shoreline. Recon Marines did everything themselves with little personnel support. Thanks to the foresight of SEAL Commander Tom Hawkins, a veteran frogman from the Vietnam era, the teams had fleet sailors to help carry the load in support positions. I continued to think on the SEALs until we arrived at the pool the next day.

The CCs marched us into a large classroom and introduced us to a first-class petty officer brandishing a gold Trident and impressive fruit salad above the left breast pocket of his uniform—military slang for the SEAL qualification badge and ribbons, respectively. He was incredibly fit with swimmer's shoulders, a small waist, and forearms that would make Popeye jealous. BM1 O'Connor was a SEAL who spoke like a business executive as he moved around the room. There was no macho posturing or tough-guy talk; he didn't need it. He carried a quiet authority that instantly captured the class's attention. Even the company commanders treated him differently.

Over a period of twenty minutes he told the class about the diving programs the navy had to offer, speaking well of each one of them but saving the SEAL Teams for last. I was completely impressed and immediately understood why the navy held them in such high regard. Then he showed something that I will never forget. During the last ten minutes, he played a short movie called "Be Someone Special." Personally, I found it to be the cheesiest recruiting film I have ever seen, but apparently I was the only one.

By the time it ended, everyone wanted to be a SEAL, just not me. However, as recruits eagerly signed up for the screening test the following week, I was summoned to the back of the room by one of the CCs. "Seaman Recruit Donald, this is Boatswain's Mate First Class Harry O'Connor," he said, introducing me to the SEAL who had just spoken to us.

"Donald, they tell me you were a Recon Marine," he said.

"Yes, sir," I answered crisply. Then came the typical string of questions special operations ask one another to verify the person they're talking with is actually who he claims to be. I could see my company commander out of the corner of my eye as we spoke and couldn't help but notice a sigh of relief when BM1 O'Connor had concluded I was who I claimed to be. I explained how I came to be there and how I just wanted to return to the Corps. However, it didn't take long for an experienced SEAL to read this former lance corporal and react in a way that would psychologically control him.

"I respect your decision, and I must say I'm impressed with your ability to accept your limitations," he said in a way that both sounded professional and poked at my ego. Then he went on, "We've had quite a few marines wash out of training."

"Those weren't Recon Marines," I said in a questioning tone, nearly interrupting him.

"No, I believe they all were," he answered back. Needless to say, over the course of our conversation he successfully reverted me back to an egotistical Hispanic kid that had no choice but go to BUD/S to prove to the world he can make it.

Nearly four weeks had passed since my arrival at Recruit Training Command, and everything was going along just fine. I had passed the BUD/S screening test, developed a friendship with Harry O'Connor, as much as the circumstances would allow, and given up on trying to explain what my recruiter had told me. Top was right; navy administration screws marines. I was a sailor now, though, and to be honest I was pleased with how things were panning out. That is, until I was called back into the company commander's office to make a decision with a senior chief petty officer I had never met before.

Turns out that once I passed the screening test for BUD/S they had to take another look at my orders. "Donald," he said—which after weeks of boot camp sounded strange to hear without having "Seaman Recruit" before it—"it looks as if someone may have made a mistake." *Wow*, I thought to myself, *what a great way to start the conversation.* Even so, I listened intently as he proceeded to tell me that although I qualified for OSVET and should have been placed into the program, somehow I foolishly waived the option and the processing command had cut my current set of orders. Unbeknownst to me, passing the screening test for BUD/S was akin to accepting orders, and BUD/S superseded everything else in the navy.

He continued explaining my options. I could be pulled from training, have my rank and pay restored, and enter the next OSVET class, which started a couple of months out. I would then continue on to corpsman school. Or I could stay, graduate with my class, and have a guaranteed shot at BUD/S but not a specific job in the navy. If I took OSVET, I would lose the opportunity to attend BUD/S before having to go to the fleet for at least two years of service, which he assumed would be with Recon, although he couldn't guarantee that either. If I stayed in boot camp, the navy couldn't guarantee me Hospital Corps School, but more than likely I would end up as a corpsman because the job was undermanned, especially in the SEAL Teams. He also mentioned that he had spoken with the SEAL motivator, who said that he would make a couple of calls to help me get to Hospital Corps School before I started BUD/S. They gave me a couple of days to think about it, but it only took a few minutes. These men had no reason to help make things right other than being a good shipmate. Instantly it reminded me of how the marines came together to get me here in the first place. I knew medicine was my calling and God would get me there, so I was keeping my promise to Harry and going off to BUD/S even if it killed me.

We graduated boot camp on Friday, and I can't explain how good it felt putting a SCUBA badge and parachute wings back on my uniform the night before. I had grown close to the men in my company the same way I did at marine boot camp, but neither the fleet Marine Corps nor the navy offered the same level of camaraderie I felt within special operations. Up until that point I never recognized how important that degree of brotherhood was to me, but having been away from it for over two months, there was no use denying it.

I looked forward to going home to visit my mom, my platoon, and a certain navy recruiter, but it would have to wait. I had one more stop before my triumphant return home.

HOSPITAL CORPS SCHOOL

United States Navy Corpsman "A" School, in those days, was a ninety-six-calendar-day course held at the Naval School of Health Sciences. The schoolhouse was built on the grounds of Naval Medical Center San Diego, but due to its location within the city the vast compound was more commonly known throughout the fleet as Balboa.

I checked into corpsman school on a Monday morning, and the process was relatively smooth except for one small bump in the road. I arrived in my navy dress blues, known to the world as "Cracker Jacks," which were meticulously pressed and, frankly, immaculate thanks to my marine training. While I was filling out paperwork, a navy nurse, rank of commander, walked through the reception area and did a double take when she saw the scuba bubble, jump wings, and marksman badge on my navy uniform. She immediately called me into her office and gave me the third degree about the "unauthorized" badges on my chest. I calmly explained my background, and she made a few phone calls to confirm it. Half an hour later, she gave me a red-faced apology and sent me back to processing.

Academically the coursework was on par with the first semesters of an associate's nursing degree, but the hands-on training conducted at the hospital was wholly dependent on which staff member a student received as daily supervisor.

Generally speaking, the senior enlisted corpsmen and the commissioned nurses, who were once corpsmen themselves, were top-notch instructors, but occasionally we would get someone on the opposite end of the teaching spectrum. I always felt like it was a bit of a crapshoot when I walked onto the ward. Would I leave trying to remember all the things I learned? Or would I try to forget the nurse who spent hours pointing out how much I *didn't* know? Thankfully, we had a great officer assigned to oversee our instruction and get us past any personality shortfalls that hindered our education.

Lieutenant Marty was a dark-haired, slightly bug-eyed officer with a boyish face and comedic charm, and folks instantly loved him. He was both a nurse version of Patch Adams and a highly proficient naval officer, making him the best mentor on the instructor staff. Teaching wasn't his only duty; he spent plenty of time ensuring we learned the material and had a good time in the process.

As class leader I usually sat toward the back with my assistant and good friend Eric Sine so we could watch the flock, so to speak. So it wasn't unusual for Lieutenant Marty to pop into the classroom or catch us on a hospital rotation to speak with us and gauge our progress. If we made a mistake during a training evolution, he'd make it right, and then he'd make a few jokes about it to enlighten the class on how trivial some of our complaints actually were. In addition to LT (pronounced "el tee," a nickname given to all lieutenants in the navy), there were two hospital corpsmen assigned to the class to act as our primary instructors. Unfortunately, they weren't both of the same caliber. It was almost a Jekyll and Hyde team that would have certainly driven us insane if it weren't for the humor of LT and Sine.

HM1 Kleinfelter was laid-back, helpful, and well versed in medicine, while his counterpart's challenging personality traits exposed envy of his partner to even the most naive members of the class. Neither man had spent time with the marines, but both were experienced with first aid and had mastered improvised methods of care necessary for shipboard medicine. I had received basic medical training in the Marine Corps, but that was nothing like what I learned in corpsman school. The first part of their classroom instruction was always by the book, but Eric and I would wake everyone for the second half, which at times was genius. Years of caring for sailors at sea had taught these two how to treat and move men in the most confined spaces imagined. I quickly learned that transporting patients was as much an art form as it was a skill, and for the first time in my life I truly felt I was in my element. In the classroom everything was so easy to absorb that I often found myself reading ahead. During our practicals the minutiae that slipped past my classmates jumped out at me as if it were saying, "Attention to detail, attention to detail!" A paradigm shift began inside me, and I felt like a new man.

Over the first twenty years of my life, I was either in a fight or training for one. In the streets of Albuquerque, I fought on the playground to defend my honor or protect my lunch money. Later, as a teen, I fought to defend my friends—and, on a couple of occasions, my life. Then came the Marine Corps, an adrenaline-charged community whose main purpose in life is vanquishing the enemy. Now, at Balboa, I was learning how to save lives and live by a Hippocratic Oath. I assisted with the delivery of babies, treated victims of drunk driving, and sat with veterans from past wars while they awaited their next dose of chemotherapy. I was beginning to understand the fragility of life and appreciate the talents of health care professionals in all the fields of medicine. From the emergency room to the radiology suite, everyone had the same goal: to save and preserve life. Just as Mom had prophesied, it wasn't *my* career choice; I was called by a higher power. Still, I did have a say on *who* I wanted to serve. Once again, fate and ambition had stepped in, and my calling was about to take on a whole new meaning.

6

BUD/S—JUST THE BASICS

*Given enough time, any man may master the physical. With enough
knowledge, any man may become wise. It is the true warrior
who can master both . . . and surpass the result.*

—Tien T'ai School of Buddhism

I stepped onto the beach ready for our class's first timed swim. This
would be one of the few timed events in First Phase that didn't
come with a must-pass requirement. We sounded off with a full
head count to the instructors. They lined us up side by side and started
inspecting our gear, first to ensure everything was operational, next to
see if we were familiar with how to use it, and finally to find if anything was improperly rigged. Of course, something was always im-
proper or fell short of BUD/S standards, and we as a class would pay
for it with a short but intense preswim warm-up. That morning was no
exception. Our "remedial activity," which was actually punishment for
a student's inadequately sharpened dive knife, consisted of an exercise
the students referred to as surf-torture, which meant locking arms,
walking out into the surf zone, then facing toward shore and falling
back into a reclining position. This was followed by calisthenics in the
sand just to make sure the granules were in all the wrong places under
our wetsuits before we started the swim. These sessions usually went

until the instructors grew tired of watching or they began to impinge on the day's schedule. Generally, the latter was the deciding factor. After half an hour of "warm-up" we gathered around Instructor Kress and received our brief, each and every one of us resembling a human sugar cookie.

Instructor Kress informed us our swim times would determine our swim buddy, the classmate who would remain no more than one arm's length away from this day forward. The concept is a simple one: No student was ever to move alone or be found alone on the compound again. Being left alone can mean being left out, being uninformed, or, worse, left behind, and that simply doesn't happen in an organization that has the word "team" in its name. That was fine for all of us. With a few rare exceptions, it was an individual journey getting orders to the renowned Naval Special Warfare Center, and the thought of having a partner made us feel like we were already a member of "the teams."

The swim was designed to pair us with someone of near or equal speed. It wasn't based on military rank, experience, friendship, or any other factor. It was solely based on a need to break us into two-man teams of comparable ability so no one student held another back. Rather, the competitiveness between two equally matched BUD/S candidates would motivate the pair to push one another harder. So it came as no surprise when our highest-ranking officer was paired with our lowest-ranking enlisted sailor. I believe this is where the strong officer-and-enlisted relationship found in the SEAL Teams all starts. If you were a fly on the wall and heard a SEAL officer and SEAL enlisted carrying on a conversation in the platoon hut, you'd have a difficult time discerning who's who. Sure, when they're in uniform at a navy function they'll follow the same military protocols that rank and tradition require; we are professionals, after all. What the world doesn't see is how they interact with one another in the team area, where only team guys are allowed access. It's not unusual for them to address one another by first name rather than by rank and last name, the tradition nearly everywhere else in the military. They discuss personal matters as if they were speaking to their own brothers. This is not a sign of disrespect. On the contrary, speaking to one another in this relaxed fashion is a sign of the greatest respect. They speak as family, as teammates . . . as SEALs, and it all stems from a personal bond that is forged when men face adversity as one.

As a former marine I often wondered why the Special Warfare device, also known as the "Trident" or "Budweiser," was gold for both officer and enlisted. Everywhere else in the navy, officers wear gold and enlisted wear silver, but not in Special Warfare. Over time I learned that unlike the rest of the navy, Special Warfare officers and enlisted go through the same six-month qualification process at BUD/S, which has essentially remained unchanged since its inception. After graduation from BUD/S the few remaining students in the class attend SEAL Qualification Training (SQT), an additional half-year advanced training program that instills the skills necessary to qualify as a modern-day SEAL. Although I cannot be certain, I believe this to be the only training pipeline in the U.S. military in which both officer and enlisted share the exact same qualification standard for their military occupation. This equality in earning the title is what allows the enlisted member to wear the gold Trident following graduation from SQT. Every SEAL and their UDT (Underwater Demolition Team) predecessors before them have endured the same twenty-four weeks of SEAL basic training. This combat-proven and time-tested pipeline is the foundation for an undying unity that exists among all members of the community regardless of their rank, experience, or generation.

There I stood at the gateway to the frog family with absolutely no idea it all started with that first swim.

Unlike distance running, ocean swims require constant diligence; you must maintain a constant state of awareness of your position in the water if you expect to stay on course. Otherwise you might find yourself swimming hundreds of extra, unintentional meters. Like runners, though, distance swimmers find a rhythm and then lose themselves in thought, some focusing on a personal mantra or visualizing a future event, like graduation from BUD/S. I had my own unique method for ocean swims: find a tempo and let the mind wander, usually to something in the past. As I made my way through the water I thought about graduating from Hospital Corps School a couple of months earlier and how it was the beginning of my journey to fulfilling a personal calling to medicine. The differences I encountered between the United States Marine Corps and the Navy Hospital Corps were extreme. The marines base effectiveness on military discipline and practice it in everything they do. Perfect appearance in uniform and execution of close order drill are indicative of their lifestyle. Navy medicine was equally professional but far more relaxed. The hardened look and crisp "yes, sir" and "no, sir" of the Corps were replaced with a smiling face and "sure, let me see what I can do." Both were effective methods, but they were dramatically different. One was for operating on the battlefield and the other on the hospital wards after the fight. Then there was BUD/S, which was all business. No babysitting here; sailors who needed it were weeded out of the system long before receiving orders to Coronado, California. At BUD/S the class is told one time where to be, when to be there, and what to have ready. If an individual can't figure it out, he has no business being there.

I was no stranger to Coronado. I was stationed there as a young marine but never bothered to cross the base into "SEAL country." I was focused on marine training but had no reason to bother the SEALs, and the SEALs certainly didn't want me there. Back in those days, I never imagined I would one day train on their sacred ground with the ambition of making that ground mine.

SEALs are a particular breed. From a distance they seem like a cross between an easygoing soldier with relaxed uniform standards and an intense prizefighter looking for his next opponent. Constantly training and never satisfied with their performance, they carry themselves with an attitude that can be interpreted as an inflated ego. Spend a few moments speaking to a team guy, though, and you'll find him humble, especially when it comes to warfare, well read, and fiercely dedicated to the community to which he belongs. Outsiders often buy into the team mystique, mesmerized by our stories and commitment to one another— but don't ask too many questions or overstay your welcome, or you risk alienating yourself from the group. It's not that we purposely try to push folks away; far from it. SEALs enjoy diversity in conversation and opinion but are intensely private when it comes to team business. It's simply in their DNA. SEALs are warriors in every sense of the word: men who actually go into combat on missions that bring them eye to eye with their enemy, up close and personal. Even their methods of insertion are extremely dangerous; parachute jumps, submarine launches, and ocean swims in treacherous seas are very serious business. I guess that's why I find it hard to accept how our society tosses around the word "warrior" when describing an athlete, businessman, or even a politician. To me the term "warrior" is a sacred one characterizing a lifestyle of personal sacrifice. A warrior's training is continuous in order to maintain a constant state of readiness, often taking him away from the ones he loves and those he's sworn to protect. A warrior does this not for reward but for a chance to join his brothers on a high-risk mission. It doesn't sound like any civilian occupation I know of.

"When you get to shore, Donald, just drop down in the push-up position with the others," Instructor Richardson's voice bellowed from one of the safety boats trailing the swimmers. I had zoned out for the majority of the swim but was still focused on the objective, a tactic that we would all have to perfect if we expected to graduate. If you can't put discomfort and monotony out of your mind and concentrate on the particulars at hand, you really don't stand a chance. Fortunately, there is ample opportunity to learn the technique during the multitude of must-pass events going on during each week of training. Those that get it right develop an ability to find a certain nirvana during the most stressful times. That doesn't always equate to success but definitely prevents pressure from being a cause of mission failure. I still recall how one of my classmates looked as if he had fallen asleep during underwater knot tying. Imagine having to hold your breath at the bottom of the combat swimmer training tank, tying one knot after another on a line that transverses the bottom of the pool. Most people would panic and bolt to the surface once they started to run out of oxygen, but the majority of the remaining students were well versed in controlling their senses and compartmentalizing anxiety, and the ones that weren't either failed or "rang out." (A SEAL who chooses to quit BUD/S voluntarily can do so without prejudice by ringing the brass bell in the quadrangle three times.)

I got to shore, took off my fins, turned in my swim time, and joined the rest of the class alternating between push-ups and flutter kicks in the surf zone. It may not sound like much, but facing waves in a foot of water as they surge up from underneath you or crash over your face while you're breathing heavily from exercise creates a water boarding effect. Add in the saltwater and the sand chafing every fold of skin imaginable while the cold water steals your heat away, and you'll begin to understand the effectiveness this training has in building mental stamina. The continual employment of the surf zone as a means of punishment eventually sweeps away any fear of drowning, leaving the navy with one hell of a resilient amphibian.

From the push-up position I looked down the line of my classmates and wondered which of the remaining eighty-four would be my swim buddy. Fifteen of them either dropped out or were rolled back into another class by the time we finished the four weeks of pretraining, and that was just the beginning. Just days earlier we had our head-shaving party and, with a little assistance from a few bottles of loudmouth, began convincing ourselves that we could be the second class in the history of BUD/S to have everyone graduate Hell Week. Of course, the instructors who supervised our celebration reminded us that we might just be like the class that had zero graduates. *The class that never was* was infamous among trainees, and for a period of time a statue sat on the quarterdeck memorializing their lack of fortitude. When I heard about that particular class, I promised myself then and there I would never quit. I might be dropped for failing to complete a task, but I wasn't quitting. I would rather die in training than ring the bell. It may sound a bit extreme, but not for me. I looked at it more as an extension of the oath I had taken for medicine and the promise I had made to the good Lord.

The Hippocratic Oath is an ethical promise that all medical providers must take when graduating from student to provider. There are various versions, some based on the educational level—doctor versus medic is a prime example—and some were interpretations of the original text, but one thing that rings clear among all the versions is the notion "to do no harm." I simply added on a personal pledge that I believe is the essence of a frontline medic: "and allow no harm to be done, even at the sacrifice of my own life." From the moment I took on the proud and honored title of navy corpsman I knew that despite my status as care provider, I would still be issued a weapon and be expected to use it. Since the dawn of time a small portion of enemy forces has always sought out the medic. Take out the man that can save the life of another soldier and possibly return him to battle and you'll have a far greater effect on a unit's effectiveness and morale than if you target a rifleman. It takes a sick mind to think that way, but firsthand stories from corpsmen and marines from Iwo Jima to today have told me there were plenty of them. Through history some countries have honored the Geneva Conventions, which offer protection to medics, while others simply have not, including our current adversaries in the War on Terror. I accepted the fact that I would both fight and heal and adopted "Trained to fight, but called to serve" as my new motto for the battlefield.

BUD/S has one of the top medical departments in the navy. Yet even with all its expertise and ability a good many of the students were avoiding it at all cost. They were concerned their attendance at sick call would send the wrong message to the instructors and their classmates alike. Dr. Pollard and Dr. Castellano, stationed at the clinic, knew this and had arranged for all the corpsmen waiting on their class to convene to work at the clinic. Despite that this was a relatively short period of time, the docs were able to build a rapport with each of us. They'd use our knowledge of our classmates' injuries as another means of monitoring the students they were entrusted to protect. If the docs felt a corpsman knew his limitations, they'd issue a small medical kit or aid bag to provide follow-up care back at the barracks. This policy not only extended their reach, but also allowed me to build a rapport with students from other classes.

As long as I kept them apprised of which trainees I treated, how severe their injuries were, and what I did for them, everything was good. So when the workday was done, I'd restock my aid bag with the necessary items for treating blisters, chafing, and other common aches and pains related to BUD/S. I'd start making my rounds in the barracks trying to patch up friction burns on macerated skin and icing joints, earning me the title of "Mom" from our First Phase proctor Phil Jannuzzi. I never cared for that nickname but made sure no one knew. Otherwise it would have been permanent; thankfully, "Mom" ended with the First Phase, along with over 70 percent of our original class.

Every few years the navy invests more time and money trying to improve the number of graduates from SEAL training. Over the years I've watched class sizes fluctuate from under a hundred students to well over two hundred. I've seen the Naval Special Warfare Center try to double the number of classes per year and make continual changes regarding the length and location of pretraining regimes. Yet the number of SEALs produced per year never changed. Don't get me wrong. These are all appropriate measures, and at the very least, they physically prepare candidates far better than in my day and prevent folks from receiving orders to training that shouldn't be there. Nevertheless, after spending nearly a quarter of a century in and around Naval Special Warfare as both a SEAL and a medical officer, I find it hard to believe that any of these actions are ever going to improve the numbers. The number of SEALs isn't based on the percentage of candidates that attend BUD/S but on the percentage of a specific type of man that exists in relation to our country's overall population.

During the first week of pretraining, also known as Fourth Phase, intentionally placed ahead of First Phase so not to disturb the historic numbering of each phase of training, each of us went through a psychological screening process. Back then the navy tried to find a way to identify candidates who displayed all the right attributes and had those qualities at the level necessary to graduate training, but I believe it's impossible to measure the amount of fire in a man through a written test or series of interviews. In fact, I no longer believe the navy makes SEALs at all. In my mind the navy can only assist in identifying the right candidates through recruiting and, once established, provide them with a means to prove themselves to serve among the nation's best.

SEALs are a unique blend of physical strength, academic intelligence, mental tenacity, and unwavering commitment. Their dedication to the mission and their teammates is unimaginable to most Americans. Despite the navy going to great lengths to continually educate these men on everything from the art of war to moral responsibility, their ethical and patriotic foundation was laid long before the navy had anything to do with it. Their family, friends, neighbors, teachers, coaches, and others close to them throughout their youth played a greater role in instilling these characteristics than the navy ever could during the short period of time it had them at boot camp or Officer Candidate

School. It's not a matter of possessing the right traits but, rather, the *degree* to which those traits exist within the man. There's only one way to find out: BUD/S. It is the navy's litmus test for commitment. Therefore, it's my belief that BUD/S doesn't make SEALs; it only validates a man's dedication to joining them.

7

BREAKOUT

We do not rise to the level of our expectations.
We fall to the level of our training.

—SOMETIMES ATTRIBUTED TO ARCHILOCHUS

It would start in a matter of hours: the noise, chaos, confusion, and pain of Hell Week. The tension was thick in the barracks, and the base was secured around the SEAL training area; except for a few patrons at the gas station and our coveted minimart, there wasn't a soul around. Soon the class would be completely cut off from the outside world. We could see the tourists on Coronado's pristine beaches and the motorists driving along on the Silver Strand, but that didn't seem to matter too much. We all knew what was coming; we would soon be in hell for five and a half days, and the outside world would cease to exist. We welcomed it, albeit with reluctance and a healthy dose of anxiety. The majority of the class joined the navy specifically for the opportunity to become a SEAL, and that meant passing Hell Week. We had worked hard for months to get to that point, and although Hell Week was the biggest obstacle we would face over this twenty-four weeks of basic training, most of us just wanted to get started.

Our class proctor, Phil Jannuzzi, came into the SEAL Teams

post-Vietnam but was trained by the men who had cut their teeth in the Mekong Delta. They knew the costs of war and had instilled this knowledge in him through intense training that demanded complete focus and 100 percent dedication. Needless to say, Phil would go on to live a storied career in the teams, protecting our country in ways the vast majority of Americans will never read about. Like many teams guys before him, he had returned to his roots to serve as "Instructor Jannuzzi," and Instructor Jannuzzi wasn't about to let standards drop.

Like all the other instructors, he had his own quirks, and his was to bellow to the class during the most difficult training times, "The Chinaman doesn't care, boys, he just doesn't care." At first no one really understood what that meant. I thought perhaps it was his way of reminiscing about his training days, going through BUD/S with instructors that battled against China's support to the North Vietnamese, but it was just a guess that seemed like a good enough explanation at the time. All we really knew was, when we heard those words training intensity would pick up tenfold, and by the end of the evolution at least one more student would ring out.

Over time we figured out the statement's meaning and how clearly it defined the BUD/S mission, so we couldn't help but adopt it as our class mantra. I once had to explain the meaning to my mother when the phrase slipped out of my mouth during a conversation. Growing up facing racial and sexual prejudice as a Mexican woman, she really didn't like the sound of it, so I tried to explain. "Mom, it means the enemies we're going to face won't care if we have to travel thousands of miles in just a few hours. They won't care that we'll be inserted by physically exhausting methods so as not to be detected, or that we'll be carrying a load that would make a pack mule cringe. They won't care if we're cold, wet, haven't slept or eaten for days. They'll only care about one thing— sending us home in flag-covered caskets, and we can't let any of those circumstances affect us. Our resolve to accomplish the mission must be stronger than theirs." She understood it but liked it even less after hearing my explanation. So I made sure never again to let the China-man leave my lips anywhere near my mother.

Decades later I, too, found out how much the Chinaman, or, as I came to know him, al Qaeda, didn't care, but neither did we—nor do the SEALs who are still out there defending us today. For any terrorists wishing to do harm to America, I want you to know it means you can run, you can hide, you can even build up your defenses, but no matter how long it takes or what extremes we must endure to get to you, if we are called upon to take you out there's not much you can do to stop it. It means pain and discomfort are recognized as just being part of the job and neither will hinder or prevent American special operations from completing its mission.

Instructor Jannuzzi knew the physical difficulties of operating all too well and reminded us that whatever we faced during Hell Week would be minor compared to what we would endure defending our country. He also knew it was the responsibility of the BUD/S instruc-tors to weed out those who lacked the ability to overcome adversity, and he wasn't about to let the community down. From our first day of training to the last Friday before Hell Week he conducted mandatory end-of-day remedial training sessions, which we affectionately called "circuses." At first everyone dreaded ending the day with an additional twenty to sixty minutes of intense exercise, but over time, and as the class began to thin out, it became more of a source of pride than a pun-ishment, kind of like Class 159's own special routine. Circuses taught us that no matter how well things went, at the end of the day bad things were coming, so we needn't spend time worrying about what we couldn't control. We were better off mentally preparing for the eventual colli-sion, "bracing for shock," as they say in the navy. I don't know if it made any difference physically preparing us for Hell Week, but it definitely built our mental tenacity and forged the attitude of the class.

This take-it-as-it-comes approach was clearly evident as we gath-ered for morning muster. Despite being on the precipice of BUD/S training, no one seemed to act any different. I'm not saying the class was free of worry; I just can't remember anxiety being the dominant emotion among the group. We all knew not everyone was going to make it, and by the end of the week it would all be decided, so no need to concern ourselves with the inevitable punishment or wondering about who might or might not be standing when the sand settled. We had work to do.

After a quick roll call, our class leader, Ensign Houck, briefed us about the day's activities. Then Drexler, our leading petty officer, separated us into our boat crews so we could begin final preparations. Although we were all busy working on our boats, stories about holiday adventures began to permeate through the ranks, and it didn't take long before some of the more colorful classmates had us on the floor laughing about their exploits. I think to an outsider it would seem an unusual way of mentally preparing for arguably the hardest week on earth, but we took it in stride. Christmas and New Year's fractured our training schedule at the worst possible time, and there wasn't anything we could do about it. When we first received 159's training calendar, everyone winced seeing where the holiday leave period fell. I remember feeling as if a sick joke had been played upon us, but it was nothing more than dumb luck. Every few years a class gets screwed over by the holidays, and this time it was our turn.

Unfortunately, we would receive our obligatory vacation just before the start of Hell Week and return only one day prior to Breakout, the simulated combat situation that kicks it off. So ensued the dilemma. Take leave and spend Christmas with Mom and Dad to refresh and recharge the batteries but risk losing focus, or stay on the island to train and spend it among classmates at the local pub, which might be far worse. For some it was a hard decision, often switching back and forth depending on how severe the circus was that day. For me it was simple. I knew if I went home to Albuquerque I would return the size of the house. Nothing's more appealing to me than traditional New Mexico cooking founded on the two most essential food groups, fat and salt. Worse yet, my Mexican mother would feel compelled to get everything for "mijo," her little boy, which meant I'd never leave the couch or risk breaking her heart. Nope, I'm staying! Actually, in the end it didn't matter too much what choice we made. Despite the fact that we all kept working out like madmen, no student alive could avoid partaking in the wondrous amounts of food, freedom, and merriment that come with the holidays after being beaten up for months on end. Without any formalized group training program, it would take one mentally strong class to be able to go from zero to a thousand miles an hour with only little more than a day between the two. Suddenly the genius of having the circuses became apparent.

After hearing a few comical stories, our attention went back to our individual boat stations and we started checking the essential components on our boats. An Inflatable Boat Small, or IBS, as it's commonly referred to around the compound, is basically a small rubber flat-bottom boat with round edges that was designed over half a century ago to allow frogmen to effectively lock in and out of submarine escape trunks. Needless to say, with the advent of newer submarines it had become an obsolete piece of gear, and it would have disappeared from navy inventory altogether if BUD/S hadn't implemented it in its training program as one of the primary means of punishment and team building.

Everyone on the Smurf boat crew—a derogatory yet affectionate term used to describe a boat crew comprised of a class's shortest members—which I was a part of, had fallen into a love/hate relationship with this black piece of head-chafing rubber. Due to the shape of the boat and our weight, we had the advantage at sea and rarely lost any of the waterborne boat races, but on land our stature almost guaranteed last place. Heck, we had to run just to keep up with the brisk walk of most of the other crews, and running with a 300-pound rubber hat bouncing up and down on your head isn't good for either the crew member or the boat. Like all other seagoing vessels, ours was quite moody and very high maintenance. If we didn't spend the time work-ing on valves, patching small holes, or just keeping her clean whether she needed it or not, she'd have a blowout at the most inopportune time just to remind us that we had misplaced our priorities and not to let that happen again.

However, this day was different from most, as all the crews were out working on their boats at the same time, and I couldn't help eaves-dropping on the other crews as they reminisced about the first months of training. What I found was that somewhere around week three or four everyone in the class had come to the same epiphany about BUD/S. There really isn't a level or scale to the misery. Sure, at first doing any-thing when you're warm and dry is much better than doing it when you're cold, wet, and sandy, but after a while, and as you learn to ignore the bleeding and chafing occurring at your armpits, nipples, and groin, the days more or less become equally unpleasant. After a while the only variable you notice is the length of time spent participating in whatever torturous event you need to pass in order to continue on, so best to just get through it the first time. I'm sure this awakening of sorts that all BUD/S students go through helped establish the well-known and of-ten overused infamous saying, "The only easy day was yesterday."

After we finished our boats we had until noon to make personal calls and kiss visiting wives or girlfriends and, for a few students, their kids good-bye. Our class had steadily dwindled down to approximately half our original size since our head-shaving party, and although we knew we would lose some more this week we certainly felt that every one of the fifty-five that remained had earned his place. I can't speak for the others, but the Smurf crew never doubted any of our eight members' ability or determination to make it through. In our minds we were all going to be standing there when the instructors secured Hell Week that Friday. Of course, the instructors felt differently, and in a matter of hours and days they would be proven right.

We all had heard rumors from previous classes about the chaos of Breakout and how having our personal gear organized and keeping good communication among the class could make a world of difference. Being a bit of an organizational freak, which I attribute to my time in the Marine Corps, I carefully positioned my gear in an arrangement that would allow me to easily find anything I needed at a moment's notice. Once I felt content with my final prep work, I sat back and forced myself to snack on one of the two tasteless box lunches the galley had made for us, one for now and the other for dinner. I knew I needed the energy, but it took nearly everything I had to consume the day-old bread, moistened by a slice of green tomato and condensation from the sandwich's mystery meat, all covered by melted government cheese and wilted lettuce. Umm-umm, good. The rest of the box wasn't any better. This box lunch would make any school tray in America seem like a gourmet meal. All the condiments in the world wouldn't stand a chance of bringing a palatable taste to this masterpiece. It had to be a BUD/S instructor special order just for the occasion—as if we weren't going to suffer enough? Thankfully, no one would need to eat the second box, since our class proctor graciously arranged for everyone to enjoy a dinner of warm soda and pizza during our final pre–Hell Week briefing.

We were ordered to remain in the barracks, so we sat in our four-man rooms while the minutes turned into hours, giving more than enough time for anxiety to set in if we let it. I was lucky. Tony, our class musician, was one of the classmates I shared my room with, and before long he started to pass the time playing his harmonica, which the instructors required him to carry to all training evolutions after they found a plethora of instruments stuffed into his locker. The solid concrete floor and cinder-block walls made the room sound like an amphitheater, and as some of the other students from nearby rooms gathered to listen, I started on my barracks walkabout. I did last-minute checks on classmates—chafing, blisters, and ailments—although in reality at this point in the game it didn't matter what I did. Not one piece of moleskin or tape was going to last more than an hour, let alone a week.

Not long after that, we were summoned to the compound. As we entered one of the large classrooms next to the First Phase office, we caught a glimpse of the instructors sitting next door going over the week's events. We'd been there plenty of times before, but I think this was the first time everyone was in a clean and dry uniform, which should've been our first omen that there was more to this goodwill gesture than meets the eye. As we approached, our mouths began to water from the wonderful smell of delivery pizza emanating from the room. The sheer sight of it on the tables hypnotized each of us into grabbing a few pieces as we walked over to our seats. It seemed reasonable: Eat it now before the entourage of instructors arrived and we found ourselves enjoying our last meal in the surf zone. Something about soggy pizza with a good helping of sand, saltwater, and seaweed didn't sit well with anyone. We gorged ourselves on the hot greasy 'za, and despite being full on just a few slices everyone kept going back for more. We knew we were being fattened up for the kill, but it was far better than our alternate dining choice—and how bad could it be, anyway? It wasn't dark for at least an hour, so we had plenty of time for our meal to settle . . . or so we thought.

Just as we finished off the last box of pepperoni, one of the officer instructors, Lieutenant Zinke, strolled into the room. Everyone jumped to attention and gave the traditional greeting, "Lieutenant Zinke." "Hooyah, Lieutenant Zinke." It didn't faze him. He just looked around as if to see if we had taken the bait and then left. A few moments later he returned with the rest of the Hell Week instructor staff and calmly went through the safety brief. After a short question and answer period, which was filled with silence, they exited the room and left us with our proctor.

Instructor Jannuzzi was an experienced, respected, and dedicated

SEAL who took everything he did to the extreme, which included his love for football. Needless to say, he focused his motivational preparation for the class around the sport, showing a movie based on the 1986 New York Giants championship football team as part of his "gut through it" speech, but by now temporary motivation wasn't going to help. You either had it inside or you didn't.

The grenade simulator rolled into the hallway hours before anyone ever expected it. Just when we realized what was happening it exploded with a loud concussive bang. Instructors began pouring into the building from every point of entry as if the ocean were filling the hull of a sinking ship. Within seconds the noise from weapons being fired and devices going off made it impossible to hear your own voice, let alone the commands being yelled by our class leader. What was once a sanctuary filled with music and First Phase sea stories had now become a chaotic hall thronged with BUD/S students desperately searching for their swim buddy and the closest exit. Even with our familiarity with the layout of the building this wasn't an easy task. Smoke and fog had become so thick it prevented me from seeing more than a few feet in front of me. Coupled with the ringing in my ears and the smell of gunpowder, it produced utter confusion. Breakout was on its way to being a complete success.

Knowing we had to stick together, we ran to the door and tried to make our way through the building and find our swim buddies. All the while instructors' hands were coming out of nowhere, grabbing one or two guys and separating them from the others. They gave them specific instructions, which they had to follow, designed to segregate the class into smaller pockets of mismatched boat crews. The information—or gouge, as we say around the watercooler—that we received from the classes ahead of us was right on the money. Communication was key, but at this point all the yelling and hand waving we were doing wasn't making a damn bit of difference. We were no longer a class of strong-willed sailors. Within a matter of minutes the cadre had turned us into a sparse gaggle of confused students desperately trying to return some form of structure to our class. For those of us who would go on to graduate, this was just the beginning of a long indoctrination process into the combat environment, but what we all took away that day to the benefit of the navy was realizing the amount of bewilderment that can occur on the battlefield if you're not ready for it.

Just then I heard Drexler's voice through a break in the gunfire yell out, "Swim fins! Swim fins!" That was all I could make out before the next burst. Were we supposed to link up with our swim buddy and head to the beach, or gather the crews at the boats and take to the water? I figured I would find out along the way and ran back into the barracks to collect my gear from wherever it now lay. Once in the room I tore off my kapok and green fatigue top, threw on my inflatable UDT vest, and jumped to the floor, searching for my fins, which I was sure were under some of the overturned furniture. I thought I saw one of the heavy black fins and was reaching for it when one of the instructors grabbed me and told me to start low-crawling out of the barracks to the center of the compound.

While under the blanket of smoke that filled the whole compound, I was able to make out the silhouettes of some of the others. Some were wearing fins on their boots, another had on his UDT shorts (frogman swim trunks) pulled over his pants, and one person looked as if he had every piece of uniform he was ever issued layered one on top of the other. My classmates were running, crawling, and moving in every direction both in small groups and individually. One thing for sure, we were all moving with a purpose; unfortunately, no one was really going anywhere.

Suddenly a smile broke on my face, and then I couldn't stop laughing. Here I was, a soaking wet, shivering, half-naked student adorned with various pieces of equipment all improperly secured to my body, crawling along the paved area we used for PT, half choking from the high-pressured water being shot in my face while I called out for my swim buddy; hilarious. As ridiculous as I looked, I wasn't as bad as some of my classmates, and I realized I was right in line with the rest of the class, learning to survive the worst of times with a sense of humor. BUD/S has a great way of doing that, breaking the ice during the most intense training times with comic relief. For those who wonder how and why SEALs can function when everything else is falling apart around them, this is why. It all starts here: a professional introduction into the world of chaos with a grounding in what's truly important and lessons on how not to let the worst get the best of you during the most dire of circumstances.

Needless to say, the night went on with more of the same befuddlement among the students caused by an ever-changing and continual shock-and-awe attack by the instructors. By now the physical exhaustion from lack of sleep and nonstop strenuous activity coupled with the frigid arms of King Neptune and the cold breath of Mother Nature had started to wear on some of the class. More and more students started to ring out, and although I didn't agree with it I understood their reasons. During Camp Surf, I was so cold that as I lay locked arm in arm with what remained of the class in the surf zone, waves throwing us around like rag dolls, I couldn't help but look up to the heavens and begin to make peace with the idea of leaving this earth. Still, despite feeling as if I were on the edge of life, I wasn't about to quit on my boat crew, my class, my family, or my country, and I wasn't alone.

At the end of day five, sixteen of us finally secured from Hell Week and limped over to medical to be evaluated for release. Laughing, I started to tell the story about how delusional I had become. Much to my surprise I found it was a common theme among the other fifteen, especially with Kent Hayes from our Smurf crew, who was carted off to the hospital that same night. Kent was now spending a week on the wards recovering from severe pneumonia, and while we were being released to waiting family and friends he was being cared for by many of the providers I had come to know from my short time in Hospital Corps. Needless to say, Kent had plenty of visitors that weekend, and although he was happy to know the instructors graduated him from Hell Week, it was hard on all of us to assemble the following Monday without him.

There is a side of me that would relish the opportunity to describe what goes on during SEAL training just to see the expressions on your faces, but the other side of me takes great pride in knowing that only those with the dedication to serve our country in the greatest navy the world has ever known and the spunk to take up the BUD/S challenge will ever possess the knowledge of what actually occurs there. Now, I know some of you are scrambling to do a comparison of your mental fortitude based on your athletic accomplishments and what your imagination has conjured up about SEAL training. I can attest that you are nowhere close to understanding the level of commitment it takes to earn the Trident, so I'll give you a bit more insight in hopes of identifying a future warrior.

Everyone who arrives at BUD/S comes from an athletic background. They have all committed countless hours to building and strengthening their body and mind. Their coaches and trainers have motivated them to push beyond their perceived limits, but therein lies the key. All of those limits are set at attainable levels. No teacher or trainer ever sets someone up for failure, except at BUD/S. There, physical abilities are something that are built upon, not utilized as a determinant. Mental tenacity reigns supreme. It depends on an individual's ability to survive the continual stress from daily pass-or-fail events that go on for months on end, all intended to take away each student's strengths. If you're a good runner, you won't be one there. The instructors will find your nemesis, be it running in the sand, the surf, or some other equalizer. If you're a strong swimmer or someone who possesses great strength or stamina, you won't be one there. I cannot tell you what will happen, only that all your best attributes will be stripped away and that you will find yourself facing challenges in ways you never imagined.

I don't know the formula for finding out who will successfully make it, but neither does anyone else. What I have found is that the star athlete for whom everything comes easy, the man who could excel in any sport due to his natural abilities, generally doesn't stand a chance. Rather, I place my bet on the kid who despite not being in the starting lineup not only never missed a practice but was never late to one either. The teammate that never complained about how long practices were because he just wanted to be among his friends during the good times and bad. The one that despite never setting foot in the limelight never stopped giving 100 percent. The one whose family, coaches, and team-mates talk more about his commitment than his abilities. That's the candidate I think has the best chance at becoming a SEAL: the man who lives in adversity each and every day, who has dealt with the stress of "will I make it," who despite the odds being against him keeps fighting. Physical fitness can be achieved, and no matter how fit you are when you get there it's never enough. BUD/S exposes every weakness on the way to transforming the strong athlete into a great warrior. It's the mindset that is most important! Life in the SEAL Teams is one sudden-death overtime period after another. A never-ending calling of internal fortitude to continue when there is nothing left to give, yet somehow finding it inside yourself to make it happen.

8

THE TEAMS

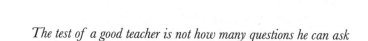

The test of a good teacher is not how many questions he can ask
his pupils that they will answer readily, but how many questions he inspires
them to ask him which he finds it hard to answer.

—ALICE WELLINGTON ROLLINS

My orders were to Naval Amphibious Base Little Creek in Hampton Roads, Virginia, now called the Joint Expeditionary Base. Little Creek, as it's known colloquially, is a medium-sized installation that sits on the Chesapeake Bay, just a few miles southeast of the world's largest naval base in Norfolk, Virginia, and roughly ten miles north of Virginia Beach's resort area. It was established in the early 1940s as a training station; its primary mission was to train naval forces on how to put a substantial number of troops on the beach while facing enemy gunfire. Ships specifically designed for this task, dubbed "amphibs" or "gator freighters," continually trained offshore with landing crafts perfecting these procedures. As the Second World War came to a close, the base's central location on the eastern seaboard and its proximity to Naval Base Norfolk's support facilities made it an ideal berthing for the Atlantic Fleet's amphibs. As time passed, Little Creek would become the home to a number of operational commands including Explosive Ordnance Disposal, the navy's Mobile Diving and Salvage Unit, and eventually, the Navy SEALs.

I had orders to SEAL Team Two, one of the two original SEa-Air-Land Teams established by President John F. Kennedy in 1962. SEAL Team Two would be my home port for the foreseeable future, and I was eager to finally get started on real-world operations. I remember arriving in Virginia Beach on a rainy Thursday night, a few days earlier than expected. The next day I tried to make use of the time by getting some personal items squared away, but just like in the Corps, I had to be officially checked on board a command, so I had time to kill. I called Tony, a classmate who had already checked on board his team. We met for beers at a local team guy bar, and I tried to pump him for intel. All I got was a sly smile and "Oh, you'll see soon enough. It's loads of fun."

On Monday morning, I arrived at the team an hour early in a perfectly pressed dress white uniform and found out the Administration Department had already scheduled a 1000 meeting with my commanding officer. I didn't have time to do anything before then, so I sat in the office watching the clock until precisely two minutes till, then walked up to the CO's hatch (a nautical term for the doorway), knocked on the frame three times, and requested permission to enter. The skipper called me in, placed me at the position of attention in front of his desk, and proceeded to flip through my ridiculously thin military record. After several minutes, he put me "at ease" and began explaining the team's mission and his commander's intent. His tone was calm and measured, ensuring I clearly understood his objectives and how the officers and senior enlisted would execute their assignments. This never happened in the Corps; young marines followed orders, rarely expecting or receiving explanations about their leaders' objectives. From the moment I arrived on base, though, I could tell things were going to be vastly different from anything I ever knew in the past. The skipper continued describing how the SEAL Teams operate on the premise that America will be at war by the end of the day and we will be fighting it. It doesn't matter if peace reigns throughout the world; in the SEAL's mind it only takes a few critical minutes to harm America, as evidenced at Pearl Harbor in 1941. To SEALs this means much more than being ready to deploy at a moment's notice; it means the CO expects his crew to think and act independently to accomplish the mission. This was a dramatic departure from the highly structured world of the Marine Corps. In the teams, our ability to think and act as individuals was not only valued but expected, as long as it supported the team's mission.

I listened intently to everything he said and even asked a question or two to clarify a few points, but by the time he finished there was absolutely no doubt he lived and breathed physical, mental, and operational readiness, and expected me to do the same.

"One last thing," skipper said before dismissing me.

"Sir?"

"Don't think making it through BUD/S proves anything to anyone. All my men have done the same thing. You haven't demonstrated anything, yet. If you stay hungry you'll earn your spot here among my warriors. Ease off and you might find yourself leaving for the fleet." His calm, steady tone reinforced the strength of his words.

"Yes, sir, I know what's required of me, and I won't let the team down."

Skipper then stood up, firmly gripped my hand, and shook it. "That's the spirit, Doc. Welcome aboard."

Next stop was the command master chief's office. He was the senior ranking enlisted member, and he knew everything that happened within the team, and then some. Master Chief Ponson was a lean and fit SEAL with a slight French accent, decades of experience, and an obsession with skydiving. He welcomed me in his office, then promptly told me I was the only FNG, or "f***ing new guy," from my class assigned to the team. He explained how the navy purposely spreads new graduates across the force to keep the number of FNGs at each team fairly low. This maintains a high median experience level while allowing for one-on-one mentoring by the team's senior members, a key training element in the SEAL Teams. Master Chief launched into an oral history of Naval Special Warfare and the teams, then drilled down on the storied past of SEAL Team Two. I listened intently and took mental notes in case I was quizzed later. In just under two hours I had learned what the CO expected of me as a member of his crew and what the community expected from me now that I had officially become a member of the frog family.

"Donald, don't worry about the rest of the check-in process today. I want you to go find a place to live right now. That's your top priority. I don't care if you're staying with another SEAL, if you rent an apartment or buy a home. I want you out of the bachelor quarters by the end of the day, if at all possible." Master Chief went on to explain how life in the barracks can lead to trouble, and that certain segments of the military challenged "the SEAL" to fill a void in their manhood that was created by their lacking the courage to try to become one themselves. He went on, "There's plenty of opportunities for fighting, but the type you'll find in town is not the type you need to be doing."

Having always lived in a crowded home, the idea of having a place of my own was music to my ears. After speaking with Tony and a few of his teammates, I knew exactly where to look.

As I rose to leave, Master Chief gave me the plans for the following days' events. "Doc, Quarters is at 0700 every morning immediately followed by two hours of PT. Since you don't have your gear issue, it's probably best you just wear your dress whites again. I'll meet you on the quarterdeck at 0645 and introduce you to the boys then. Welcome aboard. It's great to have another corpsman. It's one of our biggest shortfalls in the teams."

"Thank you, Master Chief, I look forward to meeting everyone then," I said before hustling out the door.

The next morning I met Master Chief on the quarterdeck as instructed and followed him outside for morning muster. The team was gathered in the compound, ready for another fine navy day. I was the lone FNG walking among a herd of barrel-chested "been there, done that" frogmen. Master Chief had me stand off to the side where I couldn't hear his comments to the executive officer, but I certainly heard the laughter coming from the seasoned SEALs as we waited for Quarters to begin.

The leading petty officer called the team to attention. I looked over at Mater Chief Ponson, to see if he wanted me to stay put or jump into formation with the rest of them, but he kept staring straight ahead. Then I started to hear voices softly saying "meeeeeat, meeeeeeat," referring to my being the new meat on the team.

"Alright, that's enough, get into formation," Master Chief said to the crowd. The platoon chiefs immediately reacted to his orders and instantly turned the gaggle of team guys into a military formation. "Attention," Master Chief barked as the CO walked out to join his crew.

"At ease," said the skipper as he made his way to the center of the formation. The CO's message was quick and to the point, just like the day before when I'd met with him. This time, however, his speech was followed by an inauguration ritual.

"Skipper," Master Chief said, trying to conceal his smile under his mustache. "Remember, sir, we have a new man to introduce to the crew."

"Yes, you're right, Master Chief," he replied, acting as if he'd forgotten, although he certainly hadn't. "Carry on."

"Petty Officer Donald front and center," Master Chief said firmly.

Not knowing how formally Quarters was run in the SEAL Teams, I decided not to chance it, so I marched up to the elevated walkway, making sure I did proper facing movements along the way.

"Relax, Donald," the CO said under his breath before addressing the troops. "Petty Officer Donald is a BUD/S graduate and one of our new corpsmen."

"Wow, was it hard?" one of the voices yelled from the back, followed by "Hey Doc, why does it burn when I pee?"

Unfazed, the CO continued on. "Interestingly enough, Petty Officer Donald was a marine before he joined the navy." He hadn't even finished his sentence before jarhead jokes started among the group. I was beginning to feel like the skipper was waving a twenty-four-ounce steak in front of a pack of rabid dogs that hadn't eaten in weeks.

"Calm down . . . calm down," Master Chief said, laughing under his breath. It took a few seconds, but eventually everyone quieted down. We all stood there silent for a few moments. Master Chief then looked at me and said, "Well?"

"What, Master Chief?" I stammered, looking back at him. A voice from the crew yelled, "Tell us about yourself!" I glanced at Master Chief, unsure how to proceed.

"Well, Donald, are you going to tell us about yourself or not?" Master Chief asked.

"Uh, alright, Master Chief," I answered, trying to think about what to say. Apparently I wasn't thinking loud enough to hold off the comments coming in from the peanut gallery.

"It's not rocket science, meat, tell us about yourself."

"Where are you from?"

"Do you enjoy long walks on the beach?"

"Pipe up! We can't hear you in the back!"

Completely confused, I attempted to answer. "Well, I'm originally from . . ." was as far as I got before the whole crowd erupted with team guy shouts.

"Shut up!"

"No one wants to hear you, meat!"

And the more polite "Close your mouth, Donald!"

"Quiet down and let him speak," Master Chief answered back to the men while I stood there shocked, not sure which way to go.

"Please continue," Master Chief said with a nod.

I tried again, only the second I opened my mouth a virtual tidal wave of taunts and insults rolled over me like a tsunami.

"Shut the hell up, meat!"

This continued for a few more times, until I received the message loud and clear: As an FNG, I'd better keep my mouth shut and listen to what the salty team guys say—the SEAL equivalent of "Do not speak until spoken to."

Even the skipper enjoyed watching my attempts to be heard, and I'm sure he probably would've let it continue if it hadn't been cutting into PT time.

"Attention," Master Chief called out, bringing everyone back to the reality of the military so he could officially end Quarters. "Carry on," the skipper said before he entered the building with his officers in tow.

That wasn't too bad, I thought. *A little bit of yelling to reinforce my naïveté within the community and . . .*

Thud! I was suddenly on the deck and being stretched as if I were on some medieval torture rack while a few of my teammates taped my ankles and knees together. They then flipped me over to secure my hands behind my back as if I were wearing handcuffs. I knew where I was going, straight into the drink. At BUD/S every SEAL is taught how to survive in the water with our hands tightly bound behind our back and our feet strapped together. We call it "drownproofing," and successive repetitions of this drill and many others relieve any fear a student might have of water. This was just going to be the "same old, same old," only this time I was in my dress white uniform.

They finished the tape job and hoisted me overhead and carried me to the bay as if I were some rock star who'd dived from the stage into the crowd. Everyone seemed so happy with the idea of having me take an ocean swim, I couldn't help but laugh along, wondering if I'd ever find my shoes again.

"Welcome overboard, mate!" was the last thing I heard before my right side hit the cold Chesapeake Bay. Of course, with a uniform on I immediately began to sink to the bottom, but training kicked in. I bobbed right up like I had been taught at BUD/S. I then started dolphin swimming toward the boat ramp as my new friends looked on. It took several minutes to get there and then another five to worm my way onto the dry area of the ramp.

I was lying there catching my breath when one of the team guys came over to look at me.

"Glad to have you as part of the team, Doc," he said while he cut me free.

"Damn glad to be here," I answered back as I got to my feet and shook his hand. For the rest of the week, I endured nonstop teasing, taunting, and relentless pranks that often ended up with me in the bay fully dressed, but it was all part of being a team guy. I'd earned the chance to join a platoon by finishing BUD/S. To earn the trust and respect of my teammates, I had to embrace the initiation period and drive on with good humor, even when dripping wet in a dress uniform. More importantly, I had to perform as a warrior and medical provider and prove my worth by my actions and dedication to the mission and the team. I was up for the challenge and jumped in with both feet.

MY FIRST PLATOON

SEAL Teams are broken up into smaller operational platoons, and I had been assigned to one shortly after arriving in Virginia due to the shortage of SEAL-qualified corpsmen. My new platoon had just returned from a long deployment that took them across Europe and parts of Africa. There, they helped bolster the defense forces of our undeveloped allies, with hopes they would defend themselves against threats to their governments, thereby preventing the need for a U.S. military presence there in the future. They also spent time working with the renowned British Special Boat Service, or SBS, and other allied frogmen, concentrating on improving "interaction and coordination" between our countries. This would prove essential as America headed into the First Gulf War.

It didn't take long to realize their combined experience and knowledge was extraordinary. Later, I would be awed by their ability to remain tactically sound while navigating the politically sensitive waters of international relations. It wasn't too difficult to figure out where their maturity and sound judgment came from. Like the rest of the SEAL Teams, my platoon ranged in age from their midtwenties to midthirties, each man possessing a strong intellect and a high level of education. The officers graduated from some of the top engineering and science institutions in the country, and over a third of the enlisted crew had a college degree, making me one of the least-educated members among them. They were also fiercely loyal to one another, a tight-knit tribe that did nearly everything together, including the mentoring of one young SEAL corpsman.

Thad was a formable college wrestler and a natural teacher who happened to have a bachelor's degree in history. Despite qualifying for an officer's commission, he purposely joined the enlisted ranks as the most direct route to fulfilling his life's desire, to be a Navy SEAL. It was his calling in life, and he wasn't interested in delaying the opportunity by waiting for an officer billet. In the military that would have been quite unusual, but not in the teams. Enlisted SEALs operate and kick doors for their entire career, while an officer's time as a shooter is limited. Eventually rank will push an officer out of the team room and into an office. It may be an office in the middle of a jungle or on a forward operating base in a barren desert, but it's still an office. Officer candidates realize this, so when it comes time to apply for a commission many opt for the enlisted route instead. The officers that do enter the teams often opt for extended operational time versus a promotion in rank. My SEAL Team was no different from the rest of the force. Our guys had degrees ranging from philosophy to engineering to history. We even had foreign language majors that used their skills to seamlessly blend in with the local populace when needed. This broad range of skills, education, and experience was the foundation of plenty of spirited discussions on world affairs, sports rivalries, and, of course, practical jokes.

The months began to fly by when we started our workup, the training period used to prepare SEALs for an overseas deployment. During that time I worked hard to absorb everything I could as both a SEAL and a medic. Lucky for me I had a senior corpsman to teach me the ropes. I can't imagine trying to get acclimated to special operations medicine without his guidance. I remember the frustration I felt when I received my first aid bag. It was haphazardly stuffed with lifesaving equipment and common medications that had no place in a first aid bag. Some of the trauma gear was basic, and I had mastered its use in Hospital Corps school, but other items were way beyond my abilities, and it made me wonder why I was issued these things in the first place. I was unsure what I needed to carry or even where to place it inside the bag, so I laid everything out on a table in front of me.

"What the hell are you doing?" asked Scott, my senior corpsman, as he walked into the medical department.

"I'm trying to figure out what I'm going to need. SOT didn't teach me about any of this," I said dumbfounded as I lifted a thoracostomy tube and Heimlich chest drain. SOT stood for Special Operations Technician Course, an intense diving medicine course that all SEAL corpsmen attended after BUD/S. It was a good course, and I learned a great deal, but it only concentrated on the diagnosis and treatment of dive-related injuries and not the field trauma that special operations medics encounter during training or on the battlefield.

"Don't worry about any of that, you'll get introduced to it later. Just keep it simple for now. Stick with ABC's, but not necessarily in that order," he said as he laughed at the mess I had made. I knew he was alluding to the importance of controlling hemorrhage from a conversation we'd had the day before.

I picked up a couple of ancient battle dressings and tossed them to him as I sarcastically said, "What, these things?"

"Yep," he replied, not reacting to my mockery of the bag's contents.

"These bandages look like remnants from Iwo Jima. Four linen ties sewn to the back of a cotton bandage. Now, I get the whole 'if it ain't broke, don't fix it' thing, but come on . . . you'd think by now someone would have developed a better bandage."

"I'm not arguing with you. All I'm saying is stop your bitching and get your shit ready, otherwise you'll be here all day. Besides, these battle dressings aren't that bad. You can get them on fairly quickly, and they'll control some pretty heavy bleeding—but not the way you have them now. You need to prep the right way and place them in the bag where you can get to them within seconds," he said, demonstrating what I needed to do.

Scott stayed with me for nearly three hours helping to prep and pack my aid bag. We'd stop every few minutes so he could explain or demonstrate the proper use of an item, or justify why we were throwing it out.

"These Vietnam-era tourniquets are useless," Scott said. "Now, go over there and grab some extra cravats and I'll show you how to make a device that'll hold both in and out of the water."

Scott was right; I tried using one of the navy-issued Vietnam-era tourniquets to hold my dive med kit to the backboard when I was on the support boat during SOT. It worked at first, but once it got wet it failed miserably. I knew then there was no way this tourniquet would ever stay tight enough to control a major bleed, especially if we had to extract through the water, and that's exactly what we're taught to do. The water is our home, and while others look at it as an obstacle, we view it as an ally. If our equipment can't handle the extremes of sand and saltwater, carrying it is more trouble than it's worth.

Scott continued showing me the tricks of the trade, and I couldn't have been more appreciative. Back then, unlike our army counterparts, we didn't have a formal "combat trauma" training program, so the principles of battlefield medicine were passed down from SEAL corpsman to SEAL corpsman. Over the course of the workup, I spent a lot of time with him going over everything from trauma to snotology, a term I picked up for describing the branch of medicine that deals with the common cold and other low-level complaints. I knew at some point our platoon would be split in two and half of the men were going to be relying solely on me for care, so I took every available opportunity to see patients both with Scott and at the medical clinic in the middle of the compound.

The clinic offered new learning opportunities. There I joined with other SEAL corpsmen and a dedicated doctor and learned about orthopedic injuries, allergic reactions, emergency medicine, and, of course, the treatment of hangovers. If the military offers one thing to care providers, it's variety.

I had two very distinct duties in the teams: The first was to take care of the SEALs and the support personnel as medical provider, the job I was called to do. The second was to train up as a combat-ready shooter. It created a moral paradox that would follow me through my career. Eventually, I would receive the qualifications to prescribe meds, place chest tubes, and perform lab procedures, but I also shot, swam, jumped from planes, and blew things up. I worked hard to become a valuable member of the platoon, and over our workup period I earned the trust of the team guys both as corpsman and warrior. I would soon put that training and trust to good use in the Persian Gulf.

9

DESERT STORM

*For to win one hundred victories in one hundred battles is not
the acme of skill. To subdue the enemy without fighting is the acme of skill.*

—SUN TZU

I n August of 1990, Iraqi troops invaded Kuwait, and the United
States prepared for war. The UN Security Council brought eco-
nomic sanctions against Saddam Hussein, and President George
H. W. Bush deployed troops to Saudi Arabia under Operation Desert
Shield. Saddam was ordered out of Kuwait on a strict timeline, and
blockades were initiated to prevent Iraqi ships from ferrying cargo to
and from restricted areas. In response Big Navy sent a few carrier battle
groups into the region, and my platoon was assigned to one of them. It
would be my first deployment, and I was more than ready to implement
both the deadly skills I'd learned as a Navy SEAL and the lifesaving
procedures I'd been taught as a combat medic. Years of training, conditioning, and mental toughness would soon be tested, and I welcomed it.

The USS *Saratoga* had positioned itself off the Arabian coast with orders to prevent unauthorized passage of any ship that dared break the

blockade. We were just one of the many options on the table, but since our methods didn't require sinking or disabling a ship we quickly became the navy's preferred method of interdiction.

After landing on the "*Sara*" the platoon immediately began honing skills needed for the mission. Shipboard seizures are perilous at best; if everything goes right the enemy should never see us coming, and we may not have to fire a single shot. However, if just one or two things go awry the risks exponentially increase with each passing minute. Understanding the gravity of the situation, we'd split our time between ready room briefings on potential targets, shooting practice, and the all-important rehearsal. For weeks we practiced each phase of the mission, concentrating most of our time on shipboard movement until we were able to flow through a ship's infrastructure like a train. Soon everything was instinctual; a head nod, hand gesture, or stance would silently relay the next man's role as he approached a passageway or hatch. Timing was everything, but in order to take down a ship we had to be both fast and tactically sound, which meant daily rehearsals.

As we were jocking up for one of the training missions, Senior Chief informed us that we only had one bird (helicopter) available, so each squad would be inserting separately before regrouping on the deck to finish the drill. This suited us just fine as long as we had the ability to further refine our timing requirements for inserting onto a nonpermissive vessel. Insertion was one of the most vulnerable components related to shipboard assault, and we knew if the balloon went up (a spec ops euphemism meaning execute the mission), we'd only have a minute or two to get the team on deck before losing any element of surprise.

Much quicker than rappelling, fast-roping is ideal for minimizing the time a helicopter has to maintain its hover, but it's far more dangerous. First, the pilot has to quickly find the designated insertion point, then maintain a constant distance from the ship while crosswinds push him from his position and waves shift and possibly bob the ship. The SEAL, heavily laden with body armor, weapons, and other equipment, is only attached to the rope by his grip. Once he lands, he has to resist being propelled overboard by the wind generated from the rotor blades while simultaneously readying his weapon, which was previously secured to his back. All with the possibility of receiving incoming enemy fire.

Today my squad would be going first, so after Mike rigged the helo for fast-rope insertion we crowded into the plane and lifted off the *Sara*, heading out to sea. The pilot took us out for about five minutes before banking left and roaring the bird back toward the flight deck. Once the helo was in position we kicked the rope out, and in less than a minute everyone was on deck, dispersed with weapons at the ready. Tom, our officer in charge, nodded in approval as the bird landed for his squad's run. I watched as the squad loaded up, and within a few minutes the bird was back overhead. The ropes dropped to the deck with a thud immediately followed by the signal to exit the aircraft. Hector, the platoon's fearless Puerto Rican, was the first out the door, followed by Scott. Just as Scott grabbed the rope, the helo bucked and sent him down the line in an awkward position toward the steel deck below. Fast-roping is just that: fast. From the moment he exited the aircraft it didn't look good, and he had no time to recover. He hit with the full weight of his body sandwiching his ankle against the steel deck, snapping it like a branch of a falling tree. Scott tried to stand but collapsed on the deck and rolled out of the way before the next man on the rope landed on top of him.

Once the last man touched down I tried to rush forward with the shipboard medics and assist them getting Scott to sick bay, where we could better assess his injuries, but that wasn't my job. I had to remain with the team and finish the training op. In the SEAL Teams emphasis is placed on practicing in the same manner we are expected to perform. If there's a possibility a mission requires parachuting our boats into an extreme sea state in order to get in undetected, then by damn we'll be rehearsing in those same conditions. In Scott's case it was move him to a secure area for the medical evacuation and continue on with the op. Knowing the high possibility of injury or wounding on insertion, we developed contingencies for just such circumstances and had a response team standing by on the ship. They didn't have to fast-rope from a search-and-rescue bird; they simply ran across the flattop to render aid to Scott. It was their job; that's why they were standing by as we rehearsed. It was not mine, and despite an instinctual medic's urge to stay and help my friend, my place was with the squads moving forward. No deviations from SOPs—"practice the way you play!"

At the end of the training day we were all anxious to learn the extent of Scott's injuries, so immediately after debrief I headed down to sick bay while the rest of the group restaged our gear, or so I thought. I paid a quick visit to the ship's physicians in sick bay to get the official diagnosis, but as I walked out of the medical office I saw the platoon huddled around Scott in the treatment area, ribbing him about his fall's "lack of style points." They laughed loudly as Hector continually replayed the video from the ship's closed-circuit TV that had managed to capture the event. "I knew my ankle was fractured. I heard it pop when I hit," Scott said to the group, and he was right. The X-rays confirmed everyone's suspicions. His fractures were beyond the capability of the ship's medical department. Scott would need an orthopedic surgeon if he expected to remain a SEAL.

Just as the likelihood of real-world interdictions seemed eminent, my mentor would be heading home, leaving me as the only medic among the group, at least for the interim. Despite being an unseasoned SEAL and medic, I knew I was ready. As the junior corpsman, I ran all my squad's medical issues past Scott in order to prevent making a well-intentioned but naive mistake. Although Scott could be very direct, he wasn't controlling and took pride in his ability to train me in the particulars of battlefield medicine without stifling creativity. Some lessons were obviously necessary for a medic who operates in and around the ocean, like how to waterproof medical gear well enough to exit a submarine while at depth, or how to transport a casualty long distances through the brush, over the beach, and eventually out to sea. Others were more obscure but equally important, such as knowing how to balance the ethical and tactical requirements of being a special operations medic.

Most of these lessons couldn't be found in textbooks or explained on a chalkboard; they needed to be demonstrated to be understood and then practiced to acquire the craft. Combat trauma medicine is a triad of skill, art, and knowledge that requires being able to combine speed, dexterity, and ingenuity in a calm fashion that can only be gained through practical application, and I had received plenty. The same could be said regarding my operational capabilities. My platoon was loaded with experienced frogmen with every qualification in the book, each one of them willing to pass on his knowledge, and over the course of the workup I, like my fellow FNGs in the platoon, absorbed as much as I could. I knew the level of responsibility that lay on my shoulders and wasn't about to let any of them down.

As the United States continued lobbying the world for support, Iraqi-flagged vessels slowly positioned themselves outside of the notional "do not cross" line in the sea. With only days remaining before the UN vote on Resolution 678, giving coalition forces the authority to militarily take back Kuwait, they pulled up anchor and ran the blockade. Scramble Alpha was transmitted over the ships 1MC (the main circuit public address system), sending us into action. In less than fifteen minutes we were geared up and test-firing our weapons on our way to the flight deck.

The rules of engagement were extremely strict: Do not fire unless fired upon! There was no way to "positively" know who or what was on those ships, and America couldn't risk wrecking its newly formed alliance. We may have been designed to be killing machines, but unlike the ancient boarding parties who'd lay waste to both crew and passenger, SEALs are trained to be the most precise and discriminating weapon system in the navy's inventory, and we weren't about to let the country down.

I knew this wasn't going to be some simple search-and-seizure operation. If that were the case they would have sent sailors from one of the neighboring ships. The Iraqi captain had already shown complete disregard for authority by failing to yield to any of the countermeasures the navy was obligated to try on renegade vessels. Make no mistake about it; we would be facing a belligerent crew.

As wheels lifted off we officially received the word "go" and quickly moved into holding pattern until the last bird cleared the flight deck and indicated it was ready for the assault. The helos fell into formation as they approached the target and then descended one by one to a height just above the water's edge. The low and fast approach prevented the ship's crew or radar from detecting our assault until it was too late.

"Two minutes," the door gunner mouthed over the engine noise while holding up his fingers to emphasize his point. Simultaneously the air-crew chief slid the side door open and our cast master positioned the coiled rope next to the door's edge. As the cold wind started swirling through the airframe, I quickly rechecked every piece of my gear and made sure everything was still in place. This would be my first experience facing a hostile force, and I didn't want to take any chances. "Thirty seconds!" Through the open door I could see a sniper bird and the other squad's helo cutting away as we exchanged positions.

"Go!" My hands gripped the rope and I focused on the landing area below. When I hit the deck, I saw the other squad had set security and was waiting on us to start our movement forward. As the last man touched down and drew his weapon, the train began moving toward the bridge. Within minutes we secured the wheelhouse and started sweeping through the rest of the ship. Everything was going according to plan. Although some of the Iraqi crew heard us coming, they had little time to effectively react before finding themselves hog-tied and huddled in a holding area. The hard part was done; we had stopped the vessel dead in her tracks. Now all we needed to do was bring on the marines to provide enough manpower to finish searching the vessel.

I think every fighting man yearns to be in a position to impact the outcome of a battle or the history of his nation. I know I did, but I can only speculate whether it was Saddam's intention to goad America's navy into sinking a vessel or unnecessarily harming a crew member in hopes of gaining sympathy for his cause and a "no" vote on the UN resolution. That being said, I unequivocally believe that had we, or our SEAL brothers operating in the Persian Gulf, wounded or killed someone the Arab world perceived to be "innocent," the outcome of the Security Council's vote would have been different.

History tells us a single shot by a lunatic can be the flashpoint for starting a war, but what I discovered those days at sea was that the discretion of a professional warrior might avert battle altogether. Unfortunately, Saddam never could reciprocate this sensibility, and by mid-January America's Shield turned into a Storm.

It took less than forty-five days for American forces and our allies to overwhelm the Iraqi army. Our special operations brothers on land found the Iraqis to be largely compliant and apathetic about the fight. As for my fellow warriors, we felt somewhat disappointed. After years of training, months of buildup, and flawless execution, the enemy simply folded like a cheap card table, limiting my platoon's involvement to interdiction operations. Vietnam was twenty years in the past, and I had very little frame of reference for how war should look and feel. To me, war seemed easy; America had gone up against the third-largest army in the world and soundly defeated it. It would take nearly a decade before I found out how wrong I was.

———

I ended up spending a little over four years at SEAL Team Two, where I felt I had earned a master's degree in special operations warfighting from some of the world's best operators. I would take this expertise on to my next command and a whole new set of teammates. There, other skills would be added and refined, but not before a yearlong stop with the army at the renowned Special Forces Qualification Course—18D.

18 DELTA

Prior to attending 18 Delta the intricacies of battlefield medicine were passed down from one SEAL corpsman to the next, just as Scott had done with me. Although OJT (on-the-job training) was effective, it took an indeterminate amount of time to develop a corpsman and did not guarantee equal proficiency across the force. The army certainly didn't have this problem; Special Forces had developed the world's finest combat medical training program and continually updated it to stay in step with modern medicine. Not wanting to reinvent the wheel, Naval Special Warfare Command started negotiations to send all of its SEAL corpsmen through the program. Fortunately, by the time it was my turn to rotate from Team Two all the logistical details had been worked out, so I packed my bags for San Antonio, Texas, and a short tour with the army.

The medic course was broken into three segments. The first portion was held at Fort Sam Houston and included six months of painstaking didactic instruction covering everything from anatomy and physiology to zoonotic disorders. This was followed by two months of clinical training at some of the country's most remote medical treatment facilities. Each of these was carefully selected based on the medical staff's dedication to teaching the 18 Delta and its geographic location. The more isolated the hospital, the more credible a site. Being near the top of the class I had an early pick, so I chose one of the most removed areas in the Southwest run by one of the best medical providers in all of special operations.

Dr. Warner "Butch" Anderson started his career as a Special Forces medic before becoming a physician assistant and later MD. He'd held nearly every medical position in Special Forces, but you'd never know it. His humility and knack for conveying expertise without arrogance made him a favorite among medics and physician interns alike. Yet in spite of his calm demeanor, action always seemed to follow Butch, making him the preferred preceptor for students eager to put their newfound skills to work. It took all of five minutes before I was engulfed in his medical mojo.

It was my first day in the emergency room at the Gallup Indian Hospital, and Butch had just sat me down at the doctors' station to tell me that not everything I'd see or do would be exciting. "I've heard the rumors and I don't want you to think that every five minutes an emergency is going to burst through that door." He'd barely finished his sentence when a call came over the radio from the local ambulance company. They were bringing in a man who in a drunken stupor managed to tear his chest open by stepping in front of a moving train. With little time to prepare, I immediately threw on some surgical gloves and readied myself for the inevitable mess.

Minutes later the glass doors slid open and in rolled a man with a partial amputation of his upper and lower limbs, a lacerated chest exposing his lung, and a heart that was barely beating. Butch immediately grabbed my forearm and thrust my hand into the patient's chest. "Compressions" was all he said as he placed my hand on the heart. "Doc, I guess we'll finish the conversation about how mundane this place is a little later," I said as I tried to mimic the heart's contractions. Butch smiled, then went about directing the rest of the team and paramedics. Despite our best efforts we ended up losing the patient in OR, but what I learned was that even the most traumatic situations could be managed if a competent leader was at the helm, directing, not doing.

Over the next eight weeks I absorbed an enormous amount about the practical application of medicine from Butch and laid the foundation for a lifelong friendship before heading to Fort Bragg, North Carolina. There the class would finish the course with an intense three-month trauma module on frontline care. We weren't sure what we'd encounter, but we knew this final segment would piece together the education of Fort Sam Houston and skills we practiced during our hospital rotations with the realities of war.

Having worked with Army Special Forces in the past, I thought I knew them, but it took nearly a year working side by side to earn the Special Forces medic qualification before I really understood who these men were. Green Berets didn't enlist to be special operations; rather, they joined to be soldiers, each one proudly serving in the infantry, armor, artillery, intelligence, or combat support. However, somewhere along the way each one of them had a revelation that unconventional warfare was his true calling. Unlike BUD/S, where the average rank and age were indicative of men entering the service, Special Forces recruited from within the rank and file of the army, seeking only the most experienced soldiers, which is the key to their success.

Special Forces sergeants from Vietnam to Afghanistan have led company-sized forces against hardened enemies and won. They do it because they are "intellectual" warriors using judgment and reason to develop tactics foreign fighters can implement to win in battle. For them textbook maneuvers only work if the men they lead understand the textbook, so they are often forced to develop unconventional approaches to nearly everything they do. They certainly did when it came to the instruction of medicine, and all of special operations is better for it.

10

EVACUATION

★ ★ ★

Perseverance is more prevailing than violence; and many things which cannot be overcome when they are together, yield themselves up when taken little by little.

—PLUTARCH

After graduation I was assigned to a team tasked with training our allies in South and Central America, especially those battling internal threats such as rampant drug trafficking. I'd soon find out that was only a small portion of the adventure that lay ahead.

We arrived at Soto Cano Air Base in Honduras to help the regional authorities develop the necessary skills to deal with the troubles affecting the territory. We were there as advisers; the local troops handled the heavy lifting. Immediately after touching down, we received orders for our first operation. The mission would take half of the platoon to the shore of the Caribbean Sea, just within the borders of Honduras. We were dropped off by air and set up a base near an airfield that paralleled the sea. As usual, I set up a small clinic, used primarily for the treatment of my guys but also for the foreign troops serving with us. I would also treat the locals if supplies and time permitted. We were ahead of schedule for the first few days, so Dave, our officer in charge, gave us the morning off to enjoy the sun and water. While most of the platoon got up for a morning ocean swim, I opted for alone time at the other end of the compound. I snuck away and strung a hammock made out of parachute cord and jungle netting facing away from the others. I would have hung a DO NOT DISTURB sign had one been available.

For an hour, I enjoyed the rising sun while listening to local music on a small radio and thumbing through medical journals. Just as the sun rose above the eastern horizon, a hulking figure approached and blocked it out. The silhouette told me it was Smitty, a large SEAL who looked like a scruffy Mr. Clean, but with a bad disposition.

"What's up, Smitty?" I asked, assuming he wanted me to look at someone's sprain or perhaps a nasty jellyfish sting.

"A plane crashed about fifty meters off the shore," he said calmly, pointing to the area where it happened. "LT, Norris, Bucky, and some of the others swam out to the wreck and pulled the guys to shore. They sent me to find you and get you to the local clinic." Turns out while I was looking east the plane was coming in from the west and crashed about a half mile from my hammock. Once I stood up, I could see the twisted tail, wing, and landing gear poking straight up through the receding waves. In a few hours the tide would ebb, fully exposing the plane. Being curious about the extent of the damage, I made a mental note of its location as we ran to the truck.

I closed my door just as Smitty started to explain. Apparently the guys had just finished their morning swim when a low-flying plane hit the beach behind them, finally settling in about four feet of water. Five guys swam out to check if there were any survivors. LT and Jessie dispatched the others to get the rest of the operation in motion. With only swim trunks, fins, and a mask, they pulled the severely injured passengers from the wreckage and brought them to shore. Two others were sent to commandeer vehicles, and Smitty used one of them to find me.

As we reached the main road, another unfamiliar truck coming from the opposite direction screeched to a halt directly in front of ours. It was Norris, another teammate; he'd been sent to pick up every piece of medical equipment we'd brought on this trip.

"I got your bag, Doc," Norris shouted over the noise of the engine. "I can see that," I answered. "Just get in, we need to roll!"

Like Smitty, he was clad in nothing but a wet T-shirt, shorts, and sandals, but his appearance wasn't any indication of his adeptness with trauma. Norris understood the importance of the golden hour. He had taken a couple of rounds during Operation Just Cause nearly six years earlier and wasn't about to waste time looking for apparel when minutes were worth more than gold. Nor was it any surprise to me that he wanted to help in the treatment of these men. I've always found that those who come close to losing their lives have a zest for preserving others' in situations like these, and Norris was certainly among that group.

Smitty and I jumped into the vehicle just before he gunned it and tore off down the rocky road toward the clinic.

"One guy isn't too bad, a couple of broken legs and possibly some minor internal injuries, but the pilot has a cracked skull, broken ribs, broken leg."

"He's just real f***ed up, Doc," said Smitty, interrupting Norris.

"Exactly, what he said. Anyway, LT is with them at the local hospital. What a dump that place is," Norris said.

"Gents, I hate to tell you this, but I don't have the equipment to treat these types of injuries, and even if I did, there's a good chance they're way beyond what I could do for them anyway," I said, holding on for my life. The "road" was actually a glorified cattle path that ran through a city built on a series of hills, yet Norris was driving it like a NASCAR track.

"We thought about that. Bucky's getting an aircraft right now," Norris replied.

"What do you think he'll find?" Smitty asked. Norris smiled and shrugged.

I could tell from Smitty's voice that no one knew if he'd find any-thing or anyone to fly it, so I just kept quiet for the remaining minutes of the drive, hoping the procurement of an aircraft and pilot wouldn't lead to an international incident.

We arrived at the hospital moments later, and it was just as Norris had described; a primitive three-room concrete building intended as a family practice clinic. LT was on the scene, trying in vain to calm a pan-icked midwife nurse and assist an overwhelmed doctor unaccustomed to this level of trauma. The clinic was clearly used for treating stomach-aches and snotolgy, and his staff had zero experience with blunt trauma.

The aircraft passenger was stable, so I had Norris and the LT im-mobilize his legs with fracture splints while I did a quick assessment of the pilot's condition. It was obvious the local doctor wasn't familiar with treating the severe hemorrhage that generally accompanies scalp lacerations, but he did a great job controlling the bleeding from the pi-lot's linear skull fracture just the same. However, the pilot's airway and breathing were starting to go downhill fast. Blood from a large gash to his nose, cheek, and upper lip was pouring into the back of his throat, affecting his ability to breathe. LT had placed him partially on his side to facilitate drainage and keep his airway open, but there was simply too much blood pooling in his mouth. Eventually we'd need to pack the wounds to prevent further blood loss. After conferring with the doc-tor we agreed intubation, which is the placement of a flexible plastic tube into his windpipe, would be the only way to adequately maintain his airway while we worked to control his bleeding. I'd been taught endotracheal intubation at the army's Special Forces Medical Ser-geants Course and practiced the technique with the anesthesia depart-ment at Portsmouth Naval Hospital, so I wasn't too concerned about our performing the procedure. The big problem was a puncture in his chest. Although it was only a small hole, it was large enough to allow a slow stream of air to seep into the pleural space that separates the lung from the chest wall with each breath he took. Since there was no way for the air to escape once it entered, the built-up pressure would eventually cause the lungs to collapse upon themselves.

Thankfully, when they pulled him from the water someone cleverly tried to prevent air from entering into this space by securing three sides of a plastic 4" × 4" zip-lock bag over his chest wound. This makeshift device acted as an occlusive dressing and flutter valve, allowing air to escape but not enter. However, as he continued to slip into shock his skin became so cold, clammy, and wet that the rigger's tape (olive drab military duct tape) no longer stuck to his chest. Even if it had, it wouldn't have solved the problem. He'd eventually need a chest tube, so as the doctor and I placed the airway I asked LT to pull out the thoracostomy tube and Heimlich chest drain from my bag. Then, as I reached for the suction device, I noticed how grimy the clinic was and decided it might be best to try to relieve the pressure with a needle, at least until we had time to appropriately clean and anesthetize our patient.

"You going to chest tube him, Doc?" LT asked as he pulled the equipment out of the bag and Norris splinted his limbs.

"I might, but I don't think it's a good idea right now. This place is filthy, and I don't want to risk a serious infection getting into his chest cavity or making matters worse." I looked at the local doctor as I said it, hoping to get some direction, but he just continued to secure the newly intubated tube to the pilot's good cheek while the nurse began assisting the pilot to breathe with a bag-valve device. I don't know if the doctor didn't understand what I was saying or was simply avoiding responsibility. After all, we had no idea who these people were. Regardless, getting oxygen to the tissues was still the critical issue, and we hadn't yet seen the full effect of the new airway, so when Norris brought the portable O_2 unit in from the truck, I had him hook it to the reservoir on the bag-valve device while I prepared for a needle thoracostomy.

The pilot might have needed a chest tube; I just wasn't sure now was the right time or the place. I'd learned from Dr. Anderson, my physician preceptor during the 18 Delta course, that even the simplest procedures can become complicated in an austere environment, and just because a medic was trained to perform a procedure doesn't mean he needs to do it. The body is far more resilient than most people believe, and sometimes all it takes is a little bit of help for it to save itself, so before I started barreling on to the next procedure I thought I'd wait and see the effects of the direct flow of oxygen to the lungs.

The increased flow of oxygen provided some relief almost immediately, and by the way he was starting to improve I knew my decision to attempt to decompress the chest with a needle versus a tube was a sound one.

Although I had placed plenty of chest tubes during 18 Delta and assisted with a few on the hospital ward, I'd never done a needle decompression on a live patient, so I asked Norris and LT to listen closely while I inserted the needle. "I've been told if done properly we should have a whoosh of air and notice an immediate improvement in the patient's breathing," I told them, which was fairly close to what we got. Rarely does anything in medicine prove to be textbook by either definition or result, but in this case it came close enough to give us all some optimism about his outcome.

With his breathing steadily improving, I decided to move him to the runway. I still wasn't sure how we'd get him to a trauma surgeon, but for sure he wasn't going to get any better staying here.

As luck would have it, just as we began to package the patient for transport Bucky called over the radio that an aircraft had arrived from God knows where ready to take us to Tegucigalpa. Knowing I'd be traveling with limited supplies, I tried to secure the catheter portion (or plastic covering) of the needle I used to decompress the chest in place. My thought was to allow a continued outlet of pressure to prevent the problem before it occurred. I fabricated a one-way valve from the finger of a surgical glove, just as I'd been taught in school, to release the trapped air and secured it in place before we carried him out the door. Unfortunately, the rough ride to the airport managed to kink the catheter, rendering it useless. So much for utilizing classroom tricks in the field environment. Lesson learned!

The failure of the catheter meant I either needed to place the chest tube or keep an extremely close eye on his breathing during transport, as I might need to release the pressure again and again to keep his lung from collapsing.

As we neared the airport I caught a glimpse of the small, unpressurized two-seater plane idling on the runway, and it became obvious to me that I'd be battling the altitude as well as the patient's injuries on this flight. Increased elevation associated with a decrease in atmospheric pressure produces a number of medical concerns, most notably hypoxia (a term describing the lack of oxygen in the tissues) and, perhaps more worrisome considering his pneumothorax, the expansion of gas. The physiological aspects of either of these are life-threatening enough, but coupled together they're perilous.

One thing for sure, we needed to keep this flight as low to the ground as possible. Just going from sea level to the typically low altitude where a plane like that flies can expand trapped air by over 30 percent, which could be fatal.

I knew I needed to place a chest tube and prep the patient for air transport, but time was quickly running out. The plane was on limited fuel, and burning it on the tarmac while I performed a procedure wasn't an option; we would be taking off as soon as we reached the plane. That meant when the aircraft got to altitude the change in pressure would cause the air remaining between his lungs and chest wall to expand, requiring another decompression and constant monitoring of his airway. I had to make sure I was situated in a position to address these problems but would be unable to do much else.

"SEALs don't travel alone, swim buddy," Norris piped up as the truck hit the tarmac and headed toward the plane. "I'm going with you, Doc." I needed help managing these patients, so someone had to go with me, and among the operators Norris and the LT were the best medical folks in the platoon. LT certainly couldn't go; they needed his leadership here, and his ability to seamlessly switch from being the boss to assistant as he did in the medical clinic made me realize how fortunate I was to have Dave as my officer.

"Norris, LT will have to make the call, you know that," I yelled back at him as the wind hit my face. "Hey, he loves me. Face it, Doc, I'm your buddy," he said with a sarcastic smile and wink. Just as we stopped next to the plane LT got out of the other vehicle and started issuing orders while he assisted with prepping the patients for transport. "Bucky and Smitty, load the copilot into the passenger seat," he said as I threw my medical bags in the back of the plane. "Norris, you're going with Doc. You'll need to wedge yourselves and the pilot in the rear cargo hold. They'll need your weight in back of the aircraft." Norris looked at LT with an "I'll make it work" smile.

We loaded the patient in feet first and toward the rear of the aircraft in a manner that would allow us to account for possible increase of intracranial pressure from mechanical forces from the takeoff and landing. Then Norris jumped in, kneeling between the patient's legs. Finally I crawled in toward the front of the plane and straddled the patient at his waist. The noise, vibration, and low-level flying rendered the stethoscope and other monitoring devices nearly useless, and the plane's cabin was so tight it forced me to spend most of the trip bent at the knees and waist to make sure I'd be able to reach his chest and airway.

The flight was rough but mercifully shorter than I expected. I managed the patient from the waist up, while Norris took care of the lower limbs. He also insisted on goosing me every ten minutes, either to add some levity or piss me off. I never could figure out which, but I suspect it might have been a little bit of both.

We finally made it to the major medical center and turned the patients over to the hospital staff. When the dust settled, Norris and I were left standing in front of the hospital; he was dressed in shorts and T-shirt, and I was in camouflage bottoms and a T-shirt, both of us covered in blood. I thought about how much had happened so quickly and how resourceful everyone had become in an instant. Every man in the platoon contributed to saving those men's lives, and did so without orders from some command back home. They reacted instantly and performed brilliantly, and I was once again amazed at the unselfish heroes I had the honor to serve with.

This is exactly what the skipper meant when I first stepped aboard a SEAL Team. Other COs reiterated similar guidance, but it all amounted to the same thing. Accomplish the mission!

"Norris, I don't know if you realize this but I don't have a wallet, a radio, or a passport on me," I said.

"Neither do I," he said with a smile.

"You think they're sending a car to get us?"

"I hope not, Doc. There's a casino about ten minutes from here by foot, if my memory serves me, and I think I need to show it to you."

Like all other special operations warriors, SEALs are extremely de-tailed in their planning, but they're also the most resourceful men I've ever known when it comes to executing strategy. My CO had men-tioned this when I checked on board my first SEAL Team. He encour-aged his men to have an "out of the box" mindset but within the limits of guidance from above. His words really didn't click at first, but after a series of events similar to the plane crash in Honduras, I realized just how ingenious and dedicated these men could be.

11

METAMORPHOSIS

★ ★ ★

Life is a series of natural and spontaneous changes. Don't resist them;
that only creates sorrow. Let reality be reality. Let things flow naturally
forward in whatever way they like.

—LAO TZU

When I finally made it back from deployment, I began to understand the effect my job had on everyone else in my life. SEALs perform at an extremely high level. Our country expects it from us, and we expect it from ourselves. Maintaining a level of excellence requires constant practice and rehearsals in unfamiliar environments. That means travel, and a lot of it. Typically SEALs are on the road for 270 days a year. When not forward deployed on a mission, we're traveling around the country training for one. We train the way we fight, intensely and with dead-serious focus and dedication. Our scenarios can't be canned like large-scale military exercises that continually perform the same procedures year after year. That type of Big Military approach is unnecessary and inhibits our ability to accomplish the mission.

The teams, like other special operations units, are made up of a very small group of patriots that generally stay in the community for decades. There's no need to retrain new members or leadership on action plans, or how to coordinate assets or operational procedures; we live it every day. Even a simple day of just jumping out of airplanes will have a midlevel, enlisted SEAL synchronizing with other warfare elements normally done by a midgrade officer. Now multiply that five- or six-fold. One team is on the range practicing sniping, another utilizing our minisubs to dive on ships, and a third perfecting direct action assaults at an urban training facility. Somehow we're able to pull it off day after day while simultaneously developing and running full mission profiles on probable contingencies to ensure each team is ready for war. All the while, headquarters continues to run a multitude of real-world operations fighting the War on Terror.

If you want to know what a day is like in the SEAL Teams, that's it. Unfortunately, that type of lifestyle comes with long hours and brutal work conditions separating a SEAL from the ones he loves the most. During my first five years in the teams, wives and families were few and far between. The divorce rate was high, and many of the team guys chose to wait until they hung up their spurs before thinking about putting a ring on a finger, but I wasn't one of them. I married a hometown girl five years younger and tried to make it work. Although the love was there, the experience necessary to deal with the "team lifestyle" wasn't. Tamara was a beautiful and intelligent twenty-one-year-old, so she really had no way of knowing what she was walking into, and neither did I. I guess the mystique of being married to a SEAL was as appealing to her as she was pretty to me. However, relocating to a city two thousand miles away was a lot for any young couple, especially when one of them was away from home three-quarters of the year.

Having grown up Roman Catholic and witnessed Mom's dedication to my father, I didn't want to consider the word "divorce," so I started to look closely at the marriages that were able to survive. As with anything associated with Special Warfare, the best place to start is in the "goat locker," or chief's mess. I sat down with a few chiefs who had strong marriages and took mental notes during our conversations. I even spoke with their wives during team activities to get a feel for their personalities. In the end I found all the successful "team wives" were levelheaded, discriminating with circumstances, and capable of handling responsibilities they never thought they would have to when they took their vows. Of course, there was love and dedication, too. All the wives and the long-term girlfriends had that, but their wisdom was far beyond the confines of passion. If there were one word to describe the quality all those women possessed, it would be "maturity."

Bill was my platoon chief and one of the best SEALs we had. He had been a mentor for nearly every member of the team at one time or another, so when he called for a meeting it was usually something important.

"You wanted to see me, jefe?" I said. The team used interchangeably the Spanish word for chief or boss due to the work we were doing throughout Central and South America.

"Yea, Doc. Grab a seat," he said, sitting down on the corner of the couch. "Doc, you know the baby you helped to deliver on your last trip down south?" He was alluding to a young Peace Corps volunteer who became pregnant by a local and decided to stay to personally continue her work despite losing her spouse.

"Yes, but babies really deliver themselves, so I'm not sure how much of a help I was. Why, is something wrong?" I asked, concerned about her and the child's health. Rumor had it her husband was accidently killed by criminals or the cartel, simply because he was in the wrong place at the wrong time, and I dreaded the idea of something similar happening to them.

"Turns out the skipper received a phone call from the CNO [the chief of naval operations, or head of the navy] about what happened out there," he said as he put a dip of chewing tobacco between his lower lip and gum.

"I hope it was good news." I was still unsure where this was going.

"I guess so. Seems Admiral Boorda has written a letter of appreciation to you, and the skipper is going to present it at Quarters on Friday."

CHIEF OF NAVAL OPERATIONS

22 February ▮▮▮

Dear Petty Officer Donald,

▮▮▮ I just received a very nice letter from ▮▮▮▮▮ ▮▮▮▮ expressing her gratitude for your assistance in delivering her daughter in Honduras.

Nothing pleases me more than hearing about a Sailor who has gone out of his way to help someone in need. Your assistance to Ms. ▮▮▮ is an outstanding example of how compassion and commitment can make a difference. Thank you for caring enough to go the extra mile, and rest assured that ▮▮▮▮▮▮▮▮ will never forget your efforts. Well done, and keep up the great work!

All the best,

BZ!

J. M. BOORDA
Admiral, U.S. Navy

HM1 Mark L. Donald, U.S. Navy
SEAL TEAM ▮▮▮
▮▮▮▮▮▮▮▮▮▮

Copy to:
BUMED
COMNAVSPECWARCOM
▮▮▮▮▮▮▮▮

"So it is good news?"

"Yep," he answered, then paused long enough to deposit some spit into an empty soda bottle. "But that's not why I want to speak with you."

OK, now I was really curious. What on God's green earth could this all be about?

"Doc, you've been doing a lot of talking to me and some of the other mugs about how we manage to hold together our marriages. I also know yours isn't as strong as it once was, and we both know this job isn't going to make it any easier to repair." I reminded myself to try to keep an open mind. "So I've been thinking. You always have your nose in a medical book, and when we're in town you spend just as much time at Group Medical working with Revaz as you do here."

Everything he said was right. Revaz and I had been working for Master Chief Cavolt, the SEAL corpsman in charge of Special Warfare's East Coast medical assets, on updating our authorized medical loadout for deployment, which had begun to take up a lot of time.

"I may not understand it all, but I know what you're doing is a good thing for all the force, so I want you to hear me out on this." Chief reminded me of the story I had told him about wanting to be a corpsman. Then he explained there were two types of medics in the teams, those who chose the corpsman rating and those who were assigned it. "Doc, you love medicine and you're good at it! You can't kick doors forever, but you can make a career taking care of those who do."

He looked me in the eye and said, "I know you've mentioned the idea of becoming a PA [physician assistant] to Norris, and you've started taking college courses to qualify for a commissioning program. What I'm saying is, you need to think about what's in your heart, and what's best for you and your family."

I wasn't sure what to say; a meeting that started out unclear turned into "Atta boy" and now was ending with "You need to reevaluate your priorities."

"Kevin Charles will be putting in a package for PA school later this year. I think you need to give him a call. Think hard on it, Doc. Now get outta here," he said with a smile as he returned to the papers on his desk.

On the drive home I thought about a conversation I had at the parish when I was a boy learning how to deal with all the troubles going on at home, and the cover-up that came with them. Following Mass, Mom gave me some time to meet with my favorite priest. Father Fangler listened to my problems for over an hour before finally answering my question with a question. "Marcos," as he used to call me, "you've told me you prayed, but have you been listening for God's answer?" Being a young kid, I wasn't sure how to respond. I thought to myself, *Did I fall asleep or miss this class in Catechism?* Then he went on to explain that the Lord's answer can be given a number of ways.

"When you hear a verse on the radio that suddenly wakes you from a daze to answer your question, who is stirring your thoughts? When a sentence in a book or writing on a billboard jumps out at you to answer your prayer, what is that saying? When someone answers the question you have put before God during a conversation that has nothing to do with your problem, which you never spoke about, who is actually speaking to you? Marcos, that might be God talking. We all pray. Even those with little faith pray to heaven for guidance. The question is, are you listening?"

I had been praying for an answer on how to deal with our marriage problems, especially with a child on the way. What the chief was saying hopefully would not only help my marriage but also help solve an internal conflict I had been wrestling with since I returned from a trip to areas bordering the Caribbean Sea.

It wasn't the typical SEAL operation. Instead, I was fortunate enough to join my army counterparts in Special Forces on some civic actions assisting people in villages suffering from the drug trade. Outside of the obvious poverty, it was impossible to tell there were any problems, let alone criminal activity going on, but that's how we knew the intel reports were accurate. When impoverished neighborhoods are without crime, generally that means a criminal element has taken control. However, intel was not my focus on that trip. My job was to work with the other health care professionals to provide aid for the downtrodden.

I knew the work we were doing was just scratching the surface, but we made a difference. The people were so thankful for our help, and I was immediately reminded of a powerful statement a marine captain shared with me while we were on a training mission together in California. The captain told me he had served as an enlisted sailor in the Coast Guard prior to attending school and becoming a marine officer. He spoke fondly of the rescues he participated in, and I could tell it meant a lot to him. Being naive, I jokingly asked him if he regretted his decision to leave the Coast Guard. He answered, "Yes, I do . . . I found saving lives is far more rewarding than taking them." I never wrote down the captain's name, and have long since forgotten it, but his words always stayed in the back of my mind, and now they came forward again.

I thoroughly enjoyed my time in the teams and couldn't imagine taking care of better people, but ironically, I had to leave in order to do just that. It would be a big change in my life, but I knew I had to at least give it a try.

I firmly believe change is life's biggest fear, and the more drastic the change, the greater the fear. I know men in special operations that would easily charge into a room full of enemy without hesitation, knowing their chance of survival was slim at best. Yet they would try with all their might to stay at the same command throughout their career. Some do this because it is the essence of who they are. However, others try to stay because they have become comfortable and fearful of what change will bring.

I know how fearful change can be. I went through it in the Marine Corps. I gave up a promising career that allowed me to attain more qualifications in two and a half years than most marines obtain throughout their entire career. I walked away from all my rank and a choice of orders for the opportunity to get a job I knew very little about. Now, a little over twelve years later, I found myself at the same crossroads making another monumental life-changing decision.

———

No use denying it—I had ambitions that were going to take me away from Naval Special Warfare, for the short term at least. Most importantly, I wanted to be a good father and husband. That meant no longer allowing myself to be whisked away across the globe solely because of world events or training opportunities. I might have had the self-discipline to become a SEAL, but I lacked any ability to control my selfish desires to operate rather than to accept orders to a shore command. Since my arrival I had remained in a deploying billet, jumping from one platoon to another, and with SEAL corpsmen in constant demand I wasn't about to let that change. Now I was at another crossroads, though, and I knew I had to make a hard commitment to my family by putting myself in a job that would reverse the operational tempo I had been living for over a decade. I needed something that would allow me to be at home nine months out of the year but still train to deploy in support of our country should my services be needed. It also meant I needed to find an occupation that not only fulfilled my desire for a higher level of medical practice but kept me in contact with the sailors and ground pounders that did the job the military was built to support. As always, jefe's advice was solid, so I picked up the phone and gave Kevin a call.

Kevin had taken an instructor billet at the army's famed Special Forces Medical Sergeants Course I had just left a couple of years before. The job of an 18 Delta is like that of no other enlisted provider in the military. A Special Forces medic must stay razor sharp on his trauma skills, be constantly ready for action when the bullets start to fly, and be capable of establishing trust with the local populace through medicine. This means addressing a village's health and veterinary issues, just as I experienced working in the jungles of Central and South America. When I attended the sixty-two-week medical training pipeline, it gave me a glimpse of the grueling nature of the job. These men were truly the experts at unconventional medicine, and Kevin was stationed there

training future medics as part of an integration program special operations began when SEAL corpsmen started to attend the course.

That evening I dialed Kevin's number at the schoolhouse, and he
picked up after two rings. We caught up on small talk and then cut
right to the chase.

"Kevin, rumor has it that you're thinking about becoming a physician assistant," I said, the application to PA school spread out in front
of me on the kitchen table.

"Yeah, I just got word I was picked up by the program."

"Congratulations. Do you think you made the right choice?" Kevin
was another one of those SEAL corpsmen that went out of his way to
get a corpsman rating.

"Well, after being here a while and getting back into medicine, I
just thought it was about time to move on. Why? You getting the itch,
too?" he asked.

"Giving it some serious thought, but just looking at the application
process is killing me."

"Don't spend too much time on that. I'll send you a copy of mine to
use as a 'go by.' I got it off Jessie, who did the same from Conrad Kress."

"Kress—that guy was evil as a BUD/S instructor," I said, remembering his torturous runs and stone stare that made everyone wonder
what was coming next.

"Yeah, he was, but he was just doing his job. Once you get to know
him as a team guy you'll probably end up being tight."

Kevin listened as I unpacked my degree track, and he told me which
credits I still needed, and I realized I was still a couple of years away.
After discussing it with my wife and watching her give birth to our
daughter, Tabetha, it was easy to decide what had to happen next. I'd
move into the position of leading petty officer for a SEAL platoon before returning for a tour in the medical department. It would be a long,
painful road blending academics with operating, but I'd have to make it
work.

While the teams never like to lose a frog, whether to battle, separation, retirement, or career change, the skipper did everything he could when I returned home from Panama to ensure I was able to take the remaining college courses and submit an extremely strong package. After thirteen years in special operations, I received orders to the Interservice Physician Assistant Program and returned to Fort Sam Houston, Texas.

PA SCHOOL

San Antonio seemed to be the perfect place to start a new life with my wife and daughter, what with its rich Hispanic culture and heritage. Tamara and I had been here before when we were dating and I was attending the first portion of 18 Delta, but now we would be returning as husband and wife. However, just like 18 Delta, the physician assistant program hits hard and fast. It's akin to academically drinking water out of a fire hose. It took sixty semester hours of specified college credits to even apply for a selection process that would rival most Ivy League entrance requirements. Hundreds of candidates apply each year from all the military services, including Public Health. All try to become one of the few students who'll spend nearly every waking moment working on converting their credits into a master's degree in only two years' time. The military takes the program very seriously. These men and women will act as the primary medical providers for our service members and their families at every location imaginable. You'll find PAs everywhere, from base health clinics to forward operating bases to combat surgical hospitals. A very small number of PAs serve with special operations.

The navy takes particular pride in the profession since the founder of the physician assistant career field, Dr. Eugene Stead, assembled the very first PA graduating class from a group of former navy corpsmen. Against the odds, Dr. Stead convinced his colleagues that corpsmen who'd received considerable medical training over their career, including the Vietnam War, could help meet manning requirements of primary care physicians by extending each doctor's reach through the use of competent assistants. Duke University agreed and allowed him to develop a curriculum based on the fast-track physician training programs used during the Second World War. In 1965 they graduated that first class, and ever since PAs have been practicing in nearly every facet of medicine.

I quickly adapted to the pace of PA school. The only trouble was holding my marriage together while getting through eighteen hundred hours of classroom and laboratory time within the first sixteen months of school. In the beginning Tamara and I both agreed that completing the program would afford us the best opportunity for our family to succeed, but really the classroom replaced the "team room" so little changed regarding the amount of time I had to spend with my family. After waking each day at the crack of dawn, I had to either work out or find some last-minute study time before a make-or-break test. Then I would go to class for the day, come home for dinner, and then head out to the library or study group. It wasn't at all what Tamara had expected. Needless to say things continued to sour so she packed up Tabetha and visited New Mexico trying to sort everything out while I finished the program. They came back for my graduation, and I thought we could rebuild the marriage now that the didactic portion of the program was over. Sadly, the emotional distance between us was too great for anything more than friendship.

12

TEAMMATE, MENTOR, FRIEND

*There is nothing like returning to a place that remains unchanged
to find the ways in which you yourself have altered.*

—NELSON MANDELA

Once I finished up the classroom requirements at Fort Sam Houston, we packed up our belongings and headed for my next stop, Naval Medical Center San Diego. Surprisingly, I found myself checking in at the exact building where I'd reported as an undesignated sailor for Hospital Corpsman School. Only this time no one was questioning my warfare qualifications. For the next year I would undergo all the same clinical rotations a general practitioner serving the fleet would require, not to mention monthly exams and presentations to my colleagues and journal club. I was becoming a regular academic and hoped I would feel equally as comfortable as a midlevel medical provider. In fact, that was the easy part.

No matter how successful I was in medicine, I had already failed in my mission to salvage my marriage. Soon after arriving in San Diego, we filed for divorce. It didn't matter that I knew it was coming or that it was something we both agreed upon. It didn't matter that we still cared for one another as individuals and tried to be understanding of each other's circumstances. It's still extremely painful when two people realize the dreams they once shared will never materialize.

All that would pale in comparison to being separated from my daughter. Going from holding my flesh and blood each day to not having her anywhere near me was the most painful experience in my life. I might have only had a few moments with her each day, but they were the most valuable moments in my life. Often when I would come in late from the library, study group, or hospital wards, I would go to her room just to sit and watch her sleep. Now I would have to make a twenty-six-hour round-trip to a small town outside of Albuquerque to see my little girl. I would have much rather flown than make that drive, but every penny we had was spent on bills we accumulated by either trying to save our marriage, relocating Tamara back home, or paying lawyers' fees—leaving both of us penniless. By the time it was all over, Tamara had to move in with her mother, and I barely had enough money for gas and food.

I lived close to work at Balboa in sunny San Diego and rode my bike in each day. The money saved paid the bills and covered the gas I would use traveling back and forth to New Mexico. The drives were brutal, after spending a forty-to-sixty-hour week on the hospital wards or clinics, depending on the rotation I was on. I would jump into my car and drive thirteen hours to Tamara's mother's home. Time was limited, so if traffic allowed me to get there earlier than expected, I would pull over and catch a thirty-minute catnap in the car before washing up at a local gas station. Then I would pick Tabetha up by 8:00 A.M. From there it was a drive into the city to stay with Diana or Mom, depending on how Cassandra's mental condition was at the time. It really didn't matter where we stayed. All I knew was that for the next thirty-two hours, I was going to be with my little girl.

Returning to San Diego was always even harder due to the anxiety that generally accompanies morning traffic on the California freeways. Yet somehow I always seemed to make it back to the hospital with enough time to shave and throw on my lab coat before morning rounds.

This chaotic routine took a lot out of me, and it was starting to show in my grades, but that didn't matter as much to me as the idea of having my daughter grow up without knowing her father. Every time I'd hit that long stretch through the Arizona desert, I'd tell myself that any man can be a father, but you have to work hard to be a dad.

Still, all my time in the teams, from BUD/S to Central America, couldn't change the fact that there were only so many hours in a day. Whether I liked it or not, I had to limit my trips to twice a month and every three-day holiday when I wasn't on call. I'd like to say that it was solely my love and devotion for my daughter that enabled me to keep this tempo up for more than half a year while I recovered from financial ruin, but truth be told, there's no way I could have accomplished any of this without some very close friends. Although our jobs never really allowed us to spend time together as a group, I would refer to them as my "fire team."

Derrick Van Orden was a young tadpole when I first met him coming out of BUD/S; I had the honor of mentoring his work, and that of other young SEALs, which would eventually dwarf anything I ever accomplished. Out of all the things he and the others were able to achieve, there was only one thing that I envied—Derrick's role as a husband and father. From the first day I met Derrick and Sara, I knew they had everything prioritized. After arriving in San Diego, I would escape to their home at every possible opportunity. Sara would feed me while Derrick and I caught up on everything going on in the teams. She'd then send me home with meals and groceries I couldn't afford. What I enjoyed the most was spending time with their kids. That family taught me what I needed to do in order to be Dad, and it made me never want to leave. Eventually, though, I had to get back to the time-intensive world of medicine, and with Derrick's operational tempo in the teams, and Sara managing four kids ranging from high school to elementary, anything more than a weekly visit was impractical. That's where Jim, Jerry, and Pat took over.

Jim Elliott was a reserved, fit, and clean-cut doctor who was going through his intern year at Balboa. We first met during one of my first hospital rotations and immediately hit it off. Even though I tried to hide how precarious my situation was, he was able to figure it out by piecing together my activities.

"Hey, let's go to lunch while we have the chance. You know things here can get crazy quick," Jim said one afternoon, making a joke about our current rotation on the psychiatric ward.

"Go ahead, brother. I'm not hungry. Besides, I could use the time to study."

"Nah, come on, it'll be quick, and I'll treat. I'm not going without you, and I'm starving," he said in a friendly but persistent tone.

As we walked to the sandwich shop on the hospital grounds, we casually talked about his alma mater's loss in the Sugar Bowl. We grabbed a couple of hoagies and went outside to eat under the California sun.

"Mark, we've talked about my divorce, so you know I have some understanding of what it's like to be separated from your kids," Jim said, alluding to being apart from his son and daughter. "But I also know you're broke. I see how you make the drug rep's coffee and bagels every morning, and how you try to attend each of the sponsored luncheons, too."

I kept listening despite my throat going dry as he went through a litany of circumstantial evidence. "Look, you don't have to go at this alone. No matter what you say, you're taking this," he said as he inconspicuously slid a folded stack of bills under my hand.

I wasn't sure how to respond until I remembered what my mom told me years earlier. *People want to help, mijo. You just have to let them know how.* Suddenly my eyes were tearing up as I stared off into the distance. "OK, but what I really need is help getting my mind off all of this. I can't seem to concentrate right now, and if I fall too far behind I'll never catch up."

"Keep it, we'll do both."

The rest of the year, Jim never left my side, and a couple of rotations later we picked up an ENT (ear, nose, and throat) resident named Jerry Castro and a classmate of mine named Pat Hare. Between all of them, I always had a place to stay, food in my belly, and my mind focused on school and my baby girl. None of them ever asked for anything or gave anyone even a hint about what was going on. I might have been away from Special Warfare, but with my family and friends, I was never without a team.

Following graduation from PA school, my classmates and I shipped to Officer Candidate School in Newport, Rhode Island, the final step to becoming commissioned medical officers. After twelve weeks of instruction, we were commissioned as ensigns in the United States Navy. Prior to that, we were merely officer candidates, which meant we wore the uniform but had no authority whatsoever. I always marveled at the strange looks I would receive when seasoned sailors stared at the rank on our collars, trying to figure out whether they needed to salute or not. Those days were over. As newly minted ensigns in the Medical Service Corps, we were excited to report to our very first medical clinic for duty.

Navy PAs follow the same general path, unless there are extenuating circumstances. They cement their newly acquired skills at a primary care clinic and eventually receive orders to an expeditionary command. I looked at it as navy medicine's way of ensuring each of us completed a workup before pushing forward to practice medicine in some of the more challenging environments.

My assignment was to the Branch Medical Clinic at Naval Amphibious Base Coronado, my old home as a BUD/S candidate. At Coronado, I worked under two of the best PAs in our community, one being a frogman like me.

Dave Holder was a straight shooter who served as a corpsman for several years before becoming a physician assistant. He excelled in the job and eventually took over as officer in charge of a clinic that served the Navy's amphibian forces inhabiting Southern California. His cohort in crime was another ambitious PA named Jessie Gross, a former SEAL corpsman who served with the West Coast SEAL Teams. His early career took him all across the South Pacific, and it was several years before he decided on making medicine his primary occupation. As a medical officer assigned to BUD/S, he spent countless hours with the orthopedic department at Balboa and eventually became one of the navy's top experts in sports medicine before moving on to be Dave's right-hand man.

I checked aboard the clinic early one Monday morning, anxious to get started. My first stop of the day was a meeting with Dave and Jessie in Dave's office.

After a few minutes of small talk, Dave dove right in. "Mark, you've accomplished a great deal with the SEAL Teams, but unfortunately none of that matters too much with navy medicine." I had a feeling this was going to be the tone of the conversation.

"Don't take it wrong, Mark," Jessie continued. "As a new PA, you need to continually build your medical knowledge, and to be competitive that means completing a specialty, and that means an advanced degree." Both men smiled as I absorbed the news.

Great, more school, just what I needed. I knew they were right, though. If I was going to succeed as a Medical Service Corps officer, I needed to complete a master's degree in a specialty that was useful to the navy. "I'm tracking; the best PAs have graduate degrees, but am I going to have the time to pursue one?" I asked.

"We'll work that out for you. Do you have any preferences for a specialty?" Dave asked.

"I think I would like to try something new. I've had plenty of trauma and emergency medicine in my career, but nothing really jumps out at me right now."

"Fair enough. We'll get you some face time with the different departments and see what lights your fire," said Jessie.

The mentoring session went on for over an hour as they laid out the plans for my new job and educational pursuits. Both Dave and Jessie would pick up some of my patient caseload, allowing me to split time between the clinic and the hospital. This would ensure I had an opportunity to obtain a specialty. We talked about everything from ENT to orthopedics and eventually wrapped the meeting around lunchtime, allowing me to finish the check-in process. The following day, they sent me off to the hospital to meet with the different departments, to see if a particular specialty would spark my passion and interest.

Navy physicians are generally very supportive of medical providers furthering their academic and professional development, especially those with years of experience. Early in my career I worked with Dr. Larry Garsha at the SEAL compound in Virginia. Dr. Garsha was one of the most encouraging doctors I ever met. In addition to being a Navy Undersea Medicine doctor trained in nuclear and diving medicine, he held board certifications in internal medicine, neurology, and psychiatry. His real specialties, however, were humility and inspiration. Unlike the occasional doctor who'd spend his time at an expeditionary command trying to convince himself and those around him that he was a steely-eyed warfighter, Larry embraced his role as a supporting cast member and mentor to young corpsmen. From the moment I met him he had the "what can I do for you" attitude, and it was his influence and mentorship that steered me exactly where I needed to go.

Frank Carlson ran the medicine department at Balboa Hospital. He was a senior provider who enjoyed fine dining, wine, and complex medicine. We had met years before, when I was a young student rotating through his department. Back then we would talk about overseas deployments and two areas in operational medicine that intrigued me the most: infectious disease and chemical warfare. I was still fascinated by both, and in order to master those particular areas, I needed to build a strong foundation. That morning, I sat with Frank and pleaded my case to specialize in internal medicine. The consummate teacher, he arranged for me to join the staff on alternating days between the Medicine Clinic and the Branch Clinic with Dave and Jessie. Once again, I was encouraged to succeed by a caring expert who simply wanted to help a young medical provider master his craft. Four hours into the second day, I had chosen my specialty.

Later that day, I returned to Coronado and met with Jessie and Dave.

"You've got to be kidding me, Mark! A flea!" Jessie said. "You're going to be a flea." The term is jokingly used around hospitals to describe internists. The idea is that fleas travel in packs and are always the last ones to leave the body, but I only found the first part to be true. Internal medicine is a humbling practice due to the complexities of the patients these doctors manage day in and day out. The constant consultation with their colleagues only reinforces their devotion to providing the best care possible, so the term "flea" never bothered me. In fact, I kind of embraced it.

"Yep, I'm going to work toward being a flea. At least for the interim. Who knows what could happen next?"

I plowed into my studies at the same pace at which I attacked PA school and completed a majority of my academic requirements in six months, leaving just under a year on the wards to finish my clinical time. I was really looking forward to a break and promised myself no academics for at least two years—but I've never done very well living within the confines of absolutes.

PA INSTRUCTOR

One morning I was packing my gear and heading out to spend the second half of the day at the hospital. Jessie knocked and stuck his head in the door. "Mark, can I see you for a second?"

"Sure, come on in. What's up?"

Jessie entered and closed the door behind him. "As you know, Dave's leaving, and as it turns out, I'll be taking over the clinic." I interrupted him with well-deserved congratulations and a few humorous comments about the great crew we had working there, but he held up a hand, stifling a laugh.

"Yes, I know, the crew is awesome and you're the king of awesomeness. Now let me continue so you can get out of here. I need a primary preceptor for the PA students rotating through family medicine here at the clinic, and you're my number-one choice. It shouldn't be too much of a workload since you already help teach at the clinic and the internal medicine department. I simply won't have time with all of my new duties." Jessie crossed his arms and leaned back on the door frame while I absorbed the request.

My gut reaction was to stick with my promise: no academics. However, I always learned a great deal about a subject when I taught it to others, and I really enjoyed teaching medicine; it gave me a chance to give back in a way that would make Mom proud. Besides, I owed it to both Jessie and Dave, two committed medical officers who worked hard to build the program and took special efforts to ensure my success.

"If I say yes, can I have Fridays off?" I smiled.

"Hell no, but I'll give you one Friday a month so you can attend the student presentations at the schoolhouse."

"Well, that's better than nothing. I'll do it." We shook hands roughly, the team guy way.

"I knew you would. Thanks, Mark. Now get out of here." He slapped my back as I headed off to the hospital, a newly minted instructor.

I had no idea how profoundly the teaching position would change my life.

KORRINA

Six months into the teaching assignment, my instructor duties had been expanded and I'd been reassigned to a brand-new medical clinic at Marine Corps Air Station Miramar. Despite my new location, I continued to divide my time between the clinic and the hospital and greatly enjoyed the duty. Each student had his or her own personality, and I marveled at how each one's passion for medicine and personal character would positively impact navy medicine. It was also the time I met my future wife.

Korrina was a beautiful and incredibly smart woman and single parent who was juggling the pressures of PA school while dealing with the stress of being separated from her child. She had split amicably with her husband years before and felt it best that her son stay with him while she focused on PA school. It seemed reasonable at the time, but the guilt was a major distraction and added to the difficulty of an already brutal academic course. Her only consolation was that her ex-husband was a good father and empathetic to her struggles. Following the divorce, she found herself in an abusive relationship, and the breakup that ensued only further complicated her already stressful life, but no one would have been the wiser. Korrina's grades were always at the top of the class, and her ability to reach her patients was remarkable. She was a survivor in every sense of the word, yet she still couldn't shake the weight she carried upon her shoulders; instead she reverted to doing what she knew best, and that was how to shield others. Over the weeks that we worked together we'd share stories about the difficulties of being a parent away from your child and began building a bond based on mutual empathy. Months later she graduated PA school, and while her class awaited orders to their first command, we began to date.

I read somewhere that "true love comes quietly, without banners or flashing lights," and that was certainly the case for Korrina and me.

What started out as a simple friendship quickly grew into a trusting relationship that had us spending countless hours talking about the struggles we shared being military parents separated from our children. I learned how devoted she was as a parent, which in turn made me a better one, too. I also learned how to listen to what she was really trying to say, and I began to realize how much I adored this woman.

For the first time in my life, I felt truly complete. My career was on the fast track; I had recovered from my financial difficulties and had found someone who loved and wanted me as much as I did her. Yet she had pending orders to Virginia, and we knew our lives would once again change. Rather than break up, we believed we could survive the distance if for no other reason than because neither one needed anything from the other. Our relationship was based on our desire to be together as friends, then lovers, so a mutual trust existed like never before. Years later, I would ask Korrina to marry me, and when I told my mother of our engagement she answered with her typical words of wisdom. "Marky, I am glad you are marrying someone you like. Fondness is much stronger than passion. You'll find as you go through your lives together, love, like memories, will continually fade and resurface, but your friendship will be the one constant that will hold the marriage together."

9/11

I have always been an early riser due to the military lifestyle. I'd rise at 0500 in order to get a run in by the navy's 0700 start. In September 2001, I lived a short six blocks from Balboa Park and had access to some of the best running trails in the city. I took full advantage of all of them, including on the Tuesday that changed the world as we knew it.

I returned from my morning run and opened the living room curtains and gazed out toward the San Diego airport and the bay just south of it. I followed my morning routine of calisthenics and postrun stretch while watching the morning shows, primarily for traffic and news. I was scheduled at the hospital and planned to take a leisurely bike ride through the park to get there. It was the first day for a new PA student at the internal medicine clinic, and I looked forward to introducing him or her to the staff. I'd been away from the teams for several years and had become fully immersed in the medical community and nearly forgotten about the life I'd left behind.

Just as the television glowed to life, the phone rang, indicating something was wrong. No one called that early unless it was a wrong number or bad news. Caller ID indicated the cell phone number of my close friend and fellow Medical Service Corps officer Jeff Oman. Odd, I thought. Maybe there'd been a change in my schedule and I was needed at Miramar?

"Morning, Jeff. What's up?"

"Are you watching the news? If not, I think you need to turn it on," he said in his typical low mumble. Jeff was the administration officer for the clinic; he didn't particularly like the job, but there were a lot worse places to be stationed while he waited for a medical planner billet to open up with the marines.

"I just turned it on. What should I be looking for?" I asked, walking back into the living room to see what I was supposed to be looking for.

"A plane hit the World Trade Center."

He kept talking, but my eyes were fixated on CNN's special report. I turned up the volume to learn more. Just then the second plane hit the South Tower. "OK, that's not a coincidence," I said.

"Damn right," Jeff replied. "I don't think this will change too much for us, but your buddies across the bay are going to be real busy. I've got to get to work. If I find out anything I'll page you." I continued staring at the TV as I hung up the phone, trying to put it all together. Jeff was right; the SEALs on Coronado would soon be very busy.

Like everyone else on 9/11 I had a thousand thoughts going through my mind. I mentally went over the steps that I knew were going on in the military headquarters in Tampa. I sat and listened for several minutes, fully convinced we knew who was behind the attacks. They had tried to destroy the Twin Towers in 1993 and were known terrorists to the intelligence agencies. It was just a matter of time before we identified them and took action to prevent further attacks. It was inevitable that my life would once again abruptly change; it was just a matter of when.

Something was eerily different, far beyond the anxiety that sets in when you realize something is terribly wrong. It was the same experience I would get when the helicopter inserted the team on a mission. We'd quickly exit the aircraft to a perimeter, then hold for some time absorbing the sounds of the environment while our eyes adjusted. "That's it," I told myself. "It's dead quiet." The west side of my condo was a wall of windows that overlooked Lindbergh Field and the bay. From my living room I could see every takeoff and landing and all the boat traffic heading to and from the Coronado Bay Bridge. The airport was just a few miles away, but noise was never a problem. I could hear the faint sound of engines as they readied for their landing, but not today. The silence was palpable, and as I looked out my window I noticed the runways were dead still. Not one plane was moving. No take-offs, no landings, not even a plane taxiing to the terminal. The bay was also still; nothing but calm waters. There wasn't a wake of any kind. Normally, I see a navy ship or commercial freighter heading in or out of the bay. Today, nothing. Even the vibrant Coast Guard pier was dormant. As I headed for the door, the reporter said the FAA had grounded all commercial and private aircraft, and only military fighters were in the skies. It was as if America had hunkered down in its own security perimeter and was preparing to move out into the fight.

I checked in with Korrina, then grabbed my bike and departed for the hospital. As I biked through the park to the back entrance of the hospital I couldn't help but notice several people sitting in their cars, hypnotized by the radio reports, while others were quickly moving across the empty grounds, no doubt seeking a television. After locking up my bike, I entered the medical center through the main doors of the pharmacy. Sailors were gathered around the TV that normally provided entertainment to folks waiting on their prescriptions. Only this time, instead of weather reports of a sunny warm day, we learned of a plane crashing into the Pentagon. We also heard the mastermind's name for the first time: a terrorist named Osama bin Laden. The day was getting progressively worse, and the best thing I could do at that point was carry on and wait for orders.

Three weeks after the attacks, I was at Miramar helping marine units prepare for their deployment to Afghanistan. I received a call from Steve Galeski, our PA specialty leader. Steve was a former corpsman who had served with Marine Reconnaissance before becoming a PA. We first met during Desert Storm, when he was stationed on the same aircraft carrier my SEAL platoon utilized for interdiction operations as part of the UN-mandated blockade. When Scott, my senior corpsman, was injured just before operations commenced, I was left as the sole medical provider until the team could get another SEAL corpsman out to us. Steve stepped up to the plate by supplementing the medical evacuation bird, allowing me to remain on target should we take casualties.

"Mark, thought I'd let you know I've received word from above to locate a few of you SEAL-qualified medical personnel for some specialized operations," Steve said directly.

"I figured something like this would be going on. How soon do you need a decision?" I asked.

"You have time. I have one of your SEAL classmates and friends ready to go. Just don't take too long, otherwise Big Navy may put you in a billet you don't want."

I thought about how well my life was going, how I had more time to spend with my little girl and the money to make visits much more convenient. I thought about Korrina and the limited time we had before she left on her new set of orders, so after discussing it with Steve we both felt it was best if I remained on standby.

"Mark, I can't hold off on this forever, so if you get a call from the regional POMI office [Plans, Operations, and Medical Intelligence] assigning you to a deploying unit you call me right away," he said in his typical "I know a guy" voice.

"Solid copy, Steve. You take care, and try not to ship yourself off to the war."

"I'd go if I could, but I'm chained to this desk. Take care, my friend."

The daily tempo returned to relative normal, despite the anthrax scares and other random security flare-ups. As Korrina's departure time got closer, it seemed we saw less and less of each other. We watched the calendar with melancholy spirits and said painful good-byes as she departed for a brief stint in Rhode Island and then her duty station in Virginia. It was a very difficult time for both of us, but we promised to make it work, our words taking on a far greater meaning in a time of national crisis.

Not long after Korrina departed, Jeff asked me to visit his office. Captain Ferrara, the officer in charge of our clinic, had tasked Jeff with developing a manning plan. Deploying units were requesting medical officers, and we were sending them. Yet the clinic was still very busy, and we needed a strategy to keep the clinic operating at its current numbers while meeting the needs of the Marine Corps.

I entered Jeff's office and found him staring at a spreadsheet. He spoke without looking up.

"Mark, I scrunched this with the POMI office at NMCSD a hundred times, and the only way we can continue to support both the war effort and our military and retiree population is to deploy nearly all of our military providers and have the civilians run the clinic." He looked up at me with solemn eyes. He had just told me to get ready for deployment. It was a foregone conclusion for a SEAL-qualified medic.

"We knew this day would be coming, and I greatly appreciate you and the captain giving me as much time as you did with my daughter."

"Well, there won't be a lot more, I'm afraid. You're a hot commodity and the ground pounders want you right away, and this won't be a short deployment for the infantry," he said, obviously concerned about his friend.

"How much time before you have me shipping off?"

"A couple of weeks to two months at best."

"Alright then, I need to make a call."

OPERATORS—RETURN TO SPEC OPS

I'd been away from combat units for some time, so I was sent to a training facility in Virginia to reacclimate to the special operations culture. Much had changed since my time in the SEAL Teams, especially the command structure. The Global War on Terror was fought largely with special operations forces, referred to as SOF within the community, from all of the branches and commands. In the past my platoon was assigned to an Amphibious Ready Group or the Combatant Command; now we were deploying as task forces.

It was odd returning to the high-speed world of SOF, especially after working for several years in the relatively collegiate environment of medicine. I had maintained my fitness level and friendships in the community, however, so it was more a matter of readjustment than shock to the system.

The special operations community is a close-knit family comprised of warriors from every walk of life. The average SOF operator, if there is such a thing, is highly trained and fiercely motivated to succeed, yet take away the gear and technology and what you have is a warrior who

fights more with his brains than with brawn. The physical and techni-
cal capabilities just provide a means of putting those plans into action.
I thought back to the ongoing operations when I left and how things
were quickly moving to a fully integrated working environment, which I
was reminded of upon my arrival at the training compound. I trained
with the army's Special Forces soldiers, Marine Recon, Air Force Combat Controllers (CCTs) and Pararescue Jumpers (PJs), and, of course, my
brother SEALs. The majority of the men were on active duty, while a
few others had left the military and begun working as government employees on specified defense programs in order to concentrate on specific
skills they had acquired over their years of service. Regardless of the
"home" branch or employer, each of the men had extensive operational
experience and was highly competent and committed to the missions.
They were truly America's finest, and I was happy to be among them once
again.

The training was meant to integrate the unit on current policies,
weapons systems, and mission profiles, and we worked hard to prepare
for the inevitable combat ahead. The Global War on Terror was expanding quickly in several theaters, and new government agencies and
programs were being created to obtain information and distribute it to
special operations teams in order to allow for the quick action required to
capture America's most wanted terrorist. I received orders to one of those
programs and deployed for hot missions in Iraq and Afghanistan just
two days after completing training.

13

ARRIVAL IN AFGHANISTAN

Don't be afraid of death so much as an inadequate life.

—BERTOLT BRECHT

he Chinook banked to starboard and gradually descended two thousand feet as we made the final approach. For the third time in eighteen months, I was returning to combat, this time as a "hot fill" for a position at a forward operating base that required the skill levels of a physician or PA. The helo bucked and buffeted as we crossed one of the endless mountain ranges below, then calmed as the rugged peaks ended and the rocky Afghan plains opened up as far as the eye could see. I was once again struck by the breathtaking beauty of the country and felt an odd twinge of homesickness for New Mexico, which resembles Afghanistan in many ways.

My training and experience as a battle-tested medical officer and SEAL were unique and highly desirable. As a PA, I could treat villagers and oversee care of the Afghan National Army (ANA) at the local clinic at the same standard of care we provide to our own troops. This not only helped to build goodwill but also offered some protection for the United States government as we worked to build relations with the newly formed government. My deployment tempo was very high in the early days of the Global War on Terror, and I spent numerous deployments in Iraq and Afghanistan; in some cases, they were back-to-back with little to no downtime back in the States. I suppose that's why the rugged Afghan landscape reminded me so much of home.

The fort was outside a scattering of villages called Shkin, just six klicks from the Pakistani border. I could see the firebase in the distance rising off the desert floor. It looked remarkably similar to the Alamo with a towering front wall adorned with two large gates that adjoined enormous adobe walls that had to be three feet thick. It formed a rectangular compound complete with towers in each corner and catwalks on the roofs. As the helo banked into the wind for the final approach, I spotted an artillery battery off to the side of the compound, positioned between the compound's walls and a double row of HESCO barriers. The HESCOs were stacked two high on all sides of the firebase, except for one wall facing a steep ridge. The helicopter flared to touch down, and through the back ramp I could see a series of smaller walls and fences lining a semitwisted road leading to the stronghold, preventing a direct approach and thereby providing protection against truck bombs.

The structures in the center of the compound appeared to be constructed by a combination of modern tools and ancient technology, while those that lined the surrounding walls were made of the same earthen materials used to build homes in New Mexico hundreds of years ago. The base was currently home to a company from the 10th Mountain Division, various American special operations personnel, and a motivated group of the ANA's best fighters who volunteered to serve among one of their country's special operations contingents. It was our job to train, advise, and assist them in the fight against al Qaeda and the Taliban, which required accompanying and often leading them into battle. We did so with limited manpower and supplies, on a base several hundred miles from the nearest American installation.

As the wheels settled on the large rocks that covered the landing zone, a young soldier from the 10th Mountain ducked and ran out to grab my bags. As I exited the aircraft I noticed a single flagpole atop the main entrance flying a tattered American flag and felt proud that the only color in this drab area was the flag of our country. The soldier threw my bags in the back of a worn-out Humvee and drove me into the compound, straight to a corner building that was crudely built but wired for power.

"Here you are, sir. This here is where you all work and live," he said with a smile of accomplishment.

"Well, this is—"

"A real shithole," he answered before I could finish.

"I was thinking more along the lines of austere, but I think you summed it up pretty well."

"Yes, sir." He nodded and gave another a smile, pleased with his accurate assessment of the situation. "I was also told to let you know the other spec ops guys are all in a meeting with our major, but they should be done shortly," he said as we pulled the bags out of the bed of the Humvee and dropped them against the wall of the hooch. I thanked him, asked where I could find a latrine, and then walked the compound to get familiar with my new home. As I strolled the inside compound, roughly the length of a football field, I made a mental note of the bunker location in case we were hit with a rocket or mortar attack. I also mentally bookmarked the ingress and egress routes and the positioning of the heavy weapons, as well as the many vehicles lined up in the makeshift motor pool. I would revisit the vehicles later.

As I passed the chow hall, I heard a familiar voice. "Doc Donald! Holy hell!"

I turned and saw a large, light-skinned man with a long, thick beard that would've made Grizzly Adams jealous, striding my way with an ice cream bar in hand. It was my old friend Tom, an Army Special Forces operator with a big frame and cool disposition whom I met while attending 18 Delta over a decade ago. I had heard he was in Afghanistan, but I didn't know where and never thought I would see him, least of all here.

"I heard you were coming. Welcome." He smiled as he wiped ice cream drippings on his khaki utilities before offering his oversized hand.

"Where'd you hear that?" I asked. "It's a hot fill. I didn't even know I was coming."

"We put a request in for another PA but with very specific qualifications. That meant it was either Doc C, you, or no one. Doc C just left here a little over a month ago, so we figured it had to be you."

"Makes sense. So who's here?" I asked, still trying to figure out how he had a chocolate-covered ice cream bar in the middle of nowhere.

"You'll know a few," he answered, pausing to eliminate the remaining third of the bar and scrap the stick before continuing. "Chris was here. He was a SEAL, so you probably know him. He had to leave just before you got here. He'll be back at some point."

"Yeah, I know Chris," I answered. Chris was a former SEAL who was rising quickly through the ranks of a government agency. His new job kept him in close affiliation with the rest of us; I hadn't had a chance to work side by side with him in the past but knew eventually I would. The special operations community is a lot like a small town. It's always the same names related to the same jobs. You may not live in their neighborhood, or in this case be part of their command, but you'll know the name or recognize a face when you eventually run into one another.

"There are a couple of guys you'll probably remember from South America. You'll meet the boys shortly. Was the ride in OK? Anyone shooting as you came over the mountain range?"

"Not one round. I normally prefer night travel out here, but I can't complain," I said. "One thing's for sure, I'll never get tired of the views from up there."

"I know what you mean. It's the cold that gets me. Now, where are your bags?"

"The PFC [private first class] helped me stow them outside the main hut."

"Did it have a load of wires going into the roof and a wooden porch?"

"It sure did," I replied.

"Then that's the right one."

"So what's the plan?"

"Well, Wil and the others are over there briefing the leadership for Mountain [a colloquialism for 10th Mountain Division]," he said as he pointed toward the structure 10th Mountain used for their headquarters. "After that wraps up, the team meets back at the main hooch at 1400."

"Sounds good. I assume I'll get the lowdown on how everything works around here."

"Yep. It's not that bad, really. We have a lot of autonomy, but little support since most of the equipment is either in Iraq or headed that way," he said as he turned to walk back toward Mountain's HQ. "Oh, I almost forgot. Doc C trained up a few of the brighter Afghani troops as medical assistants. They're standing by to help you at the clinic once you're up and running."

"Thanks, but aren't you a medic? Or did you cut something off someone that you shouldn't have?"

"Funny. You've still got jokes. I was cross-trained as a Foxtrot [referring to the Army's Special Forces, Assistant Operations and Intelligence qualification] and haven't touched a stethoscope in ages. I can still patch the wounds, but I shouldn't be dispensing meds. We can't risk an international catastrophe. That's why we have you, right? Catch you at 1400." Tom smiled and popped me on the shoulder, then ambled off trying to get the sticky off his hands while I continued my own personal recon.

I spent the next couple of hours walking the compound, speaking with troops from 10th Mountain, and thinking about what Tom had said. He was wise to avoid the distribution of meds. Medicine advances quickly, and just because we're out in the middle of nowhere doesn't mean we won't encounter modern disorders. I remember our initial concerns when entering Iraq were centered on cholera and other basic ailments. However, once we took control of the country we realized medications for the treatment of diabetes and hypertension were needed. Thankfully, Doc C's reports had me prepared for the unique medical challenges in the Afghan wilderness.

I knocked on the door of 10th Mountain's medical clinic, which had been inherited from the Ranger Battalion, who had turned the sand castle into a fort. It had all the modern amenities you would need on the battlefield but was housed in a primitive, camplike room. Talk about a clash of eras. I spent time talking with their PA and a handful of army medics and learned they were there specifically to treat their men. Everyone else inside the walls, including my team and the Afghani troops, was my responsibility. I was also the go-to medical provider for the nearby villages. I thanked him for covering our guys after Doc C left and apologized for not getting there sooner. Like all the PAs I had worked with in the past, the army PA was more than happy to help out any way he could. We sat down on folding stools that accompanied his army-issue field desk, which was really just a box with drawers and a lid that turned into a tabletop, to talk about the medical problems he'd encountered during his time there.

"So what are you, army, navy, or what?" He asked. It was understandable; we all had beards and wore mismatched uniforms that best allowed us to adapt to our environment. "I thought you all were Special Forces, but then I heard some mention of SEALs, so we have an ongoing bet in medical."

"Not trying to be rude, but I don't think I can help you settle your bet. How about you all just call me Don," I said as I reached out my hand.

"I'm good with that," he replied as he smiled and opened one of the wooden drawers of his desk. I had seen this type of smile many times in the past. The most recent was at a special operations base in Europe when the surgeon pulled out twenty-year-old Scotch, but who knew what to expect this time.

"Now, Don, don't let the secret get out, because it's hard to get supplies out here," he said as he placed a French coffee press and biscotti on the top of the desk. *Really?* I thought. *This is the big secret?* I thought the heat and seclusion had melted his brain, but being an avid coffee drinker and knowing how much it meant to him, I rendered the courtesy of sharing a cup of joe.

As we sat, I told him why I was there, being careful not to violate security limitations. No use holding back information from someone I knew I would need assistance from.

"Well, other than being here to enjoy the ambience of eastern Afghanistan, I have three distinct duties while at Shkin: to keep my guys healthy, keep the Afghan army healthy, and carry out missions [as a spec ops operator], which includes treating the villages and their elders in and around no-man's-land."

"That sounds about right, but you'll want to be careful of returning to the same area too often." He went on to explain that the Taliban had learned Westerners would return to the same area after a few weeks to check on the ones they treated. The Taliban set up ambushes and would wait for the medical teams to return. "There's no respect for the Red Cross out here. It's more like a target, so just keep that in mind when you plan the village visits."

At 1400, I entered the main hooch and was greeted, spec ops style, by those in attendance. Tom was right; I did know several of the guys, including Chief, a sizable Native American whom I found to be one of the hardest men I've ever known. Then there was Vic, an air force officer with extensive combat experience and Brad Pitt good looks. Vic was the assistant team leader and greatly respected by the men, and they showed it by teasing him relentlessly for being a "metrosexual operator." Then there were the other Toms, all of whom had nicknames in order to keep everyone straight. There was Muscle Tom, a Recon Marine built like a professional middleweight boxer with wavy hair and an obsession for surfing; Ranger Tom, a quiet, trim, and no-nonsense operator that still lived by the motto "Rangers Lead the Way"; and, of course, my friend and former 18 Delta classmate, whom they called Big Tom. Finally, there was Wil, our team leader and Special Forces combat veteran, who had known Chief since the beginnings of their careers in special operations.

"Doc, I'm so glad you got here. My hemorrhoids are killing me," said Chief, trying to instigate a ruckus.

"Don't just tell him about it, show him," Big Tom said, adding his two cents to the conversation.

"Stop it! Can we have a meeting without any childish antics, please? Do you think that's possible?" Vic asked.

"This isn't about your movie choice, is it? Because we all forgave you for that disastrous 'humor' flick that lacked both a plot and laughs," said Muscle Tom.

So there it was. The guys were stirring the pot from the night before. I was just thankful Vic stepped into the circle to allow me to duck out. He broke a golden rule in spec ops: If someone is in the center of the harassment circle, don't go in after him, and definitely don't trade places. While they started out busting my chops, they quickly switched to something most troops thoroughly enjoy, hassling their junior officer. The hijinks continued until disposable coffee cups and pens began to fly.

"Enough," said Wil, trying to rein it in without letting on that he instigated Chief's and the Toms' statements in the first place. To an outsider, the scene would have resembled frat-house grab-assing, when in reality it was a group of highly trained professional warriors blowing off steam in a very isolated and dangerous place.

In a split second, the team recalibrated and focused on Wil as he got down to the brass tacks. He informed us that Chris would be staying stateside longer than we initially expected so he could tend to some issues, and that I would be pulling double duty as both medic and shooter. He also tasked me with ramping up the clinic as quickly as possible, with a goal of treating some of the locals within forty-eight hours as part of an ongoing civil affairs mission. He then briefed us on several training evolutions scheduled for the Afghan commandos, which was one of the core missions of our team. Glancing around the room as Wil continued to speak, I noticed each member of the team listening intently and scrawling notes in small notebooks. There was no grab-assing of any kind. That's how SOF operates. With a flick of a switch it can go from one extreme to another. Exceptional in every way, especially when it came to compartmentalizing work from play, or family back home.

"Doc," Wil said, catching me a bit off guard. "I know you worked with the ANA up north, but I can tell you the guys we have here are much more committed." He was referring to the Afghan National Army regulars who protected Kabul, who were primarily recruited from outside provinces, which meant they weren't dedicated to protecting Kabul as they would their own villages. Afghanistan was more tribally centered than national, and we all felt it would take decades or even a century or more to change that. I was glad to hear our ANA commandos were wired tight. Wil explained they were fierce warriors, passionately committed to expelling the Taliban from their homes. A true rarity.

An hour later, Wil wrapped the meeting by announcing that as the FNG, I would be taking over movie duties from Vic. I wasn't sure what that meant, but I thought it was about to put me in the center of the circle.

As the team wandered out to carry on with their respective duties, Wil walked over and offered a hand. "Good to see you again, Doc. Last time I saw you, we were passing each other in Virginia. You were on your way to Iraq, so I was surprised you were available for this assignment."

"The deployment schedules have been crazy. Very hard to predict, little downtime, and all that, but here I am, ready to try to fill Doc C's shoes," I smiled.

"You know we purposely requested—"

He tried to finish, but I interrupted him. "I know, Big Tom told me."

"Well, I try to build a good team and keep it that way," he said as he winked. "In any case I'm glad you made it."

"Thanks for having me, Wil. Sounds like we've got our work cut out for us."

"Roger that. I'm counting on you to get that clinic up in a couple of days. Ned, our Afghan commander, has the ANA ready to help, and the medics at 10th Mountain offered to pitch in."

"I met their captain earlier, and he mentioned his willingness to help. We'll get it done."

"Come on, let's go outside and talk about it over a smoke."

"You know I only smoke a cigar once in a blue moon, and I don't have any here with me," I said, knowing I was about to be overruled.

"You know I don't smoke alone, and I'm your boss." Wil always took someone on his smoke breaks with him, and as it turned out that would generally be me. We'd stand outside on the porch for ten minutes as he discussed current situations and weighed his options out loud. It wasn't as if he was looking for an answer from me. I think he just wanted to hear himself think, and having me prevented him from looking like a lunatic, walking back and forth and ranting through puffs of smoke. Thinking out loud isn't anything new. I used the technique myself and recommended it to my students, firmly believing a person has a greater ability to learn or understand complex problems when it comes from his or her own voice.

"We've got a lot brewing right now, and there may be another opportunity coming down the pike, so don't be surprised if we all get stretched real thin," Wil said as he lit up his cigarette.

"Not to worry, boss. I don't mind pulling eighteen-hour days," I said, trying to allay any fears he might have about the clinic not getting done. I have always been a workaholic and planned to continue the trend, especially since I was sitting in an ancient fortress on the Pakistani border.

"It won't be that intensive, Doc, but it'll keep you busy." Wil then switched to the Afghan commandos and explained how far the troops had come and their expanded role performing surveillance and reconnaissance deep in Taliban and al Qaeda country. "Muscle Tom and the others have really done a great job training the ANA, but it hasn't been all roses." He told of a recent ambush the Afghanis encountered escorting a resupply convoy that took the life of one of their newest members. "He was a huge Afghani, Goliath size. He was a natural leader and positive influence on the others. His death really shook the rest of his platoon, but having a medical presence on the battlefield with them should help calm their nerves." As a medic, I'd heard that before; no matter how well trained and hard core you are as a warrior, there's a feeling of relief knowing that someone is there to keep you alive.

Wil finished his cigarette, turned, and started to walk back into the hooch. "Boss, I've got a request. If you don't mind, I'd like to work on the vehicles when time allows." I'd learned a valuable lesson from my time in Central and South America. Vehicles keep men alive.

Wil shook his head and laughed. "You know, Doc, we're on land, and those are 'army' vehicles, and they don't need the same habitual maintenance as your 'navy' boats," he said, laughing, while he thought about his decision. "Sure, Doc, what the hell, knock yourself out. Just do me a favor—let's get the clinic up and running first, and don't forget to let

Vic know what you're up to. He can get a little touchy when it comes to the comms equipment in the vehicles."

"Roger that," I said as Wil ducked back into the hootch.

With the help of the army medics, the Afghani clinic was operational within twenty-four hours. For the first time in nearly two months, I held an official sick call for the Afghani troops, and it was an instant hit. I worked nonstop for two days straight. Overall the Afghani team was in great shape, with the exception of a few repeated sprains, related to patrolling through the rocky terrain, and dental problems. We also treated locals from the nearby villages and found them to be humorless and skeptical of our intentions. I wouldn't expect any different, with the clinic's on-again, off-again schedule. Sometimes it was enemy rocket attacks that shut it down; other times it was our inability to have an American medical provider constantly on station. The primary problem was not having a competent Afghani provider as the mainstay of the clinic. We'd tried in the past, but every time we hired someone to run it, either the Taliban would chase him off or he simply couldn't be trusted. The man I replaced, Doc C, actually left the Alamo and went to Kabul to address that very issue.

When not attending to patients, I was in the hooch with Wil, Chief, and the Toms, learning the critical details of the missions and reviewing intelligence reports. Our primary mission was to train up the Afghan commandos, but we also had certain standalone missions that would be carried out by small teams of Americans from our group. As a SEAL, I was accustomed to such small-unit operations and experienced a surge of adrenaline when they were described in detail.

In my limited free time, I worked on the various vehicles around the compound. There were Humvees, old Soviet-era trucks, and Toyota Hilux trucks like those favored by the enemy. I became somewhat obsessive about maintaining the vehicles, perhaps as a subconscious way to ward off the inevitable injuries and death that come with battle. The other guys joked mercilessly about my mechanic's fixation, but deep down they knew my compulsion might actually save a life, and that's what medics do.

I grew close to my teammates in those early days. They were smart guys, all of them college graduates, with life experiences most average folks could never fathom. We spent the off-hours, usually at night, engaged in conversations ranging from politics to religion to sports and beyond. On occasion, one of the soldiers from the 10th Mountain would bring his guitar to our side of the compound and play while we stared up at the deep purple sky, the bright stars illuminating the ground below.

My first fire team: Sergeant John Shafer, now Colonel, *(top right)* and Erik Little *(not pictured)* devoted hours of personal time training me in the pool until I was ready for Amphibious Reconnaissance School. *(Courtesy of the author)*

Amphibious Reconnaissance School with Erik Little *(center)*. *(Courtesy of the author)*

Heading to Catholic Mass and later telling Mom about my wanting to transfer to the navy to become a corpsman. *(Courtesy of the author)*

Graduation Day from Hospital Corps School. Eric Sine *(far left)* and Lieutenant Marty *(center)*. *(Courtesy of the author)*

Head shaving party before classing up for BUD/S. *(Courtesy of the author)*

Surf torture during Hell Week. Just a part of the slow indoctrination of losing any fear of drowning while gaining a great deal of respect for Mother Nature. *(Courtesy of David Gatley, Gatley Photography)*

Graduation from Basic Underwater Demolition/SEAL Training. Now onto months of advanced training, a never ending process within special operations. *(Courtesy of the author)*

Preparing for deployment as part of an Amphibious Ready Group. At that time we had no idea Saddam would invade Kuwait. *(Courtesy of the author)*

Striping off the gear and storing it for the next call in the ready service locker after returning from a ship takedown in the Red Sea. *(Courtesy of the author)*

On board the USS *Saratoga* (CV-60) after another successful ship assault in the Persian Gulf War. This picture doesn't do justice to all the officers and crew that made sure we had the support we needed to be successful. I learned then, how we're just a small specialized cog in a giant machine, something every new guy needs to experience. *(Courtesy of SEAL Platoon member)*

My first taste of operating in the jungles of Central America. A dangerous, beautiful environment filled with inhabitants hidden from the rest of the world. *(Courtesy of the author)*

Diving operations in the warm Caribbean waters as we prepare to head back to Central America for another deployment. *(Courtesy of the author)*

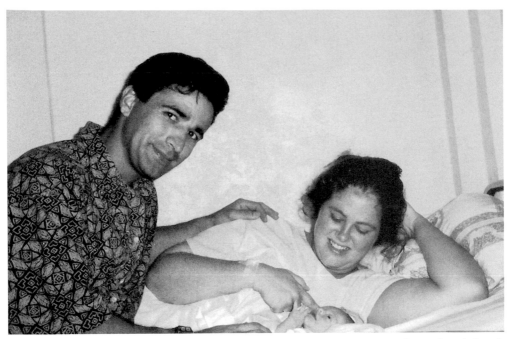

The day after assisting in the delivery during one of our many trips to Central and South America. I pray mother and child are still doing as well. *(Courtesy of the author)*

Low tide exposed the full extent of a plane crash in Central America. It was a wonder my teammates were able to rescue the men inside. I always felt that if there were bystanders record-ing their actions they would have received the Navy/Marine Corps Medal for saving those men's lives. *(Courtesy of the author)*

Early days of Operation Iraqi Freedom with the fires still burning from battles the night before. *(Courtesy of the author)*

Air dominance helped American forces cover great distances in record time. This Iraqi tank never made it through the first day of the invasion. *(Courtesy of the author)*

One of only a handful of navy flags (crossed anchors in upper corner) Saddam had for his fleet. *(Courtesy of the author)*

The 3' thick and 20' high mud walls that surrounded firebase Shkin kept it from being overrun, but they weren't enough to shield us from the rocket attacks coming from across the border. *(Courtesy of the author)*

Visiting the border checkpoint only a short distance from firebase Shkin. This outpost constantly received enemy fire, but its location made it ideal for building a medical clinic for treating the locals. *(Courtesy of the author)*

Rarely did rockets make it inside the compound, but when they did the effects could be devastating. Within minutes a structure could be destroyed and fires spread. Fortunately, this hut was empty when the rocket hit and hurled shrapnel and flames into the compound. The top picture was taken from under the awning that covered our vehicles, less than 50 meters from our hooch. *(Courtesy of the author)*

Battle tea. We are sharing a cup of tea with Ned, the Afghan Commander, and others after having to be a quick reaction force to an attack on our border checkpoint. *(Courtesy of the author)*

Checking on Ned after his return from the Combat Support Hospital following the deadly ambush in Khand Pass. *(Courtesy of the author)*

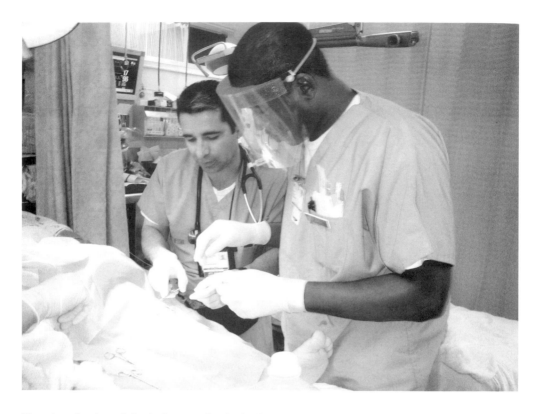

Traveling back and forth from multiple deployments only highlighted the stark contrast between the two emergency medical departments. *(Above)* Naval Trauma Training at USC's medical center. *(Below)* The medical center for firebase Shkin. *(Courtesy of the author)*

Getting ready to depart the firebase in order to make it home for Christmas. *(Courtesy of the author)*

Awards ceremony with Secretary of the Navy Donald Winters. *(Courtesy of the author)*

Saying good-bye at a retirement luncheon for my skipper, mentor, friend, and thirteenth "Bullfrog" for the SEAL community, Captain Pete Wikul. (*Courtesy of the author*)

Steve Cobb dressed in the Military Order of the Purple Heart regalia for my retirement ceremony. Steve was a persistent pundit for America's wounded and a key individual in getting me to meet and talk about my experiences with other combat vets. (*Courtesy of the Office of Naval Intelligence*)

Deputy Surgeon General for the Navy Admiral Thomas Cullison *(left)*, presents a letter of gratitude to my mother during my retirement ceremony. *(Courtesy of the Office of Naval Intelligence)*

My family waited a long time for this day. This is my first official duty as a civilian—cutting the cake at my retirement reception. *(Courtesy of the author)*

My family and I assisting at another event supporting our troops. I pray America can keep up this level of support over the years. Today's service members and wounded are tomorrow's veterans. *(Courtesy of the author)*

14

BATTLE OF KHAND PASS

*It is only those who have neither fired a shot nor heard the shrieks
and groans of the wounded who cry aloud for blood, more vengeance,
more desolation. War is hell.*

—William Tecumseh Sherman

I spent several days inventorying and restocking the clinic outside
of the firebase, with the assistance of the 10th Mountain physician
assistant and his senior medic. It didn't take long before the foot
traffic from local villages was keeping us busy, but it was still only the
tip of the iceberg of what needed to get done within the area. If we
were going to have any real impact, we needed to get out to some of
the remote villages before the winter snow. Now seemed like a perfect
time; fall was just settling in, and the brutal heat was subsiding, which
resulted in fewer cases of heat exhaustion and dehydration. Still, traveling up and down the steep, rugged mountains in 70 pounds of body
armor and weaponry kept that threat alive.

We began by frequenting the local villages and building a rapport
with the population before pushing out to remote areas where we were
needed the most. Wil or Vic would lead the group, which generally
included one of the Toms and myself. I would concentrate on treating
the locals, some of whom had never met or even seen Americans.

Afghans by nature are a very insular people and trust very few people outside of their tribes, including our team and the 10th Mountain personnel who accompanied us. Because of the distrust on both sides, we'd often meet on the outskirts of the village rather than in the village itself, which is normally where I'd set up my medical clinic. It was inconvenient for the villagers, but it afforded us additional protection. Relations began to thaw over a series of visits, and the villagers' trust eventually grew to the point where we were allowed to attend some of the local jirgas, a sort of town meeting of tribal elders. There I learned a great deal about the distrust they had for both the Taliban and the United States. In their mind their village was a separate entity unto itself, making everyone an outsider. I understood why Doc C kept stressing the importance of establishing a medical clinic that would reach both sides of the border, and the need for putting an Afghani physician in place to run it. If these people were ever going to feel the need for national unity it had to come from their government proving the benefit it brings to their lives and not by the work done by a foreign military force. We had the ability to get it under way but were unsure if the Afghani government could continue it, especially since it might take decades for it to take hold.

A month after my arrival, intel started flowing in from nearly all the villages. I kept up with the latest reports by going into the comms hooch at least twice during the day. During one of my afternoon visits, Wil asked me to join him.

"Hey, Doc." Wil smiled as I entered the hooch to find him alone, marking up maps pinned to the crude plywood walls. "Pull up a chair." He motioned to one of the plastic patio chairs commonly found in stacks outside Walmart. "Great work on the clinic. You got everything you need?"

"No, not really, but we're making do."

"Good man. That's all I ask." He pulled up a plastic chair and joined me at the plywood table that lined the front wall. "We've had a mission on the burner for the past few months and scrapped it twice. It just went to boil again, and I'm putting you in Chris's place. You've got the skills we need, especially as a medic and shooter. It's an added bonus that you were a radio guy." Wil gazed at me levelly, then gestured for me to speak openly.

"I'm good to go. Can you tell me about it, or do you want to brief everyone at once?"

Wil smiled and then started searching for his pack of cigarettes, which he'd lost under the rat's nest of maps and materials on his desk. He continued speaking as he searched. "The other guys are up to speed and have been itching to roll on this for months. We've learned of a target holed up about thirty miles from here in a place just beyond Khand Pass. We know he's been coordinating the transfer of troops and weapons from Pakistan into Afghanistan, and we believe his orders are coming from top al Qaeda leadership. We're going in to put eyes on him, assess his current location and troop strength, then call in the cavalry to grab him."

"Thirty miles? I assume we have good intel on the area?" I asked as I slipped from PA mode into SEAL mode. Because special operations teams are composed of such a small group of operators, everyone wears multiple hats; actually, mine was more like a sombrero. Unlike trauma medicine, clinical medicine had a tendency to envelop me and shade me from the outside world. Caring for smiling children dressed in brightly colored gowns would often take me away from the cruelty of war, but the evils of al Qaeda always dragged me back to reality.

"We've got the best intel possible this time around. Chris, Chief, and Muscle Tom were out there a few times earlier this year, and they all know the area well." Wil was alluding to the inaccuracy of past intelligence reporting; naturally any team would prefer to have firsthand knowledge of their AO (area of operations), and thankfully we did. "We're also receiving collaborating information from multiple other sources, including several Taliban captured last month." He paused long enough to hand me some pictures, then continued looking for his cigarettes. "The satellite imagery seems to back everything up."

Special operations missions rely heavily on intelligence reports, especially when the troops involved are in small groups and far from base. Human intelligence, acronym HUMINT, is the information gathered from people on the ground, and it's not limited to local populace; anyone with eyes and ears can be an asset. Signal intelligence, acronym SIGINT, is collected by eavesdropping on radio and telephone transmissions, or any device that produces a signal, and geospatial intelligence, acronym GEOINT, is derived from satellite imagery and related sources. There are other intelligence disciplines, but those were the ones most important to our mission, and Wil was a master at interpreting its value.

"Unfortunately Chris won't make it back on time to go on this pump. That means you'll be picking up his duties for the op."

Wil, who was normally meticulously suspicious about missions, was much more at ease for this one, so the intel must have been strong about Khand Pass. It wasn't that he was risk averse; it was simply that he valued American lives more than he believed in the outcome of this war. Vietnam veterans who built the special operations community mentored Wil during his early years, and despite their valiant service and mission success rate, the conflict didn't end the way America had intended. I think he was concerned this war would turn out the same.

"So what's next?" I asked, ready to get to work.

"Aha," he said, finally finding his pack of cigarettes. He picked up a laser pointer and turned to a map tacked to the plywood wall. "The team will be rolling out in approximately three weeks, along this main route for the first few miles, then off the grid for the rest." He traced the route with a red dot while simultaneously jabbing a cigarette in his mouth.

"You'll get a warning order when we receive final approval." He turned to me. "Doc, I wanted to let you know why I'm pulling you away from the clinic after you pushed so hard to get it up and running," he said, now searching his pockets for his lighter. "It'll be you, Vic, Muscle Tom, and Chief on this one. Vic will be team leader and primary comms. You all will be leading a platoon of the Afghan commandos, along with Ned and three terps [interpreters]." Ned, the Afghan commander, was a fierce warrior with extensive combat experience. He was raised in Kunar Province but educated by Westerners in Kabul. His English was nearly perfect and his courage unrivaled. I was happy to hear he would be wrangling the commandos. "Come on," Wil said as he motioned for me to head outside with him for a smoke. I followed him to the porch and watched him light up. He then continued. "Time to dial back your time at the clinic while we wait for the green light. I spoke with the major in charge of 10th Mountain, and he'll have his PA take care of it for now."

"I appreciate the heads-up."

"Get with Muscle Tom if you have any questions on what personal gear you might need. I'm sure it'll be approved by the end of the week, and we'll have a formal brief then. Did I leave anything out?" he asked, taking a hit from his cigarette.

"No, that about sums it up."

"Not a problem, Doc." He patted my shoulder and nodded.

"Wait, there are a couple of other things," I said.

"Fire away."

"I noticed we have some ballistic blankets in the armory. Can I use those on the vehicles? Also, I'd like to get some more medical supplies on the next resupply for additional medical kits. If we're going deep into Indian country, I want to be prepared for anything."

Wil smiled and flashed thumbs-up as he turned and headed back into the hooch. "Done and done!" he yelled over his shoulder.

A decade prior to my assignment at Shkin, I attended a briefing by two Special Forces medics who, after returning from the streets of Mogadishu, set out on personal journeys to share with all of special operations the lessons learned from that battle. One of the more salient points was the need to be able to return to sticks and rags in the treatment of casualties "because eventually you're going to run out of supplies, and you will need to improvise." The SOF medical community heeded their advice and adapted their training accordingly. In addition to reinforcing the basics, the units also began building their own medical resupply to an existing system, called "kickout bundles." The idea of throwing essential equipment or resupply out the door of a hovering helicopter or a slow-moving aircraft, or cross-decking from one patrol boat to another, wasn't anything new, at least not for beans or bullets. The medics' briefing just made it more commonplace for teams to use kickout bundles for Band-Aids, too. I reaped the benefit of their experience during the early part of Iraqi Freedom, so I was damn sure I was going to try to have some backup equipment ready for this mission as well.

I knew Wil would move mountains to find the gear I requested, but as a SEAL and a spec ops veteran of Central and South America, I thought I'd utilize an old friend from a Special Forces Group that specialized in that part of world. He had recently joined an Army Special Forces team operating in a small base outside of Khowst, only five klicks, or roughly three miles, away from the air base, so I contacted their medics to ask if they would build a couple of bundles and drop them off at the helicopter medical evacuation teams for me. They gladly obliged. I had no reservations asking for help even though it meant adding more work to another team's plate; if they needed help, they would have asked me, and I would have gladly pitched in. In the SOF community, we took care of one another like family.

While awaiting the warning order, we capitalized on every free minute. An extremely important element of special operations is the preparation, cleaning, and function check of every piece of equipment, starting with the team's gear, with everyone pitching in to make it happen. No matter your rank or position, you get your hands dirty. Once the team gear is good to go, the operator can start prepping his own personal gear. It's all part of the team mentality that's instilled from the first day of training.

Like the others I started going through my gear, ensuring everything was clean and fully operable. An odd feeling of uncertainty settled into my chest as I checked my weapon's laser sight and my night-vision goggles, or NVGs. It wasn't fear but rather a sense of internal compass recalibration as I shifted more and more from caregiver to frogman. For years, I'd been focused on healing the sick and injured, and thoughts of firefights were water under the bridge, and now I was reverting to the training I'd received as a young Recon Marine and SEAL. I felt no fear of the pending mission and knew I'd perform just as I had in Iraq and on other missions, but something felt different this time. Since returning to the spec ops community, I'd felt an internal conflict knotting up deep in my core. Once again I would carry my medical bag and M-4 with a good chance I'd need both. I was no longer a medical officer in San Diego, treating patients in a sterile clinic. I was once again a combat medic, and inside, caregiver and warrior were beginning to battle for my soul.

Wil called us together and announced the mission was a go. We all helped formulate the plan and then rehearsed day after day for the next three weeks until we knew our parts so well we could perform them in our sleep. On downtime, Big Tom, Vic, and I tuned the vehicles and augmented the armament on each. We placed ballistic blankets over the seats to add an additional layer of protection against incoming rounds and land mines buried in the road. Modifying the vehicle was a delicate balancing act. We needed protection, but we also needed power and speed. It didn't matter how much armor the trucks had if they couldn't get us off the *X*. We focused on weak points exposed from previous battles and added armor to fragile areas on the doors and along the floorboards.

I had become obsessed with vehicle maintenance, and the others knew it. It was as if each one had become a patient of mine. Even when they were completely tuned and tightened, I would spend hours going over them. I would perform a detailed physical exam, testing and refining every component. Just like any good medical provider, I greatly valued the tools of the trade. I kept my mechanic's tools clean and organized like surgical instruments. I even made my own tool roll-up from an old blanket that resembled an oversized surgical instrument pack. If they weren't in my hands, I hid them away from the others so I'd have them when I needed them.

In typical SOF fashion, my teammates quickly discovered one of the best ways to annoy me was to borrow a socket wrench and bring it back covered in axle grease or, worse, not return it at all. Since the dawn of special operations, teammates have used humor to lighten the stresses of the job or impending combat, and my colleagues were no exception.

Early one morning while I was at the clinic checking on one of our wounded Afghan soldiers, Chief crept over to my sleeping hooch and swiped my tools. He took them back to the comms hooch, where he posed with them stuffed down his pants. He then returned them exactly as he found them, careful not to reveal his shenanigans. Later that evening, when the team sat down to watch a movie, the "previews" were actually picture after picture of my tools going toward some very dark places. Although I wanted to laugh my ass off at the dastardly deeds, I knew any reaction would only fuel the fire, so I sat and viewed the movie's preview stone-faced as the rest heehawed like jackasses. They had me and they knew it, and the next day Chief stopped by to "borrow tools" and have one last laugh as he watched me soak each one in chemical sterilizer. Needless to say, I kept them under lock and key for the rest of the deployment.

Once my tools were back in acceptable working order, I joined the Toms, along with a few of the ANA soldiers and our terp named Ali, and we prepared the vehicles for the mission to Khand Pass. We attached new equipment mounts on each of them, which would allow immediate release of the medical kits and stretchers yet still withstand the constant bouncing from the terrain. Then we moved the spare tires, replacement parts, tools, and even the five-gallon water cans into positions that would provide some protection against fragmentation or penetrating rounds. Ali was a Pashtun from Kabul who was a sociable man with a wiry build but a bit too skittish. It was obvious he was there for the extra money, which was much better than what he earned at his past job with the State Department in Kabul. I was unsure how he'd hold up under fire, and it concerned me. His English was good, however, and he had decent proficiency in Dari, which made him a valuable asset.

On the day before launch, we met with the leadership of the 10th Mountain and went over the basics of our mission. Operational security, or OPSEC, prevented us from telling them all the details, but they knew enough to assist us should it come to that. They were the closest ground troops available, and it was important we maintained communication with one another. We had our own QRF (quick reaction force) troops standing by at one of the major bases, but they were hundreds of miles away and relied on air support to get there. We needed a contingency plan, and 10th Mountain provided that for us. They would be traveling by ground, which also meant they would be bringing large-caliber machine guns and automatic grenade launchers to the fight. Initially, I had doubts when I heard the 10th Mountain had replaced the Rangers that helped establish this outpost, but it didn't take long before I grew to respect the men of the 10th Mountain Division. Since my arrival I had watched them defend continual attacks against their patrols and the firebase with the same proficiency I was accustomed to within the special operations community. The 10th Mountain had lost three good soldiers in less than a month, which can shake any military unit, but their leadership was strong, and men followed suit. We supported them and they us, and each man on my team was confident they'd have our backs if things got heavy.

Chris had recently returned from the States and sat in on the briefings, providing valuable input to supplement the intel. He'd been in the target area several times over the last twelve months and gave critical advice about navigating through the rough terrain. After the meeting wrapped, Chris pulled me aside and wished me the best. He was clearly disappointed that I was going in his place. We all understood what he was feeling, especially since he'd spent so much time training the ANA soldiers from the initial stages of this program. However, there are golden rules in the special operations community that simply aren't broken. Most notably, if you're not part of the workup, you don't go on the operation. It doesn't matter how good an operator you are; if you don't rehearse, you don't go. Chris knew this but felt he was abandoning the very men he raised up from the ranks of ANA. He helped select the men, eliminated the weaker links, and trained the remaining few until they were a formidable fighting force. I believe he felt obligated to be by their sides, especially on the more dangerous operations. This one certainly fit into that category.

We launched at dusk and headed slowly east across the flat, rocky terrain. The unit was comprised of nine vehicles with roughly four men in each: four Americans traveling in swim pairs, a mechanic, two terps, the Afghan leader, who also worked as an interpreter, and twenty-four Afghan commandos. Each vehicle had a man designated as the vehicle commander, a driver, a machine gunner, and someone to work comms— except, of course, our vehicle, which held only the three of us and our terp. We all wore beards and dressed in patchwork uniforms and local dress with no indication of unit or even nationality. Most of the men wore manjams, free-flowing one-piece robes commonly worn by Middle-Eastern guerrilla fighters and Afghan tribesmen. If I didn't know better I'd swear they were Taliban. The vehicles were two American Humvees and six Toyota Hiluxes, which looked exactly like those used by the enemy, and the mechanic's truck. Each vehicle was fortified with ballistic armor and blankets, and carried a camo net that could be pulled over it to disguise it during our daytime lay-ups.

Our soldiers looked and traveled like the enemy, which was no accident. From a distance, we knew they resembled a ragged caravan of Taliban fighters or criminals, which gave us a small but critical advantage should we be observed from afar by a shepherd or farmer.

The plan called for us to travel for two consecutive nights and lay up at preplanned hides during the days. On the third day, we would break up into squads, move into our positions by foot to gather the intel, then quietly retreat back to the vehicles and later our firebase.

We had learned on earlier operations that helicopter insertion into those areas had its limitations, often precluding their use, especially if we wanted to get in undetected and remain there for a long period of time. It didn't matter how many false insertions we did, the noise from the chopper blades was so distinct it always alerted the locals that coalition forces were afoot. Word of a possible American presence would eventually make its way to the Taliban, which inspired the enemy to fortify defenses and conduct widespread security searches across the area. Insertion by combat boot, or LPC (leather personnel carrier), as I jokingly referred to it, was far less obvious, but it took days or weeks to approach an objective, putting us all in danger for much longer periods of time. Our answer was a combination of vehicles and LPC. It wasn't the preferred method, but it proved successful on similar operations in and around Orgun and Khowst, so we had good reason to believe it would be just as effective in this region as well. We also had a distinct advantage. Chief and Chris had been to the exact area we were going to, as had many of our Afghan soldiers, so we had a ground truth on which areas we needed to avoid in order to prevent early detection.

The target was located along a main road that led into the village. There were rough trails that flanked the town on three sides, and none were used by shepherds due to the lack of foliage for their flocks. We took the longest of the three flanking trails in order to avoid the main road.

The first two nights were uneventful. Our slow, deliberate pace allowed us to keep a watchful eye across the barren wilderness with our night-vision goggles and thermal scopes. We settled in remote areas during the day and evaded unwanted eyes by parking our vehicles in wadis or among large clusters of boulders. We placed each one in a position that would allow for immediate escape and covered them with camouflage netting, which rendered them nearly invisible from elevated positions. Half the team stood watch while the other half slept under the vehicles or in shady areas beside large rock formations. Everyone carried personal weapons, and each vehicle had a crew-served machine gun. While the terrain was flat and we could see for miles in every direction, the tension was always high.

The nights were cold, turning the water we carried in our canteens to ice. Before settling in, I would make my rounds and check the condition of each man and remind him to stay hydrated even though the water was difficult to drink. As I bounded from truck to truck I noticed our tribesmen turned warriors had adapted naturally to their ancestral surroundings, and I was confident we'd make it to the target without being seen.

The flat Mars-like terrain that we covered on the first two nights changed dramatically as we neared the target. Sharp, jagged rocks and sporadic trees sprang up across the hilly countryside, making it much more difficult to see an approaching vehicle or enemy ambush. To make up for the disadvantage, we pushed our reconnaissance vehicles much farther out with Ned, the Afghan leader, in charge. It wasn't unusual to come around a sharp turn and find yourself at a Taliban checkpoint, so we needed a cool-headed decision maker leading a group of locals to get us past such situations.

We arrived at our last stop four hours before dawn on the third day. We pulled the vehicles into a narrow wadi sandwiched between two twenty-foot rock faces. We drove in minutes apart from one another to ensure we didn't make a commotion as we positioned the vehicles. From there we would move out on foot, so we took extra precautions to conceal the vehicles. As I prepared my hide site, I noticed the southern cliffs in the moonlight. It looked just as Chris and Chief had described during our brief, which told me we were danger close. The village was less than half a night's walk from our hide, and we had no new intel, which made me feel a bit uneasy. The only thing worse than no intel is old intel. You think you understand a situation when in reality everything might have changed. Our last update by any source was nearly two days old, which meant there was nothing to report or there was no longer a source left to report it. We situated our gear and began preparing the Afghan commandos for a hump to the objective, or an expeditious exit should things go bad quickly. While speaking to one of the terps I noticed Vic and Ned lying at the edge of the ridge and peering out at the southern cliff face through their binos. Several minutes later they slid down carefully and stood face-to-face, deep in conversation. Ned was gesturing toward the mountains, and Vic was taking it all in. They spoke for several intense minutes before Vic walked over to me.

"Doc, I need to speak with you and the rest of the boys," he said solemnly. "Meet me at my vehicle in five."

"Roger that," I replied.

Five minutes later, we were gathered around a map spread on the hood of Vic and Muscle Tom's vehicle. Chief was pointing at something on the map and talking to Vic and Tom when I approached.

"Doc. Chief and Tom saw movement on the peaks. Ned and I glassed it and definitely saw people up there, but impossible to tell from here who they are," said Vic.

"Could be goatherds, but I doubt it," Chief said. "There's no reason to be up there except to set up an observation post. If they're enemy, they certainly aren't trying to stay along the military crest." Chief was referring to the area just below the ridgeline that allows someone to see the surrounding area without silhouetting himself to their enemy.

"The moon definitely highlights two men. The question is, are they bad guys?" Vic asked. The distance was too far for our night vision to be any use, which left us to the mercy of the field glasses or binoculars.

"The last time I was out here, Chris and I saw a lot of shepherds in places we never thought they'd be. It's hard to be sure," Chief said.

"The fact that they're running around on those ridges tells me those ain't shepherds. It's too much work to run animals over those mountains," Tom added.

I watched as Vic digested the information. His career was built on analyzing intel and making tactical decisions, and this was right in his wheelhouse. I had grown close to Vic over our time together and knew he had already made a decision. I also knew he would throw it to us in case he missed something. Vic had too much respect for Chief and Tom not to.

"Let's assume we've been spotted. We've got a couple of choices. Lay up today, hope for the best, and see what happens. Or we turn around and head home. In either case we stand a good chance of being attacked. Am I missing something?"

We stood quiet for a moment and contemplated the situation. No one wanted to go home empty-handed, but we weren't about to put ourselves into a position that we might not be able to get out of.

"Are we sure we've been spotted?" I asked.

"No one knows for sure, Doc. No radio chatter so far," Tom answered. No reports of radio or phone activity. *That's a good thing*, I told myself.

"Based on the assumption we've either been spotted or will be come first light, we need to pull out of the area, but we can't go out the same way we came. It's too risky," Chief said.

"I can send some of my men out for intel," Ned suggested.

"It's not worth it, Ned. We need to keep the team tight for now," Vic said.

"Look, if we push out now we'll still have some cover of darkness.

The road here is going to split," Chief said, pointing to a fork in the road on the map. "What you don't see is, this road, the one we're on now, is going to bifurcate and feeds into these hills and then back onto the main road." The original maps for this part of Afghanistan were terribly out of date and poor quality, so we added roads and other features each time we went out. This real-time adaptation of our computer mapping programs gave us a fairly good understanding of what to expect.

"What does that mean?" Ned asked.

"I think what Chief is saying is, if we've been spotted by the enemy, we'll be ambushed any way we go." Tom paused to see if Ned was following him. "But if those guys on the mountain are uncaring nomads, we may be able to push on to the target and get eyes on before having to abort and head back toward base."

"See, right here," Vic said as he directed Ned's attention to the map. "If we go this way it also puts us on the main road heading directly toward Shkin. Traveling during the day we can move much faster, and it should only take us half a day to get back."

"We're not far from the target. They won't expect us to come in from the north, through the wadi. It's pretty rocky there. Going deeper in might just be the safest route out," Chief said as his finger moved along the route he described.

"What do you think, Tom?" Vic asked. "Turn around and head back, or pull out and move to the target?"

"You're both right—more than likely we're going to get hit either way, but if we go this way we can approach just below this ridgeline, then move down the saddle into the wadis below, which should provide some cover," Muscle Tom said, pointing to the map and aerial photography. "We didn't come this far to quit."

Vic turned to Chief and asked, "Continue on, or turn and head home from here?"

Without missing a beat, Chief replied, "Are you kidding me? Push on. We may have to abort before we get there, but I agree with Tom. If the enemy has spotted us, we're fucked any way we go. The best way to avoid an ambush is to avoid the roads and trails. This route gives us some protection and more time to assess the situation when we get there." Vic then turned to me. "Doc?"

I just looked at him and said, "I got nothing."

Vic replied, his face showing stress, "Come on, Doc. I don't have bandwidth for any bullshit. You always have something to say." He was under serious pressure and thought I was yanking his chain.

"What ya got, Doc?" Muscle Tom asked, knowing there was something more to my answer.

I looked at each of them as I explained. "Truth be told, I'm the medic on this mission, which means I go wherever you go, even if you're going through the fires of hell on a Sunday morning." Ned looked confused but kept quiet while we worked it out. "If I say turn and go home, you may question if I have the nerve to go out and get you should the shit hit the fan. If I say push forward, you might wonder if I've forgotten my role as a medic. All I can tell you is you don't have to worry. If the rounds start flying I'll be a shooter first and a medic second, but that doesn't mean I have to choose one or the other. Where you go, I go." Chief looked at me and knew exactly what I was trying to say. We'd had a lot of conversations about our families and personal beliefs. He knew about my calling to medicine and accepted me for who I was from the moment we met. "None of us know the right answer, and since I go where you go all I have to say is . . . how long until we pull out?"

Vic glanced at Chief and then Muscle Tom, who patted my shoulder. He then looked at me for two beats, shook his head, and smiled. "Damn, Doc."

"You're one strange bird, Doc," Chief said quietly as Vic continued on.

"We're going toward the target. We'll be approaching from the northwest and navigate through the wadis. Once we get there we'll reassess the situation. In the meantime I'll inform Wil about the men on the ridge; hopefully he'll be able to have a QRF standing by. Ned, I'll need you, Chief, and Tom to brief the Afghan soldiers on the changes."

"Got it," Tom said as Chief started making a terrain model on the ground to brief the rest of the crew.

We gathered around Chief as he described what was about to take place. I kept watching Ali and the other terps to see if they understood. We counted on fast and accurate translations of orders should we come under fire. Any hesitation or mistranslation could turn a bad situation into almost certain death. Chief knew this all too well, so without hesitation he asked Vic to pull Ned from the lead vehicle and put him back with us. Chief and Tom covered the basics—convoy formation, communications, actions on ambush, specialty teams, and each vehicle's sector of responsibility—before briefing our new route. Ned made sure he translated our plan to each vehicle commander to ensure they fully understood.

"We're moving out in five. Maintain the distance with the vehicle in front of you but don't fixate on it. Remember where we are. If you see something, don't sit on it, report it back, and we'll sort it out."

We loaded up the nine vehicles and slowly exited the hide site as carefully as we entered. The first vehicle in the caravan carried four commandos and one terp. The second was all troops, and the third was Chief and me in our soft-sided Hummer with Ned and Ali. Our vehicle adaptations gave us decent protection against enemy rounds, but I certainly would have preferred an up-armored Humvee. Chief drove and served as navigator due to his familiarity with the route, and I rode shotgun as assistant driver and worked comms. Ned was behind me, and Ali, the terp, was behind Chief. Next in line were two trucks, each filled with commandos, then another Humvee carrying Vic, Muscle Tom, and their terp. Behind Vic were another four men and our mechanic, while two trucks of four trusted commandos with heavy machine guns brought up the rear. We broke camp and rolled toward the objective, eyes alert as the horizon began to glow deep purple and burned orange. We passed a few farms in the distance as we headed toward the ridgeline trail that would eventually lead us into the valley below.

Our movement took us much longer than any of us expected, and the sun began rising in the east. The light was definitely going to expose us, but it also allowed the convoy to navigate the mountain pass. The trails were steep and plagued with potholes and sharp turns. Navigating those treacherous obstacles with NVGs would be extremely difficult for us and suicidal for the commandos to follow. As we drove along, each bump reminded me I should have rearranged my gear for the trip. Jolt after jolt forced my smoke grenades deep into my side. I reached around and pulled two of the culprits out of my harness and placed them in a pouch I had fastened to the dash in an attempt to stop the continuous kidney punches to my left flank.

We stopped at the top of the ridgeline to scope the wadi below. The trail was dangerously narrow and forced the trucks to remain ten yards apart, which meant Vic and Tom were unable to jump forward for a look. Chief and I glassed the valley below with our weapon-mounted scopes.

"What do you think?" Chief asked.

"Looks like we're going to have to widen our distance the rest of the way down."

"I think you're right," Chief answered. Before he could finish his sentence Vic came over the radio. I continued to scan the hills while listening to Chief, Vic, and Tom discuss the situation. It was clear to me why everyone wanted to use that route. It wasn't the type of road someone would use to set an ambush. The wadi twisted and turned multiple times, preventing a clean shot by anyone at the whole convoy. Unless the ambush was set up perfectly, it would give an opportunity to the attacker to be flanked by the men they wished to destroy. If we did get hit, at least the terrain would give us a fighting chance.

As the rest of the team continued to chatter, I told Ali to have our commandos readjust any gear that might have shifted. Rough, rocky trails have a way of rearranging everything, and that can cause problems. Before we left the hide, every piece of equipment and ammunition resupply fit tightly together like a weekend suitcase that would barely close. This made it easy to find everything we needed in a critical situation. After several hours on the goat path, everything loosened up and was sliding around. Exactly what we didn't need. Not only would it be difficult to find critical gear if the shit hit the fan, the heavy weight shifting back and forth as a vehicle negotiated a slope would wreak havoc on a driver.

With the assessment done, we climbed back into the vehicle, and I handed Chief his helmet. He'd taken it off earlier when the sun rose and he no longer needed to use his NVGs.

"I'm not wearing that," he said, pointing to the roof with a grin. The ballistic blanketing we added for extra protection had taken up what little headroom he had, so when he wore his helmet he would have to drive with a bend in his neck.

"You sure you don't want to reconsider?" I jokingly asked.

"I think I know what I want, Shorty," he said with a wink. Ned laughed in the back as we started bouncing down the slope again. I didn't want to argue, so I followed his example and rigged for comfort by moving my med pack from the floorboard and resting it next to his helmet, making a great armrest between the two of us.

When we finally hit bottom it was all business. No one said a word as we listened for radio traffic from the lead vehicle. Everyone kept a close watch on the hillsides. The caravan crawled slowly over a rough path cut through the jagged foothills. Each turn presented a new set of terrain features that we'd quickly scan for movement. Chief's dark eyes primarily concentrated on the lead vehicles and the rocky hills ahead of them while I monitored the terrain from the ten and two o'clock positions. Ned focused on the mountainside to the west, and Ali watched the hills to our east.

The sun was now shining brightly over the hills to our east, raising the tension in the truck. Two hours before, I was wearing NVGs, and now I needed sunglasses to keep focus. The constantly changing conditions gave me an eerie feeling that I'm sure the others felt, too.

We bumped along the winding path at a snail's pace, each vehicle roughly three to four car lengths from the next. The wadi was a relatively flat, rocky area with sporadic patches of sand. It was cut between a big mountain to our right and several large rock formations on the left. These joined together to form an intermittent ridge roughly twenty to thirty feet high and hundreds of yards long. At the base of the mountain to the right, outcroppings of rock formed alcoves along the mountain wall, giving the wadi a snakelike shape. This caused the ravine floor to vary from fifty to one hundred feet wide as it weaved back and forth around the massive rocks.

The first two vehicles crept ahead as Chief wrestled our truck through a deep pocket of sand. Ned and the terp watched from the back as Chief and I silently communicated our observations to one another. Chief sensed something strange about the hills to his left, and through the corner of my eye I saw him sweeping his head back and forth, scanning them carefully. In the sideview mirror, I saw nothing; the vehicles directly behind us hadn't made it past the elongated turn we had just exited. Our vehicle crunched over a group of rocks that came together to form a ramplike structure, which lifted the front left corner of the truck into the air. Chief gripped the steering wheel and was preparing to drive down the rock ramp when I noticed his head snap toward the hills to his left.

"Movement?" I asked, but his response said it all.

"Contact left, contact left!" he yelled out in a controlled voice. Before any of us could react, an RPG (rocket-propelled grenade) blast echoed through the canyon walls. The vehicle had been raised at a 45-degree angle, and I didn't see how close the round had been. All I knew was that the enemy was dangerously close, by the near-simultaneous sound of the rocket launch and the burst of the projectile. The shock wave from the blast forced the vehicle to buck up like a rearing horse, and shrapnel crashed into the undercarriage. I knew then the time we spent lining the floor with the ballistic blanketing had paid off.

A second later, the vehicle slammed to the ground with a force that threw us around like rag dolls. At some point during that ten-second sequence, I hit my head on something in the truck, although I couldn't tell you exactly what. Adrenaline kicked in, and I shook off the pain while Chief grappled with the steering wheel and gunned it. Ned and I struggled to hold on to our weapons while Ali ducked in the back-seat, screaming frantically in Pashtu.

I looked back toward the wadi and saw a second incoming RPG, its trail heading for the vehicle in front of ours. Although I couldn't see the outcome, metal, dirt, and rock rained down upon us. Somehow Chief was able to concentrate enough to keep the vehicle upright. The good news was short-lived, as the ridge to our left erupted in small-arms fire. I could see bullets and RPG rounds tear into the vehicles in front of us and wondered how many seconds we had until the enemy would focus their guns on us.

Time has a way of compressing and expanding in situations of ex-treme duress. During the first moments of the battle, I felt time slow to a crawl, and I swear I could see everything going on around me with perfect clarity. Our truck was still on all four wheels, but we weren't moving, and that was our top priority. One of the fundamental rules of ambush is to get out of the kill zone, also known as the X, and Chief was doing everything in his power to do just that.

Suddenly Vic's voice came over the radio, but it was masked by the thunderous noise from Ned's weapon. Ali had slumped to the floor-board, giving Ned room to shift over and fire through the window. The sound of an AK-47 is loud enough to affect anyone's hearing, but when it's fired inside a confined space it's deafening. He was the only one in a position to return fire, and he took full advantage by pushing his muzzle out the left rear window and unloading everything he had. I'm not sure what he was shooting at, but the sound of return fire made me feel good. Just as he put in a fresh magazine, the vehicle surged forward, throwing Ned back toward his door. Somehow Chief got us back up and running and heading off of the damn *X*.

Chief punched the gas again, and the truck rocketed forward. The fire was now coming at us from our left rear, approximately thirty feet up on the ridge. It was obvious we had surprised the enemy while they were setting up, but they were quickly zeroing in their guns, and our vehicles were in the bull's-eye. The disabled Hilux in front of us blocked our exit, leaving Chief with two choices. He could let the truck fade northwest into a small outcropping of rocks, providing him some cover but exposing Ned and me to a withering barrage of fire, or he could execute an extreme right turn and place the truck into a dry stream bed, providing me a short jump to cover but leaving him exposed. The first option followed the natural flow of the canyon and would only take a few seconds before he was safely behind a group of boulders. The second would force him to wiggle through the cab with all his gear in order to abandon the vehicle, but Chief wasn't thinking of himself. All he cared about was giving us the best opportunity to make it.

One of us would have a long sprint into incoming fire as we tried to reach cover, while the other would have a five-yard jump to safety. We both knew what this meant. One of us was going to have a great chance at survival, while the other would be making a great sacrifice.

"Fade right, fade right!" I yelled, pointing toward the scraggly tree in front of the boulders.

"No!" he said, glancing at me. "Hang on, Doc, and be ready to bail out when this thing stops!" I knew there wasn't going to be much time, so I put my left arm through the strap of my med pack and positioned my rifle so that it wouldn't get in the way. When I looked up I saw Chief forcing the wheel to the right. I looked directly into his eyes.

There are times in life when we know the inevitable is near, but somehow we still try to deny it. I had experienced this a few times on the hospital wards in San Diego and in the triage area of a combat hospital in Iraq. Loved ones and medical providers, including myself, pray for miracles and work the case until the very end. We know there is no denying the outcome, but we reject death because deep down inside we know their courage is our strength. Chief knew what he was doing, and I honestly believe he thought he could make it out of the vehicle, but one thing was for sure: He'd be giving me the best chance to live.

"Get ready to bail, Doc!" He punched the gas, and the truck leaped into the streambed before stalling out.

"Bail out?" I yelled just as the front tires collided with a mound of rock and dirt.

"Go! Bail out!" Chief replied. I threw open the door and jumped out, my M-4 in my right hand while my left held the bottom of the arm strap of my medical bag as I tried to keep it on my back. As I stepped out I could hear the sonic crack of bullets all around me, too damn close for comfort. My first step hit solid surface, and I aimed for an alcove of rocks, and as I took my second stride I noticed a black object whizzing off the left side of my body armor just before I felt a slight punch to the chest. I would later learn the blur was my GPS being torn from its chest mount by an enemy round that also sliced into my magazines and grazed my chest plate. I dove behind some rocks at the edge of the alcove, and as I hit the ground I could see Ned's door open, but there was no sign of Ned. My first priority was to return fire; I crawled quickly six feet up a rocky hill and prepared a shooting position.

As I readied my weapon, I heard Ned yelling orders to his men in his native tongue and Ali screaming shrilly from the back of the truck. Just then I thought to myself, *I need my damn smoke grenades!* They would shield everyone from view just long enough to move to cover—but my back pouch was empty due to my foolish concern about comfort. This wasn't the time to beat up on myself; there would be plenty opportunity for that later. I needed to get rounds downrange, so I turkey-peeked over the ridge of the hill and tried to spot the enemy on the opposite side. They were backlit by the rising sun, making them nearly invisible, at least until the muzzle flashes from their PKM machine guns firing at our three vehicles gave them away.

I raised up on one knee but was careful to stay off the ridgeline to limit my exposure. I took aim through my scope and released a volley of rounds into the flashes on the opposite ridge. I don't know if I hit anyone, but there was a brief break in the enemy's fire before a second hail of bullets was heading my way. Their return fire was heavy but peppering the hill a few feet below the crest, giving me confidence to stand my ground until my magazine ran dry. I slid down a few more feet on my back to reload, making it easier for me to reach my magazines from my chest pouches. The first one I tried to pull was trapped in place by the rounds that tore off the GPS. I shook a second magazine loose and slammed it home. I looked over my left shoulder and saw a flood of bullets and an errant RPG round raining down on the front of the convoy. I then realized that if things didn't start turning around none of us would make it out alive. Radio traffic was crackling in my earpiece, and I heard Vic radioing for air support while Tom was mobilizing the back of the convoy to counterattack. I then wondered where Chief was.

"Chief! Chief!" I yelled out toward my open door, but the only voice I heard was Ned telling me he'd been hit. I knew I had to get to him quickly, but I needed to suppress the enemy's fire; otherwise we wouldn't stand a chance. I half stood, still covered by the hill, and saw Ned lying on the rocks next to his door. It was evident he'd only taken a step or two before the machine gun fire had taken him down. He lay perpendicular to the vehicle, moaning.

"Ned!" I called out to him.

"Doc, I'm hit!" he yelled back.

I knew that I could reach him, but after assessing the situation I wasn't so sure we'd make it to cover. His best chance for getting out of the line of fire would be for Ned to move himself. The enemy wasn't firing at him. They had either forgotten about him or left him for dead.

"Ned, listen to me," I yelled. He replied, then listened as I told him what to do. He paid attention to every word and pulled and rolled himself under the vehicle, where he would be somewhat protected from enemy fire.

With Ned situated and a fresh magazine in place, I slapped the bolt release home chambering a round before moving back to the top of the slope. In my mind I pictured the enemy's position, just as I had seen it a moment before. I readied my weapon and popped over the ridge and released a volley of fire. I got off a couple of bursts into them before an enemy round smashed my front sight, causing it to explode and the rifle to kick back in my hands. Small metal shards peppered my face and ballistic glasses. Half a second later, I felt a slight impact on the side of my head that sounded as if I'd been slapped. It was a ricochet or grazing blow; a direct hit would have killed me. The rounds were too damn close, and I had to move. I crawled off the ridge, then rolled over on my back and slid down the rock bank to the outcropping near our vehicle as enemy fire continued to tear up the ridge above me. My heart was jumping out of my chest, and trickles of blood slowly rolled down my cheek.

I quickly examined my rifle, then fired a test round to ensure it worked. Except for the scope everything functioned fine. Thankfully, someone had the wisdom to put an iron sight on the top edge of the scope. It might not be very accurate but it was better than nothing. It dawned on me then that I *did* have a colored smoke grenade. It was meant for marking our position for an incoming bird, but it would do just fine under the circumstances. Knowing I could screen my movements gave me a mental lift. I immediately drew it from its holster, pulled the pin, and tossed it over the hill into the center of the wadi between the vehicles. It took a few seconds for the smoke to billow enough to conceal my movement, so I threw my aid bag onto my back and returned to the group of rocks I originally fell behind when I exited the truck.

"Chief! Chief!" I continued to call out but got no response.

Vic was coming across the radio asking for a report, but I ignored him while I crawled out to get a better look. I could see Ned nestled tightly under the vehicle, protected by the rear tire and back end of the truck. He was bleeding from the chest but was able to speak clearly between deep breaths, letting me know he was stable, at least for now. As I turned toward my door I saw Chief's hand hanging below the door frame. I was unsure how many minutes had gone by; it all seemed to happen so fast. If Chief was hit, I had to get to him quick, whether we had turned the tide of the battle or not.

Battlefield triage teaches a medic to separate the casualties and focus care based on overall survivability. It isn't that simple on the front line. You can reach some men quicker or easier then others, while others are nearly impossible to retrieve due to enemy fire or location. You can't pass by the ones with the less serious wounds; otherwise you risk destabilizing the very foundation of trust built between the solider and the medic. Then there are times like these.

I knew Ned was alive, and I could reach him much easier than Chief. I realized the chances of Chief being alive were slim, and the opportunity for Ned to bleed out was increasing with every passing minute. But Chief was more than my friend, he was American. I had no choice; I had to go after my teammate. I grabbed the Afghani radio and ordered the terps to have all the men focus their fire on the ridge directly across from me for a few minutes. I then ordered the troops in front of us to watch the northeast area so we didn't get flanked. Once I heard the cover fire open up, I ran out, turned toward the open door, and lunged into the cab.

Chief was sprawled facedown across the seat with one arm dangling out of the passenger door. I landed on top of him and desperately tried to spin myself around in the tight space. Chief was unresponsive to my voice and the weight of my body moving over him, so I suspected he was mortally wounded, or close to it. I dropped my weapon onto the floorboard and opened the driver's door and crawled out the other side. Once on the ground I took off my aid bag and threw it near the front tire, allowing me more freedom to move around.

I crouched by the driver's door and pulled Chief up to a sitting position. His gear was snagged on equipment bolted to the truck, and I could see where it might have trapped him as he tried to slide across to the passenger door. I freed his gear from the snags and lowered him back down between the seat and the center console. With his left side pointed skyward I had enough room to move back into the cab while the rounds ripped into the driver's door and back of the vehicle, making a thumping sound as shrapnel hit the ballistic blanketing. As I crawled over the seat, I could see the passenger seat where his upper torso once lay. It was full of blood, but not a drop anywhere else. I reached over and checked for a pulse, and for an instant I thought I felt a weak and thready heartbeat, but I couldn't be sure. When I pulled my hand away, I noticed blood slowly flowing from the base of his neck. As I felt around, my finger lodged in the entrance wound. Chief had taken a shot in the neck, the bullet severing a major vein. I still believed I could save him, so I immediately reached for my personal medical kit, broke out the gauze, and began packing the wound. Enemy rounds were peppering the roof of the Humvee, and I needed to get out of there before they broke through.

Once again I called out to Ali, who was still on the floorboard behind the driver's seat, ordering him to call for more fire support from the commandos. At the same time Vic came across our radio and assured me aircraft were inbound. I had to move but knew I would draw fire as soon as I did so. I told Ned and Ali to get as low as possible and stay put until I moved Chief to a secure area. I grabbed my smoke grenades from the dash and put one into my pouch, then blindly rolled another under the vehicle, hoping it would find its way to Ned.

"Doc, I got the smoke," croaked Ned.

"Throw the damn thing, will you! Throw it!" I yelled, frustrated and scared by the whole damn situation. Ned pulled the pin and tossed it perfectly. His movement caused the enemy to shift fire toward the rear of the vehicle, but not before I heard the familiar soft *pop* that activates the grenade followed by the fizzing sound the canister makes as it generates its smoke. I hoped it would hold long enough to shield us from the enemy's fire, but I feared the worst.

The smoke rose horizontally as designed and spread throughout the wadi. I pulled Chief out of the driver's side and dragged him by his tactical vest into the ditch at the front of the vehicle. It wasn't ideal cover, but the truck and surrounding ground protected him, and that's all that mattered. With the safety of the smoke I unfastened his chest plate from the back of his body armor and started cutting away his clothes. I moved at lightning speed, desperately trying to find other wounds. I was determined to save the man who was willing to sacrifice his life for mine. *Where is it? Where is it?* I kept asking myself, convinced there had to be a second wound. Once I found it, I'd be able to plug the hole and turn things around, but damn it, there was no other wound. My friend had slipped away; I just hadn't accepted it yet. The man saved my life by deliberately dumping the truck into that very ditch he now lay in, putting himself in the line of fire to allow me an escape route—and there I was, helplessly kneeling beside him, unable to bring back the teammate who saved me. As a SEAL and a medic, there is no darker feeling in one's soul. *Crack, crack, crack.* The sounds of gunfire rang all around me. A round hit the top flap of my aid bag, and the sound snapped me back to reality. My first instinct was to cover the patient, and as I spread-eagled low to the ground, I felt an odd sensation at the back of my clothing, which I later learned was bullets tearing through my gear.

"Doc, this is Vic, over." Vic's voice crackled through my earpiece on the internal channel. I know there are men out there who feel they can stand alone against any adversity, but I'm not one of them. I'm not ashamed to say I've always needed the help of others, so hearing Vic's voice renewed my spirit.

"Vic, this is Doc," I answered, then gave my status report, the one I knew he'd been anxiously awaiting. I also had to break the news about Chief, although I hated saying the words.

"Vic, this is Doc, I have one American KIA."

"Say again last, over," Vic said. Either he wanted confirmation or he hoped he misheard my last transmission.

"Chief is dead," I said bluntly, incapable of answering with anything but the painful truth. The radio went silent for a second or two, and I knew Vic was absorbing the shock.

"Understood, one KIA," Vic said professionally, his voice cracking slightly from the pain that was surging through his heart. After a short pause Vic continued on for a couple of minutes, telling me Chris was leading the 10th Mountain as our QRF, and attack helicopters would be on station within "One-Five Mike," meaning fifteen minutes. That in itself should have given me some feeling of security, but it didn't. However, Muscle Tom was also on the radio network, and I could hear him directing his commandos in the background, which did raise my confidence. Tom was a warrior through and through, and the landscape put him in a perfect position to assemble his men and flank those that killed our friend. Vic closed by telling me to hang in there and switch to the main frequency. Channel-hopping while managing two radios during a firefight was a bit much to handle.

"Doc, remember everyone's talking and listening on the main channel. Keep comms short and only what needs to be transmitted. See you on main channel, Vic out."

"Doc!" I heard Ned cry out in pain. He'd taken another round, and I knew I had to move fast. It was a miracle he was still alive. Normally, an ambush lasts long enough to accomplish the mission, which could mean harassing the enemy with a single IED (improvised explosive device) or complete destruction of the entire force. Clearly the enemy was going for the latter, but we'd interrupted their plans by surprising their forces. We would later learn men were still patrolling and collecting intel when we rolled up on them, but that was ancient history in firefight terms. The enemy had recalibrated and would soon execute the second phase of the ambush. They had the high ground and would attempt to envelop us on three sides and destroy the vehicles and annihilate every living being in or around them. They would also try to capture key pieces of valuable equipment and, worst of all, the corpse of an American. I said a half-second prayer over Chief, picked up my weapon, and concentrated on the men who were calling my name.

The smoke had dissipated by the time I turned the corner of the vehicle and I fired full auto back at the enemy's position. I slung my weapon to the side and pulled Ned out from under the truck. I held his wrists and ran backward toward the area where I'd left Chief and positioned him between the ditch and the front of the vehicle. I pushed on his shoulder and hips and maneuvered him slightly under the front of the truck, putting the engine block between Ned and the incoming fire. I stripped him down while listening to him talk; the sound of his respirations allowed me to assess his ability to breathe and maintain his airway. A round had penetrated his body armor and entered his upper chest but exited midflank. The immediate fix was simple—place an occlusive dressing over the wounds and move on to the next one—but if he was going to live, it was going to take more than a piece of sticky plastic. His leg wound was more complicated. Bone fragments could be heard grinding on themselves through the boot. Ned took the second round just above the ankle, and the once brown boot was dark and puffed out with blood. I placed a tourniquet above the wound and cut away his pants to see if it was in the right position before I finished tightening it down. Ned surged up with pain as the band collapsed around the viable flesh, but it did its job. I was contemplating removing the boot, arguing with myself on its effectiveness as a splint, when rounds starting coming in again.

As I lay flat over his body, shielding it from the incoming rounds, I noticed a tumbling movement at the vehicle up ahead. I looked up and saw another Afghan commando fall to the ground. He screamed for a split second and then started to call out, "Doctor! Doctor!" desperate for someone to help him. It was obvious he had received a round to the upper body, but I couldn't see much more than that. Ned needed additional help, but he was stable, and I needed to move on.

There was nothing but chaos at the trucks ahead of us. I had to rally the troops or else the enemy would flank us. What started as a hasty linear ambush would soon turn into a deadly L-shaped enfilade if their reinforcements took control of the high ground northeast of our lead vehicle.

"Ned, I have to move to the others. Stay still."

"I can hold on, Doc, but I am out of ammo." I knew he could hold on, and he would have lied to me if he couldn't. Ned was a courageous fighter who would have easily sacrificed himself for his men.

"Don't shoot! You'll just draw fire," I said to Ned as I moved the weapons away from him and threw my aid bag on my back. "Take this and throw it when I call for it." I handed him the second smoke grenade from my harness.

"Yes, yes," he answered.

I stood in a crouching position, careful not to expose my body, and ordered Ali to move up to the next vehicle when I gave the word "go." Hell, it was a miracle he made it this far without being shot. For a split second, I wondered what in hell we had packed behind his seat that was absorbing all those rounds. It didn't matter; I had to move.

I started in a low run toward the lead vehicles but was stopped ten feet out by AK-47 fire. The enemy had stopped spraying the vehicles but instead was concentrating their rounds on our movements. Realizing I needed to get down, I dropped to the floor of the canyon and rolled to my right, landing in the same ditch our vehicle sat in. The trench twisted slightly left and right but eventually worked its way up to the vehicles in front. Rather than run across a lane of enemy fire I chose to rapidly belly-crawl up to the men. I heard the sonic crack of small-arms fire snapping overhead as I moved along the trench. As I crawled along, I felt a flood of cold liquid flowing along my lower back and upper thighs. I reached around to my medical pack to determine its origin. As a medic, I realized men can be shot or fragged and feel nothing due to the adrenaline running through their veins, but in my case a bag of saline had been ripped open by an enemy round. I was unsure if the enemy could see my medical bag, thus telegraphing my movements, so I shrugged it off and threw it to the side and continued low-crawling. The closest vehicle was only fifteen yards out, but it seemed like half a mile with the rounds cracking overhead.

While I was pulling Chief from the vehicle, Vic had moved to high ground, giving him a bird's eye view of the battlefield. This helped him direct air traffic to cover Tom's assault on the hill, as well as my movement to the forward trucks. His position also exposed him to enemy fire, but that didn't stop him from watching over us. Every few minutes I could hear him speaking with every available aircraft in country, asking them to get on station and prevent enemy reinforcements from flanking us. The fighting was too close for a bombing run, so we needed Apaches or SuperCobras on station, and needed them fast. We had worked closely with both airframes out of Khowst and in Iraq, and they were experts at supporting ground troops. Make no mistake about it, the strongest man on the battlefield is the one with air support, and those who control the skies generally win. That made Vic our biggest gun and the most important man on the battlefield that day.

I arrived at the vehicle in front of ours and found one Afghan clearly dead in the driver's seat. He'd been shot multiple times and was covered in frag wounds. Two other commandos were shot and lay

prone beside the vehicle, barely covered from incoming fire and im-
mobile. The fourth man was the vehicle commander whom we nick-
named "Dogface." We told him it was because of his tenacity, but it
was really because of his appearance.

Dogface had come off his gun and was staring at his wounded men
in a trancelike state when I got to him. Despite repeated medical training and time on the battlefield, he had never experienced the gore associated with combat wounds, so it wasn't surprising to find him in a state
of shock. A vehicle accident can cause terrible injuries, but the mechanism of injury on the battlefield is much more abhorrent. Combat weapons are designed for the sole purpose of extreme lethality. There really is
no easy way to say it; tools of war do their damage by shearing, tearing,
and ripping the body apart. The difference between hunting and combat
is night and day, and in special operations we understand it all too well.
The need to be familiar with carnage and the immediate care it requires
is one of our most important training requirements. Removing any opportunity for hesitation might be the difference between bringing a son,
husband, or father home.

I pushed Dogface aside and quickly placed a tourniquet above the
wound on one of the casualties while Dogface continued to stare into
the unknown. The other man had sustained a gunshot wound to his
back and RPG fragments to his left side, requiring much further attention, but we needed to suppress the enemy's fire before I could do
anything more.

"Dogface," I said, grabbing at his arm and looking into his eyes.
"Shoot! Shoot!" I kept repeating as I reached for my weapon and began
pointing my rifle in the direction of the enemy. The enemy's rate of fire
had once again picked up, and we had nowhere to go. Earlier, I'd told
Vic the enemy was adjusting and would soon place flanking fire on our
positions. I just didn't think it would be happening so soon. I could
have moved to the ditch for protection, but that meant leaving my casualties behind, and I couldn't do that. There was simply no way for

Dogface and me to move them without getting torn to pieces, and I didn't have any more smoke grenades to conceal us if we tried. It was either leave the men or stay and die. To some it sounds like a simple choice, especially since they weren't my countrymen—but like many things in life, it's easier said than done.

The bonds that form in battle are made of steel, and since the ambush started the Afghan commandos had fought by my side. I don't know when they were wounded; I can only surmise based on where they lay. Their wounds could have occurred when I asked for fire support, giving me the ability to reach my friend and their leader. *They* could have been the reason I made it that far. There was something else, though, something far bigger than any of us, and that was my oath, an oath to preserve life even at the cost of my own. I felt I had partially forgone that promise when I left Ned and helped Chief instead. Regardless of the outcome, I was going to stay with the men and fight it out. I'd like to believe any soldier in my shoes would have done the same. It is the reason we fight. Sure, politics, religion, or in this case attacks against our citizens send us to war, but when the rounds start flying and death is closing in around you, it is the calling of your fellow man that makes a soldier risk it all for another.

Thankfully, Dogface felt the same and snapped back to the fierce fighter we all knew. He readied his weapon and looked to me for guidance. I motioned our plans with my hands, and he nodded, ready for the fight.

"Now!" I called out. Dogface and I raised up from behind the bed of the truck and fired on the enemy. The counterattack, however, was short-lived. I had run out of magazines, and within a few rounds so did Dogface. I glanced into the bed of the truck, hoping to see the ammo boxes within reach, but they'd been lost after the first series of blasts. I was down to a couple of fragmentation grenades, which would have helped earlier in the battle but were useless now. With no ammo at hand, I flipped back to medic mode and worked on the men's wounds.

We were in very dire shape. Rounds were incoming from the ridge across the wadi, and the enemy was setting up a flanking attack. The thought of giving up never entered my mind. I just had to stay on point with my patients and trust in my teammates to pull me out of the mess. As I rendered aid, I could hear the helos, which were inbound and closing quickly. Through the radio, I heard Muscle Tom assault the hill out of sight to our rear. We just had to hang on a little longer, so we all huddled together in the only available corner of cover and waited as the bullets crashed into the dirt, just inches from us.

Then, just as quickly as the ambush had started, the enemy rounds stopped. It had to be Tom; there was no way the enemy would have quit that abruptly with rounds falling right on top of us. I rose carefully and looked across the wadi, and indeed it was Muscle Tom. He had led a squad of men directly into their fire and destroyed their ranks. Concerned only about his teammates, he ran ahead of the others up the hill and flanked the enemy that had killed our men and pinned the rest of us down. He moved along the ridge, shooting controlled bursts from his M-4 while on the move, crushing the enemy shooters and saving my life and the lives of the men under my care. I radioed Vic and let him know we were secure.

"Doc's good to go," Vic said to Tom over the radio.

"Solid copy, we're going to circle around the ridge and see if we can flush out the remaining fighters," Muscle Tom replied.

I watched as he signaled his men into a formation and headed into the mountain shadows across from us.

"Doc, can you get those casualties back here? We've got a CASE-VAC [casualty evacuation] on station in One-Five Mike, and be sure to relay any casualty updates to the bird."

"Roger that, and I'll get everyone moving to your position."

I ordered Ali to break out the stretchers and pass word to the other ANA fighters to do the same. Otherwise they were to stay put with Ned. The second vehicle was still operable, so I had Dogface turn it around so we could transport the wounded to the CCP (casualty collection point) Vic had established near his vehicle. I then moved to the lead vehicle to assess the men.

The lead Hilux was severely damaged and the driver dead, cut to pieces during the opening volley. The rest of the men, however, escaped with only varying degrees of fragmentation and no serious trauma. As I treated a laceration on one fighter's arm, I shot a look at their vehicle and wondered if they had failed to drive off the X as we had rehearsed, trapping the other vehicles, or if the truck had immediately been disabled by fire. As we pulled a stretcher from the bed and started back toward Dogface, I resigned myself to the fact I might never know. One thing was for certain: I wasn't going to question their actions. They were seasoned fighters who had proven themselves under fire, which is why they were at the front of the convoy. Combat is constant chaos; things rarely happen sequentially, and everything comes crashing in at once. This causes soldiers to react to the person, object, or activity they register as the most immediate threat. That's why two men standing side by side firing in the same direction see and remember things differently. I experienced this myself and have listened to others debrief and describe what happened during their battle. Members of the same team often contradict one another on how things went down. On one occasion video feed from a UAV proved that two men fighting together in close proximity remembered two very different scenarios, and both of their memories were slightly different from what the video recorded. That is why our all-volunteer force continues to flourish; our critical judgment is reserved for the circumstances that led to the fight, and not the actions of men and women who were caught up in it.

Two of the commandos carried their fallen comrade by stretcher toward a Hillux we used to evacuate the casualties while one stayed behind and pulled out anything that was salvageable. Dogface had loaded the deceased in the backseat, and the wounded were lying in stretchers placed horizontally across the bed of the truck. He stood by the driver's door watching and listening to the fight on the far end of the ridge, then spoke to the men in Pashtu, telling them to load their KIA in a backseat. We then moved slowly toward Chief and Ned.

Ned wasn't doing well when we pulled up, so we placed him on the hood of the truck and prepared to move out. I could hear the CASE-VAC bird only minutes away, so I ordered two men to stay with Chief and guard the convoy's previous twelve o'clock position. We rolled out toward the CASEVAC area. Ali and I trotted next to the truck and held on to the stretcher handles, preventing it from sliding off the hood. He told me he heard over the Afghan radio channel that Muscle Tom's team was following a wounded enemy soldier, but he was unsure if that was good news or bad. I didn't answer. I knew he was talking about the fight on the opposite ridge that we'd heard earlier while tending to the wounded. Word then came over the team channel that Muscle Tom was receiving sporadic sniper fire. He began speaking directly with the pilots and told them to watch for his smoke. He popped it, then told his men to take cover. He then authorized the birds to unleash hell, and that's precisely what they did. Seconds later, Hellfire missiles screamed from the birds and annihilated the mountain walls on either side of the wadi.

We watched for several seconds, then returned to the task at hand. We had to get the men on an evac flight to the Combat Support Hospital if we wanted to save their lives. I could only do so much on the front lines. The badly injured required a surgeon's knife and a sterile hospital, and any delaying treatment usually ends badly.

We arrived at the CCP, and four commandos began unloading the wounded and placing them in an open area so that I could begin to triage, treat, and dress them for transport. Once the wounded were squared away, the commandos pulled their fallen brothers from the truck and placed them in an area designated for the deceased. Without a word, Dogface grabbed Ali and headed back to recover Chief. I then began working on Ned's chest wound, placing IVs to dispense pain meds and push fluids. I caught movement out of the corner of my eye and turned to see Vic walking down from his vehicle. As he approached, I could see pain in his eyes over the loss of our friend.

"Good work out there. You OK?" he yelled over the noise from the approaching bird.

"I'm fine, Vic. These guys are going to be fine, too."

"The CASEVAC is landing in five. We'll make sure they take Chief on the way out." I just looked up and nodded, then returned to my job. Vic, like the rest of us, was torn up inside. Even though Chief's death was a consequence of an ambush. Vic was the team leader, and leaders always seem to have a way of blaming themselves. Vic saved all our lives out there, and I just hoped he understood it. I watched him turn and head back to his vehicle to coordinate the evacuation and track on 10th Mountain's movement. We were three hours into a very long day and still needed to get back home.

Minutes later, the CASEVAC bird arrived. The injured commandos were loaded first, and the aircrew then unloaded the kickout bundle the team packed earlier. I then asked the crew to take Chief's body, but the aircrew chief flat-out refused, nearly sending me into a rage. I explained that I realized Chief was deceased and this bird was designated to evacuate living casualties, but that didn't matter to any of us. He was our teammate and needed to receive the dignity his honorable service deserved. Few men ever reach the level of service this man had, and I wasn't about to let the plane take off without him.

Vic saw me arguing with the aircrew and quickly jogged over. He guided me away, then turned around and walked directly into the pilot's line of sight at the front of the bird. They spoke quickly by radio. Vic was an Air Force Combat Control officer with a legendary reputation, and he knew what to say to the pilot, and it worked like magic. A minute later, the aircrew chief was apologizing to me and loading our teammate's body onto the helo. Vic returned to the CCP without comment.

Soon after the bird lifted off, Muscle Tom returned with his patrol.

He pointed toward the battlefield, where he'd placed commandos on watch.

"I put two guys up there and over there with PKMs to provide some overwatch for perimeter security. The rest are in teams of two in a perimeter around our position."

"Good call," Vic answered before updating us. "Chris radioed that he reached the entrance to the pass. They're bringing four up-armors and two soft skins loaded to the hilt." Vic paused before continuing. "Doc, we need to fix the vehicles that can be fixed and have everyone ready to move out soon after the QRF arrives."

"I'm on it." The QRF was an hour out. The vehicles were seriously damaged, and I had to get them up and running within that hour.

"What's the status on the east side of the mountain?" Vic asked.

"The rock face on this side is clear. The birds crushed everything along the eastern ridgeline, but it looks like some of the ambushers got away. We found a blood trail heading toward the east and followed it for a while, but there's a lot of ground to cover out there." He paused for a swig of water. "Steep cliffs, rock formations, and a wadi that seems to go on forever. Basically, plenty of places for bad guys to hide."

Once Tom finished his assessment, Vic told us how he directed aircraft to take out an enemy Hilux loaded with men, as well as a foot patrol approaching from the southeast. Not only was Vic saving our lives, he was falling back on his CCT expertise and taking the fight directly to the enemy.

"Tom, I'll need you to come up with a plan to sweep the area when Chris arrives with 10th Mountain." It was a wise decision to let Tom formulate the plan since he was the only one out of the three of us who'd seen the whole battlefield. "Doc, be sure to check on the men, and when you get the chance try to take a break yourself. You look worn out." Vic returned to his Humvee, then assumed his position on his perch overlooking the area. Tom returned to his commandos and assigned several to ready the convoy for the trip back to Shkin. I checked on Dogface and the front three vehicles. Miraculously they were able to get my vehicle moving and had stripped out everything from the lead Hilux.

It seemed the threat had subsided, at least for the time being. I grabbed an empty rucksack and filled it with water, spare ammo, and AK magazines and headed out to each of the sentry positions. I started with the overwatch positions, taking an extra two-hundred-round PKM ammo box to ensure they had plenty. I also wanted to get a full view of the battlefield. Each time I reached the men I'd get a count of their magazines to make sure everyone was fully loaded while they drank up. If they had been wounded, I'd do a quick reassessment, fix what needed to be fixed, and move on. I returned to the staging area two more times to restock my pack and stopped only when I felt the men were ready. After the final run, I sat with Vic and shared an energy bar and water. I realized I was exhausted. We quietly sat together, our silence speaking volumes about the loss of so many lives while we waited for our reaction force to arrive.

15

QRF

★ ★ ★

The tragedy of war is that it uses man's best to do man's worst.
—HARRY EMERSON FOSDICK

Chris arrived with a platoon from 10th Mountain including an air force tactical air controller assigned to the company and a medical team made up of the battalion surgeon and additional medics. Chris was in the passenger seat of the lead vehicle, and we saw his blond hair from a mile out. Vic immediately called a meeting with Tom, Chris, and me along with the officers and senior enlisted from the 10th Mountain. We gathered at the spot where my vehicle sat just hours earlier and briefly explained to Chris and the others what happened. After Vic was through he turned the floor over to Tom. It had been over an hour since we received enemy fire, so we assumed the onslaught of air support that Vic wielded on the enemy ended any desire to continue the assault.

"Captain, I know we all would like to get out of here, but we'd like to sweep the area and gather what intel we could off the enemy dead if you'll allow it," Tom said to the officer in charge of the QRF. The captain's sergeant major nodded in support. Tom suggested the 10th

Mountain platoon leader take a couple of armored vehicles and head toward the southern ridge while another squad joined up with a group of our ANA and followed the blood trail on foot.

"Doc, you're the only other American familiar with the layout of the battlefield. Why don't you take Hamadullah's fighters and the staff sergeant's men and push out toward the east. Chris, grab a couple soldiers"—he paused to see if he had approval from the captain—"and check the bodies on the ridgeline for intel. I'll take some of my men and cover the flank." I could see that Chris was annoyed with his assignment, and when everyone moved away he asked to speak with Tom and me.

"What's up?" Tom asked.

Chris removed his ballistic sunglasses. "I didn't come out here to scour the dead. Frankly, these are my men, and I'm a little pissed I couldn't be here with you all when this happened." I could see both the pain and intensity in his eyes. He was right, he knew these men far better than I. He'd trained them from the beginning and led them under fire on numerous other occasions, and I knew exactly what he was feeling. I had to stay behind on previous operations when insertion platforms or other parameters changed at the last minute. It wasn't a good feeling, especially when the team took casualties. Each special operations warrior has something inside him that screams, "I can be the difference." It's not arrogance or ego; it's simply an unwavering belief in ourselves. It's part of the internal drive that gets us through training and those times when the odds are stacked against us. Unfortunately, it's also what haunts us when our teammates fall. Tom looked at me as if the decision were mine to make. Chris was a top warrior, and the mission had completely changed, so missing the rehearsals was a moot point. I had no problem with Chris taking the patrol.

"I'll do the assessments," I said firmly. "I could use a breather."

With the plans in place, we regrouped and listened as Vic addressed everyone. "Doc's doing the assessment. Chris and Tom will lead the patrols, and Lieutenant, you'll continue as planned. I'll move up to that point and direct traffic. Questions? Good."

Chris and Tom peeled off and rallied their men. Vic walked back toward his perch to discuss plans with the 10th Mountain leadership, and the remaining soldiers reinforced the perimeter. I prepared to visit the dead who had tried to kill me just a few hours earlier.

Chris and Tom led their teams over the ridge and into the wadi, both groups changing patrol formation to suit the terrain. Muscle Tom and his men broke and moved off to the left, while Chris and his men, including a trusted Afghani named Lal, headed straight down the wadi.

I approached the corpses lying on the ground. Their ethnic appearance indicated al Qaeda; it wasn't the Taliban that attacked us. These men were well armed with equipment that rivaled that of most armies. They would have had an enormous advantage on us had they been ready when we turned the corner, but their footprints and empty bullet casings confirmed our suspicions. We had surprised them, and they rushed to try to trap the convoy while the rest of their men filtered into the area. I realized how much of a hero Vic really was. Had he not maintained the discipline to hold his ground in the face of enemy fire and direct air support on the men flooding into the valley, none of us would have made it out alive.

I searched each body for information that might help us locate some of our most wanted high-value targets. As I approached each body, I pictured the man's movements in my mind. A group of men were lying double arm's length from one another in a fighting position that was only a stone's throw away from our vehicle. Another was crumpled next to his RPG launcher with the empty canvas RPG backpack still slung over his shoulder. It was obvious he'd been hit when he came up to unleash his last rocket. Thankfully he only carried four RPG rounds and was unable to keep his cool as he hurried his shots at the vehicles. He might have been the best shot among their group, but the real skill is being able to contain your emotions in battle, and that's not as easy as it sounds, especially when the men you're shooting at will be firing back the minute you give your position away.

I finished my work and joined Vic and the others to watch Chris and his men move toward a fork in the wadi, which in turn splintered into two lanes on the east side of the fork. The three-story walls that lined the wadi had slowly decreased into a series of shoulder- and waist-high berms.

Suddenly a single gunshot echoed through the wadi, sending Lal falling to the ground on the left of the hill in front of them. "Contact front!" was repeated by numerous voices on the radio, notifying the rest of their patrol where the fire was coming from. Chris returned fire off to the right as he moved forward to help render aid to his fallen comrade. The exchange of gunfire made it difficult to tell how many enemy were out there and where they were. Chris moved forward and then suddenly fell, as if he had stumbled or tripped, which gave me hope. Normally a fatal shot would drop a man like sack of potatoes, but if someone is able to brace his fall, he's not only alive but generally aware of everything around him. I grabbed my aid bag and threw it over my shoulder.

"Medic, medic." The call came over the radio from one of the men from 10th Mountain. I got the nod from Vic, and off I went. The chatter over the airways was extensive; Vic received the casualty report over the radio and requested another round of air support. Two men were wounded, and one of them was Chris. I knew I had to get there fast but wasn't sure which way to go. I met up with one of the army officers at the base of the hill and moved forward a short way until we reached a few more of his men. It was obvious these boys hadn't seen what was going on but rather were reacting to sounds and radio chatter. Hellbent on getting there, they tried to move as fast as possible, forcing me and one of their platoon leaders to slow them down in order to prevent a bad situation from turning worse.

"It's like a maze! Which way do we go?" asked one of the soldiers, who looked fresh out of high school. I keyed my radio, but the officer, who didn't look too much older, was already on it, receiving guidance from the perch above.

When the call came back to move, I turned to the men next to me and said in a low voice, trying to temper their adrenaline, "Stay low and keep your eyes open. We don't know who's around the next turn."

One of the primary aspects of special operations training is how to remain calm during periods of pandemonium. Excessive yelling and erratic movements only invoke a frantic state, but keeping your composure instills confidence. A warrior with an even-tempered disposition moving at a controlled pace is often moving as fast as a situation allows, especially when moving into the unknown. It gives you time to analyze the situation and prevents accidentally placing yourself or your men directly in the line of fire. I've seen young medics do it all too often. Unfortunately, Hollywood has them imagining themselves instantly running out to save their fellow man when that might be the absolute worst move. Moving quickly but *cautiously* gives you the ability to formulate a plan for how to approach the casualty and gather support, which is what we needed to do right now.

With help from our eyes on the ridge, we safely navigated the wadi and reached our destination. The majority of 10th Mountain was spread across an open area near us but covered by the wadi walls. The enemy had a clean shot at anybody who meandered into the field between us, so we stayed put. This time, the battlefield looked markedly different. From this vantage point it was impossible to see how the right side of the wadi bifurcated, which might have been the reason Chris was taken off guard. I was unsure if there was another way around, so I turned back to speak to the men behind me and noticed enemy machine-gun rounds ripping into the trail we'd just came from. "Alright, they're on both sides now," I said aloud, trying to visualize the layout of the battle space that I'd been watching while sitting with Vic before this whole thing started. I crawled forward and saw the first sergeant lying with his gun facing toward the enemy, while another American soldier tried feverishly to control the bleeding coming from Chris's chest. We could also hear Lal just ten feet away, writhing in pain as he pressed his blood-filled hands against his belly.

"Vic, you got an eye on me?" I said into my radio mic.

"I've got you, Doc. Hang tight at your current pos. The enemy is right across the wadi."

"I got that part already figured out, but are they located at any other locations other than my ten to two o'clock?" I asked.

"Negative, I don't see anything," he replied while guiding gun-ships into the wadi on a separate radio. For the next few minutes we yelled across the wadi and spoke by radio, forming a plan to retrieve our wounded.

The 10th Mountain opened up with a pair of machine guns and raked the wadi with a wall of hot lead while the rest of the soldiers concentrated on any of the areas they missed. Once we knew a solid rate of fire was keeping the enemy's heads down, the first sergeant who recovered Chris from his initial fall while under enemy fire and an-other man bolted forward to recover Lal while an army medic and I grabbed Chris. We dragged the wounded to the only area in the wadi that shielded us well enough to work on the men.

Chris's face and arms were pale from the lack of oxygen-rich blood. I worked fast on him while the army medic next to me focused on Lal's abdominal wounds. Rounds cracked over our heads and into the ground in front of us as the soldiers continued the fight, yet we were laser-focused on our patients. As I cut away Chris's body armor I felt a notch in the upper right corner of his chest plate. The body armor deflected the round from striking his heart but didn't stop it from nicking the major vessels directly under his clavicle before entering his lungs. Once again I worked hard to pack a teammate's mortal wound praying I would somehow manage to control his bleeding. Chris's body was working against him, however, in its fight to stay alive. The more blood he lost, the faster his heart pumped as it tried to get oxygen into his cells, but the faster it pumped, the more blood he'd lose. It was a vicious cycle that I watched unfold in front of my eyes with no way to stop it. As I worked on Chris I could hear Vic push a pair of Apache helicopters to one of the 10th Mountain officers kneeling only a few feet away, who then directed fire at the enemy.

I unrolled a package of gauze and began pushing it into the wound, attempting to tamp off the bleeder as I called out to Chris, hoping for some kind of response. He had moved forward in order to prevent death from taking the life of his teammate, only to find death closing in on him now.

Despite the extreme pressure I exerted on his chest as I forced the bandage into the bullet hole, I couldn't elicit a response from him. I told myself he knew we were doing everything we could to stave off the inevitable, but I'll never know for sure. Over and over, I reached back into the aid bag, pulling out another bandage or device in my attempt to control the hemorrhage, but my efforts were becoming futile. I then realized the only thing I could provide was comfort. Suddenly my mind raced back to a conversation I had with my father when I was a very young boy.

Like all the kids in the neighborhood, my brother and I played army, running around with toy guns and wearing my father's military equipment as if we were conquering heroes. I would imagine I was the soldier who turned the tide of the battle, emulating scenes I had seen on the silver screen, oblivious to the real horrors of war. Later in the evening as I joined the others at the dinner table, still wearing my father's steel pot helmet, I asked him what was the scariest thing a soldier will ever face. Without hesitation he looked at me and said, "Dying alone." His delivery was so chilling it stopped everyone at the table. His words return to me with every death I encounter, but never with such impact as when I kneeled beside Chris. As I listened to my friend's final breath I was proud that he had his fellow warriors by his side, and I felt fortunate to be with a hero during his last moments on earth. As I wiped away the blood from his upper chest and looked upon him, a great sadness filled my soul. He might have passed, but he looked as if he were only resting. I felt helpless and wanted to reach back into my aid bag and pull out something, anything, in order to restore life, but I knew there was nothing anyone could do.

The sounds of the helicopters flying low overhead woke me from my trance. Pass after pass they fired their guns and rockets, but nothing seemed to slow the enemy's fire, until the young army officer called them in danger close.

I could tell on the approach it wasn't going to be good for any of us. Vic tried to warn over the radio by shouting, "Incoming, incoming!" but the Hellfire missile had already whooshed over our heads, landing forty feet away on the other side of the hill. The blast showered us with rocks and small fragments of shrapnel as we instinctively covered Chris and Lal with our bodies.

"Holy shit!" I shouted out loud. I doubt anyone could hear me because our ears were ringing. Despite the risk, he'd made the right call as the enemy guns finally went silent long enough to allow 10th Mountain's litter teams to move in and retrieve Chris's body while the medic and I carried Lal.

Ideally a litter team would be comprised of four soldiers per wounded man, but the narrow terrain often forced us to carry them two at time, delaying our ability to exfiltrate from the area. Within a few minutes the sounds of sporadic enemy fire once again echoed throughout the canyon, compelling each of us to bend at the knees and waist in order to keep our heads below the hills that sandwiched the trail.

With all of us in a fighting withdrawal, Vic took back control of the Apaches and ordered them to redirect fire to the opposite mountain wall the 10th Mountain's MK-19 grenade launchers had been firing at minutes earlier. The Apaches fired again, and a full layer of the wall disintegrated in a shale avalanche, burying the enemy soldiers below.

The Hellfire missiles calmed things considerably and gave us the opportunity we needed to return to the vehicles, including Muscle Tom's patrol. When I got back to the triage area, I joined the battalion surgeon and his team, who were treating the small fragmentation wounds and other assorted injuries. I then prepared Lal, Chris, and a couple of others for the Casualty Evacuation circling overhead, and once the patients were secured, I collapsed to the ground and drank a quart of water, exhausted beyond words.

Once all heads were accounted for, Vic called in a scorched earth strike, and two A-10s roared down from their holding pattern and turned the entire wadi and the surrounding mountains into a charred, smoking hell.

We then loaded up the vehicles and headed back to the Alamo, this time taking the main road and rolling as fast as possible. Vic requested air support, and with the Apaches overhead the return was relatively uneventful except for one vehicle breaking down halfway home. We stripped it of critical equipment, then watched from a distance as an Apache lit it up with a Hellfire missile, leaving nothing to the enemy. The adrenaline wore off on the way back, but I knew I still wouldn't be able to relax when we got there. It had been a full twenty-four hours since we drove into the wadi and took fire, but it seemed like a lifetime.

16

RETURN TO BATTLE

*There is no great sport in having bullets flying about one in every direction,
but I find they have less horror when among them than
when in anticipation.*

—Ulysses S. Grant

Following the mission at Khand Pass, we spent several days restocking ammo and supplies, repairing equipment, and writing up after-action reports. Life was as close to normal as it can get, and when things become "normal," it means change is inevitable. On one particularly hot Tuesday afternoon, I was typing away on one of the computers when Wil walked in and said, "Doc, looks like the team is going to be pushing out again."

I didn't bother to look up. I knew what it meant—we would be leaving soon, and where we were heading wasn't going to be anywhere good. I asked, "How much time do we have?"

I tried to concentrate on typing, but all I could think about was how I felt the day we returned from Khand Pass.

"Not sure, Doc, it could be twelve hours, maybe thirty-six. Go ahead and sync up with the guys."

"Right, I'll get with the rest of the team," I said absently. I flashed back to that day when we limped in after twenty-four hours of hell, the gates closing behind our mangled vehicles as we pulled into the compound, Chief and Chris no longer with us. I never thought a warning order could be so traumatic, but somehow that one was.

"That'll be good, Doc. Let's meet here at 1400," he said as he wrestled with the jumble of papers piled on the table that we used as a desk. I took a deep breath, forced myself up from my chair, and headed toward the door.

"Alright, I'll let everyone know," I replied.

I headed over to the only vehicle that was under the canopy, thinking I'd drive down to the Afghani camp and let the rest of the team know. When I got to the truck, though, all I could do was stop and stare. It looked dramatically different than when we drove it in that October day. It was cleaned up and all battle damage repaired. Except for the bullet holes, you'd never know that day had ever happened—but I did, and that was all that I could think about. When we returned to the firebase, I walked up from the rear of the convoy and looked over each vehicle and realized how close we'd all come to death. I looked into one of the trucks and stared at the blood splatter that covered the seat and at the spent cartridges covering the floor. I remember standing there wondering which of the casualties was sitting in this vehicle when the rounds started piercing the metal. I ran through the list of wounded and killed, mentally reviewing their injuries and desperately trying to figure out which one it could have been.

Now, I found myself doing the same thing. The vehicles triggered raw memories, and I was overtaken by emotion. It was as if I were losing one of our guys all over again.

"What's wrong?" I asked myself. "You've seen all this before; this is nothing new." Yet it was new! Things were different. No one was shooting at us, and there had been nothing for me to do since our return except reflect on the dead, the wounded, and our mortality. I stood there frozen like a statute, unable to move except for my heart, which was racing at a hundred miles per hour.

I have never denied being scared in battle, but those were fleeting moments generally occurring during an opening volley or a break in the fighting, expunged by incoming fire or calls for help. However, being in the safe confines of the firebase gave me a new perspective about our October battle. I found myself scrutinizing each bullet hole, wondering who was the recipient of the damage caused by the round. This wasn't the typical prebattle apprehension a warrior feels when being inserted into a firefight. The emotion I was feeling was fear, plain and simple, but not fear of the firefight; it was a fear of something *else* that I couldn't quite define. I hid it from the others, but there was no use denying it to myself any longer.

Ironically, this wave of introspection was brought on by the tranquillity we experienced after our return from Khand Pass. During our hotwash after-action meeting, a sonic boom from a bomber overhead had us all jumping for cover and scrambling for weapons, but since that time there had not been a rocket, a round, or a loud noise anywhere near the camp. Each patrol left and returned without a word of enemy action. At first the calm was welcome. Then it became a bit uneasy. None of us trusted the serenity, but over time stillness became the status quo and peace a daily routine. It gave us time to think, not just on the missions ahead, but the friends we'd lost on previous ones.

I praised the firebase walls as we drove into camp that day, but now all I could do was curse them. I knew that had we stayed out there, I would have remained focused and intense, but the walls allowed me let to let my guard down, and upon hearing Wil's news about our upcoming mission, I suddenly found myself questioning my ability to do my job. I couldn't understand it. It wasn't like I was some novice to combat or hadn't faced death before. I had more than my fair share of close calls long before that fateful day. Yet here I was, doubting my ability to save lives. From my first day at BUD/S to the last day of SEAL training, confidence was instilled as a key factor for success. My self-confidence was crumbling, and I knew I had to do something to turn that around. In a desperate attempt at self-therapy, I began talking to myself out loud. I walked to an isolated area of the base and walked and talked to myself, wrestling with the waves of doubt. Then the truth suddenly came out: "I can't watch another man die!" With that, the fear was revealed. I feared having another's life slip away in front of me. I feared losing my teammates. It was my job to care for these men, but somehow I transformed this mission into one meaning that I had to bring them *all* home alive. Logically, I knew this was an impossible burden to bear. No one from either the special operations or military medical community ever said or implied anything of the sort. This was simply a duty I took upon myself. Over the years I spoke with other frontline medics and discovered I wasn't the only one, but now the rucksack of responsibility had grown too heavy to carry, and it wouldn't be long before I'd collapse under its weight.

I should have known better; I should have seen it coming. Like anything else tied to emotion, though the most difficult things to see are always those that are right in front of you. These feelings didn't start with Wil's words. They started decades earlier with my personal promise and a Hippocratic Oath. They were reinforced the moment we returned from Khand Pass, when I began my mental isolation from the others. Wil's words were only the catalyst that set it all in motion.

I gathered my composure and thanked God no one had seen me raving like a madman in the far shadows of the Alamo. As I walked back toward the hooches, I heard the distinctive grinding and popping sounds a vehicle makes when driving across dirt strewn with large rocks.

Muscle Tom was returning from a day of training with the Afghani troops. Ever since the Khand Pass mission he had been feverishly working with the replacements for his commando team, trying to ensure everyone had a solid understanding of the tactical maneuvers. They'd lost a number of skilled fighters that October day, most of them ones Tom had personally selected and trained. He knew that if America was ever going to be able to call this war in Afghanistan a victory, these men had to defeat their enemies on their own with the same swiftness and violence of action they displayed when we led them into battle, and he wasn't about to let the Afghanis slip backward in their newfound capabilities.

"What's up, Doc?" Tom joked in his surfer voice, which always carried a smile in its tone.

"Looks like we're heading out soon, not immediately, but real soon," I said. I think he sensed what I was feeling, but he just smiled and looked at me like he'd expected the news. I helped him gather the gear out of the truck and transfer it into our makeshift armory before walking with him to our living quarters.

"So what's the story, Doc?" he asked.

"I don't know, Tom, but I'm sure one of the targets just popped up on the radar or something along those lines."

"Well, it eventually happens. Plenty of bad guys out there," he said as we approached the building.

"I hear ya."

When we reached the door, he stopped, turned to face me, put his hand on the back of my shoulder, and said, "Do you? Do you, Doc?" He was reading me like a book. I stood there speechless. He looked me directly in the eyes and said, "Eventually things are going to happen, and there's nothing *anyone* can do about it. Not even a SEAL medical officer."

He then gave me a half of a hug, the way warriors do when they survive a battle but realize they may still die in the war. Tom had saved my life once before when I was pinned down and out of ammo, and once again he made his way back to me—only this time to save me from an emotional ambush of my own doing.

One battle was over, but the war of combat stress between my mind and soul was just getting started.

"Let's go," he said as he turned and entered the briefing room where the rest of the team awaited us.

———————

Wil started from the top. 10th Mountain was going to push into an area the group had wanted to get into for some time. Because they were expecting strong resistance, the army would be dedicating both artillery and air support to their operation. This would be key because intelligence assets in the area informed us that one of our objectives was residing in a village stronghold that we believed al Qaeda was using as a staging area. Corroborating sources supported these claims, but due to the intense terrain the effectiveness of aerial photography and drones was limited. That meant someone had to be in place before the main force started to move in. Normally a mission like this would have been too risky for a group our size. We had already felt the effects transit time had on air support and the quick reaction force during a prolonged battle, and no one, especially me, wanted to experience that again. Having fire support and 10th Mountain's forces immediately available tipped the odds in our favor.

Our mission would be reconnaissance, more or less. We were to coordinate and travel with a small element of Afghani forces familiar with the territory to a position that would allow us to put eyes on target. Once in place we would establish a virtual catch net to snare fleeing insurgents by guiding in intercept forces. This meant we had to be a small force, so that we wouldn't draw attention from a distance. We also had to move quickly in open terrain and have the capability to maneuver through the mountainous narrows. Yet at the same time we had to be large enough to establish multiple observation posts necessary to cover all the possible escape routes. What that meant to me was getting back into the same damn trucks I was fixated on only an hour earlier and returning to the badlands that we just fought our way out of a few weeks ago. I felt my guts tighten as the anxiety set in.

Wil finished the operational overview, looked at the group, and then made personnel assignments.

"Tom," he said, looking at Muscle Tom, "you and Ranger Tom will guide the team into place and run the Afghani fighters. Remember, with Ned still recovering from being wounded at Khand Pass, you're going to need terps with you to make sure you can direct those men should things start to turn south."

He continued with assignments, but I didn't pay too much attention. I just sat there anxiously waiting to hear if I would be going on the op. A month earlier I would have given anything to be included, but now I wasn't so sure.

"Doc, you'll assist them, but you know better than anyone why we'll need you out there."

I looked across the room at everyone, catching most of them by the eye before I turned to Wil and said, "Check."

He went on, and I sat there taking in what he and everyone else had to say while staring intently at a map on the wall behind him. As I focused on the area of operation, I thought back to a conversation I had years earlier with one of my mentors. Doc C was an old Special Forces medic turned Ranger physician assistant. Wounded on more than one occasion while caring for his men, he had become a legend and someone I would follow into the gates of hell without hesitation.

"Maarkk," he said in his thick Italian New York accent, "everyone is concerned how they'll perform the first time they come under fire, but what you don't hear about is the battle that goes on inside a medic until he gets back there again."

Then he told me a story from Vietnam emphasizing his point in an effort to save me from the abyss I found myself entering. Back then, I thought I understood his message, but in reality I had no context to put it in. Unfortunately, that was no longer the case.

The horrors of war have a way of changing something inside of you that words simply can't explain, and those who never experience it will never be able to truly grasp the pain. Emotions tear at you from the inside, trying to find their way out at the expense of your sanity.

I would rather die than have my teammates go into battle without me. Yet the thought of having one of those men suffer horrible wounds or die in front of my eyes was killing me. I took a deep breath and concentrated on how Doc C's lesson ended.

"We all go through this, Mark, it's our unspoken bond," he had said. I thought about it and realized Doc C was right. No matter how agonizing it is, it's just another rite of passage. I had made a promise and taken an oath like all those medics before me. Death would've been the easy way out, but it wasn't in the cards. Soon I would be back where I was supposed to be, on the battlefield fighting side by side with my teammates and maybe picking up some of the pieces of me that never left.

I tuned back in to Wil. "You're going to initially move out with 10th Mountain, then break away as you start to near the area of interest," he said. "Vic is going to be the on-scene commander, so from this point forward, get with him on the finer details. Any questions?"

"When is army projected to pull out?" Tom asked.

"0400 on Friday. That gives us just under thirty-six hours to get you all ready."

There were a few more questions, but nothing of significance for the group, and with that everyone rose from their seats and headed to the door. I could hear the typical conversations about what needed to get done first, spiced with the usual wisecracks that reflected our group's trademark sick sense of humor.

"Doc, you got a moment?" Wil asked. Vic was standing next to him.

"Of course," I replied.

I walked the short distance separating us and stood facing the two of them. Vic looked at me and said, "Doc, I know how you feel about Muscle Tom, but because I'm going on this mission, I need the guys most familiar with the area up front, so I'm putting Tom and Tom together." He paused slightly before continuing. "I'll need you to be my driver in the middle of the pack."

I know this may seem like an insignificant conversation, which guy goes where, but it was anything but that to me. We had all saved each other's lives out there at Khand Pass that day, but I had watched Muscle Tom save mine. Somehow, it made me feel a little closer to him. I looked at them both, gave a half smile, and said, "Not a problem."

As I started for the door, I realized how lucky I was to work for men who knew me well enough to tell me that news in private, and suddenly a great deal of the weight was gone.

The convoy was remarkably similar to the Khand Pass mission: nine vehicles, four men in each, packed tight with weapons and gear. Ranger Tom and Muscle Tom would alternate as the lead vehicle with the Afghan platoon leader. Afghan commandos manned the following vehicles, putting the vehicle manned by Vic, two terps, and me in the center of the pack. Behind us were four more Hiluxes filled with Afghan commandos, several of them new replacements for the valiant warriors lost on the Khand Pass mission. There was one distinct difference this time, however.

Our target was an al Qaeda senior leader holed up in a small village carved into a sheer mountainside, roughly fifty meters above the wadi floor.

The access route to the target was a rugged washboard trail along a rocky ridge that shook our heavily laden vehicles like toys, tested even the most robust suspension systems, and challenged the arm strength of the drivers. The path was dangerously narrow and squeezed by a steep mountain face to our immediate left and a deadly cliff dropping straight down to our right. I could barely open the driver's door, and anyone exiting the passenger side had two feet of earth, then nothing. I felt uneasy knowing the horribly precarious situation we faced on this trail heading toward the village, which lay across the wadi on the opposite ridgeline. If there had been another route we surely would have taken it, but this was the only way to the objective.

Those who have experienced the outlands of Afghanistan are familiar with the treacherous, unforgiving terrain; perhaps the most difficult on earth and certainly the worst I've ever encountered. The harsh conditions would often force convoys to move at speeds no greater than fifteen miles per hour for hours on end, often telegraphing their approach and allowing the enemy, sitting on mountaintops miles away, the time they needed to establish an ambush or set an IED.

That day was no different, and the slow speed at which we traveled likely compromised our element of surprise. I had firsthand experience with ambushes and prayed we wouldn't encounter one, although I knew we probably would.

As we continued toward the pass, Vic studied a map spread across his lap while I kept eyes on the Toms' vehicle near the front of the convoy.

Vic spoke into his radio. "We're coming up on the entrance into the canyon, and it might get squirrelly. Keep it in the road." The treacherous road was covered in the mission briefing, but it was nice to have a running update from the boss.

The fifty meters of road leading to the pass was fairly wide and relatively flat, and my confidence was high. Then the Toms' vehicle abruptly vanished as if they'd fallen off the face of the earth, and I knew a steep drop-off was just ahead. Their radio chatter told us they were doing fine, at least for the moment, but when Vic and I finally saw what lay ahead we couldn't help but look at one another and let out a disturbing "you've got to be kidding me" laugh. We then saw the Toms' vehicle ahead and below us, approaching the treacherous S-curve that served as a gateway to the flat wadi floor.

We inched down the gravel path and hit the sudden drop-off, sending the pucker factor off the charts. The smaller rocks were like marbles under our tires, forcing us to ride the brakes and curse through clenched teeth as we wrestled the vehicles down the path. The vehicles, packed with troops, armor, weapons, and supplies, were very heavy. When combined with gravity, the heavy load strained the brake systems, requiring us to stop every few minutes to allow the pads to cool. It was clear the "road" had been cut into the side of the canyon centuries ago to allow merchants and armies access to the wadi below, and little had changed since then. As I pumped the brakes and eased the truck down the path, I whispered a prayer of thanks for the highly popular spec ops driving course I'd taken. If it weren't for the enemy forces hell-bent on killing me, I might have enjoyed the ride, but the threat of ambush was very real, and we all felt it.

As I wrestled with the vehicle, Vic kept his attention on the opposite ridgeline and began to announce our intended route. As he spoke, I added my own mental commentary:

"Doc, once we hit the hairpin turn at the bottom and roll into the wadi, we'll need to head northwest *(once again exposing ourselves to the open area we just left)* for a few hundred meters toward the road on the opposite ridgeline *(which appears to be equally as dangerous as the one we're currently on)*, which will take us up to our recon hide on the outskirts of the village *(the village filled with bad guys, who definitely hear us coming and will try to kill us)*." I always enjoyed riding with Vic, and I like to believe he felt the same, so I generally kept comments like that to myself. I'm sure he didn't want to be reminded of those particulars just then.

Halfway down the steep path, we stopped briefly to cool the brake pads. We were still relatively high off the wadi floor and, as the middle vehicle, had a good view of the vehicles in both directions. Vic ordered the convoy forward, and as we descended the road became increasingly more treacherous. It was as if the ancient mountain were mocking our attempts to drive her paths with our modern machines. Vic looked down to the wadi on his right, then up toward the village on the opposite ridge, and whistled quietly. A silent blanket of uneasiness fell over everyone, sharpening our senses and reminding us to keep moving through a very precarious situation. Vic's gaze returned to the point where the path met the wadi.

"The Toms are navigating the hairpin now," said Vic, his eyes scanning the rocks above the hairpin, clearly tense. Several seconds of silence followed.

Muscle Tom radioed a SITREP via the secure team radios. "We're through. The last turn is a bitch; take it easy. We'll move forward and guide the rest of you down."

The Toms drove thirty meters up the wadi, dismounted, and quickly scanned the surrounding area with their weapons optics. Both men were battle-hardened special operations warriors with extensive combat experience, and each had a sixth sense that saved many lives. We were fortunate to have them on point.

The second vehicle of ANA commandos then exited the hairpin, turned north and crawled up the wadi, and then parked just beyond the Toms' vehicle. The third vehicle was nearly through the hairpin turn as the fourth neared the entrance; we'd be next.

Just as we prepared to crawl forward, Ranger Tom's voice crackled in our earpieces.

"Looks like a stick man wearing fatigues on the opposite ridge, far north end," he stated in a flat professional tone. Ranger Tom was like ice on the battlefield. "I think we need to move!"

Within seconds, we heard a bone-chilling sound we knew too well: a blast followed by the distinct whizzing sound and subsequent explosion of an enemy RPG. I felt a cold grip in my gut but shook it off and guided the truck behind a small rock formation that provided a few feet of shelter to our midsection. RPG rounds were now falling around the formation, but none on target. It was obvious the enemy intended to disable the front vehicle and trap the rest of us on the mountainside, allowing the gunmen to pick us off one by one. It was a classic ambush technique, one we shouldn't have survived. If the tables had been turned, the battle would have ended quickly and decisively. Thankfully, they had nothing close to our level of military skill and executed poorly.

While the enemy could be fierce and fearless, they fought as individuals rather than as a unified fighting force. They had little grasp of the team concept and made the same mistakes time and time again, battle after battle. Their incompetence worked in our favor and gave us precious seconds we needed to react and fight through their inept execution of their ambush, which on this day was the key to our survival.

As the initial blast echoed through the wadi, Vic consulted maps and coordinated with the Toms by radio. I reverted to training that was ingrained in me early on: Get off the *X*, pronto.

The Afghan commandos were on a separate radio channel and didn't hear Vic's commands. Many of the ANA traveling with us weren't on the intersquad radio channels, so I began shouting to those around us, "Off the *X*! Keep moving. Get off the *X*!" Getting out of the kill zone was all that mattered, and there should have been zero hesitation doing so. We had rehearsed it countless times, and its practical value was bolstered at Khand Pass. Perhaps our living through a deadly ambush, which no one should have survived, reinforced bad habits. For some unknown reason, however, the ANA troops exiting the turn discarded their training and were nearly killed for it. As they reached the turn at the canyon floor the driver moved to the center of the wadi, stopped his vehicle, and dismounted his troops. They took cover behind their vehicle, and later nearby boulders, as the RPGs rained down upon them. Their AK-47s were ineffective at that angle and essentially useless, and the PKM mounted on top of their exposed vehicle gave the enemy a perfect target to zoom in on. Rather than break it free and hand-carry the weapon they abandoned it as they drew the enemy's fire. Their leader's foolish tactic could have signed his men's death warrants, but to them, it didn't matter. They were driven by a sense of ancient tribal pride. The Afghan warriors who made up our ANA detachment were hardened fighters raised in a land that has experienced warfare since the dawn of its existence. From the moment they were born, they were taught that one's survival equates to one's courage in the face of battle. A man must stand and fight, and to run away demonstrates cowardice. This was the modern battlefield, however, and we needed them to stand and fight, *just not there.* Vic was on top of it and immediately ordered all the men to get back into their vehicles and off the *X* while we still had the chance to do so, although I'm not sure they heard him. They continued to unload their weapons and swear loudly in their native tongue.

Just then a dangerously close RPG blast hit the ground below our vehicle, sending shards of rock and shrapnel straight up in the air. Moments earlier the cliff was a hazard; now it was a shield that propelled the fragmentation up and away from us. Had the round been a few feet higher, a few of us certainly would have been mortally wounded. The RPG reminded Vic and me that we needed to act fast and to get the hell out of our bullet trap as well. I jumped out the door and grabbed a machine gun out of the back of the vehicle and began returning fire. I wasn't sure where they were, but we needed cover fire, so I bombarded the area where I thought they might be. Vic's door was useless considering the cliff on his side of the vehicle. He was wearing body armor and enough equipment to make even the thinnest individual a wide load, yet he flew across both seats and exited the vehicle like a gymnast. Bullets are excellent motivators. Once out, we moved to the front wheel well and the protection of the engine block. It's amazing how two grown men wearing full battle gear can compact themselves into a safe position when RPG rounds are bouncing around.

PKM rounds ripped into the terrain around us and peppered the unshielded portions of the vehicle's exterior. We were relatively safe behind the thickest part of the vehicle, so we assessed the battle space and quickly formulated our plan. We were experienced fighters in the region and understood how long it would take for air and quick reaction forces to respond. In order to act, we had to know the enemy's exact location; otherwise we might turn a bad situation into tragedy. Muscle Tom and Ranger Tom had moved from their position in the wadi down below to an area that afforded some protection as they looked up at the opposite cliffs, trying to get a bead on the enemy. As at Khand Pass, the enemy was backlit, and the sun made it nearly impossible to locate their position, except this time it was the late afternoon and the sun would eventually fall behind the opposing cliffs. Vic was busy calling for air or artillery support while trying to get our Afghan warriors in front of us back in their vehicles and on the move so we all could get the hell off the X. That left it to me tackle one of the most difficult aspects of counterambush in the mountainous terrain of Afghanistan: locating the dug-in men who were trying to kill us. In Afghanistan there is a seemingly endless amount of ground to cover when looking from ridgeline to ridgeline. Throw in caves, boulders, sunlight, distance, and a hundred other external details, and the task of finding a small group of men is a daunting one.

I moved from the position with Vic to the rear of the vehicle and squatted behind a tire. I did a mental inventory of what we knew: There was a scarecrowlike figure on the opposite ridge. Their fire was relatively inaccurate, which meant they were probably either hurriedly assembled or impatient and undisciplined. I knew the general direction from which they fired and had a good idea of their numbers. It was probably a small contingent of men; otherwise we would have been shredded during the initial volley. I did the mental math, took a deep breath, and stood for a three-second peek over the wheel of the vehicle. "OK, they weren't where I thought they were," I said to myself out loud, an odd habit of mine while under fire, "time for another look . . . perhaps a bit higher on the ridge?" I knew better than to come up in the same spot twice; I learned that lesson from the metal fragments that peppered my face during the Khand Pass ambush. I moved to a different part of the vehicle and took another three-second glance at the opposing ridge. I saw the muzzle flashes of a PKM clear as day, even with the sun shining directly in my eyes. Bingo, I knew where they were. I jumped back behind the rear wheel well just as another volley of PKM rounds ripped into our location. Had I stood half a second longer, one of the 7.62×54 mm rounds traveling at 800 meters per second would have taken half of my head clean off. I sat back and quickly pulled out the map, trying to get a decent set of grid coordinates for Vic. I looked over and saw him reporting in to air controllers, with hopes of getting some support here sooner rather than later. Vic was locked in; he had been in this situation before, and his calculating demeanor had taken over. I knew if anyone could conjure up fire support it was him. I relayed the coordinates to Vic and described the natural and man-made fortifications being used by the enemy.

Vic finished his radio conversation, then turned to me. "Doc, air support is inbound, but it may be a while. We need to get this damn convoy moving." He glanced over his shoulder toward the front of the convoy and made a command decision. "I'll work on the vehicles up front; you take the rear."

"Roger that" was all I said as turned around and moved toward the rear of the truck. I crouched behind the wheel, waited for a brief lull in the gunfire, and then sprinted up the road toward the vehicles at the rear of the convoy. As I ran along the path, enemy rounds crashed into the cliff wall, and bits of rock stung the exposed skin on my face and neck. They were close, but not close enough.

My first three stops along the road were with ANA soldiers who'd taken cover behind their vehicles and surrounding rocks. I low-ran to each cluster of men and treated a few minor wounds while directing their fire onto the enemy's position. In some cases, I had to pull them from behind the rocks so that I could point out specific targets on the opposite ridge. I also had those within effective range concentrate fire on the enemy gunmen to provide Vic some relief as he tried to get the front vehicle moving. At each vehicle, I ordered the driver to start it and let it idle so the convoy would move quickly when the time was right. The rear of our convoy was almost out of the enemy's range, so when I reached the last Hilux I stood up straight, stretched my back, and caught my breath. Just then the QRF from 10th Mountain arrived. I pointed out the enemy positions, but the experienced American soldiers had already tracked the muzzle flashes from the hilltop and were setting up a counterattack. The sun was beginning to set, and now more than ever we needed to get moving. I couldn't imagine trying to navigate those mountain goat paths in low-light conditions.

During my mad dash, Tom and Tom gathered the few men they had from the vehicle that made it to the bottom and moved them out of the wadi. Ranger Tom assembled a maneuvering element while Muscle Tom began to set up the 60 mm mortar that he always carried in his vehicle. The 60 mm is a versatile, lightweight, high-angle-firing weapon specifically designed to support close-in fighting. It was a perfect choice for the terrain of Mangritay. This weapon had the ability to clear the natural obstacles our enemy was hiding behind and maintain the destructive force necessary to penetrate their defenses when it dropped in to say hello.

Back at the rear of our convoy, I briefed the 10th Mountain officer on the plan Vic and I had put together. He then added his suggestions, and we called it in to Vic and the Toms. It was fairly simple: I would start back down the mountain, ensuring our personnel and vehicles were ready to roll. When 10th Mountain saw me nearing my vehicle, they would let go with the M-2 .50 caliber Browning machine gun, aka "the fifty," and the MK-19 automatic grenade launcher, concentrating their fire on the enemy's position. They would maintain a constant flow of return fire that would naturally start to die off when each group of ANA fighters climbed on board their vehicle to move out. Once everyone was mounted up all of our vehicles would move forward, except the last one. It was far more sensible for 10th Mountain to tow it backward over the initial hump and have the men remain with them until we were able to link back up at a later time, rather than expose them to fire. At the front of the convoy, Vic would somehow get the stalled vehicle moving and clear the path for the rest of us. Muscle Tom, meanwhile, would start a flanking maneuver once we were safely out of their direct fire. Somewhere along the way down the mountain, I would pick up Vic, unless he was piloting another vehicle.

On Vic's command, I sprinted down the mountain, once again low-running from truck to truck. The incoming fire was still sloppy and undisciplined but also very dangerous. I reminded each of the ANA fire teams of the plan, then continued toward the front of the convoy. As I reached the last vehicle before mine, the mountain behind me erupted in a thunderous explosion from 10th Mountain's gunners. Up ahead, Vic cleared the stalled vehicle and ordered their asses off the mountain before returning to ours. I opened the door, and once again he scrambled across the seats as I jumped in behind him. "Get us down the damn mountain, Doc. Don't be shy." I gunned the engine and threw it into gear and bounced down the path toward the wadi floor below. I was monitoring radio traffic as I drove and was relieved to hear the 10th Mountain guys report the convoy behind me was mobile. I wrestled the truck around one of the curves as I rattled down the mountain just before 10th Mountain's return fire fell silent. As powerful a weapon as the MK-19 was, it always seemed to jam at the most inopportune time. For some reason the .50 cal went silent, too.

"You just keep your eyes on the road," Vic said as he looked behind us, relieved to see the ANA troops were following the plan. "Good, good," he said as he turned back and focused on the path in front of us.

"Roger that!" I gassed it and tore into the final curve in the path.

We reached the bottom with such a thud the doors of the truck flew open and Vic nearly tumbled out. "Hang on, boss!"

"*Now* you tell me? Did they teach you that in SEAL driving college?"

Just before the initial attack kicked off, the Toms and a couple of ANA vehicles had entered the wadi, turned right, and moved out of the enemy's range. Once the ambush started, however, the wadi became the *X*, and we were approaching it quickly.

Having seen the vehicle in front of us fall into the enemy's crosshairs, I yelled out, "We can't turn right. They'll shred us with machine-gun fire!"

"Roger that," Vic yelled back. "Hang on!" The truck rolled into the wadi, and I bolted straight forward across open ground as rounds rained down from the opposite cliff. They had expected us to turn right, and our amended plans threw them off. When we reached the halfway point, the 10th Mountain boys unleashed hell, having got their guns back online. The brief break in incoming fire allowed us to unclench and concentrate on finding a safe area out of the enemy's range. Ironically, the safest place was against the opposite mountain face, directly below the enemy's position.

As soon as we parked the vehicle, Muscle Tom's voice came over the radio net. "Doc, I can see you from here. That was the right call."

I rogered up, exited the vehicle, and reminded everyone to watch for grenades from above. We took cover behind a large rock formation along the edge of the wadi as the ANA vehicles continued to exit the curve and move to our position. Meanwhile, Vic was working air support.

"Birds are incoming. We're staying put for now. I'm pushing control of air support to Muscle Tom," he said calmly.

"Good copy. I've got air support," responded Muscle Tom.

A few minutes later, two army SuperCobras arrived on station, and Muscle Tom directed them in to the enemy's stronghold. We quickly deployed bright orange VS-17 signal panels and stretched them across the hoods of our trucks so the gunships would know we were there. For good measure, Vic contacted them and advised them of our position. Seconds later, the birds lit off their weapons, turning the ridge above us into a smoky hell.

Twenty minutes later, we rallied at the far end of the wadi with Tom and the first trucks that pushed through.

During the battle, Muscle Tom quickly placed a pressure dressing on the hand of one of his ANA soldiers, which warranted further attention. The round tore away the majority of his fingers and part of his thumb and palm. Although I was able to control the bleeding, he would eventually need the care of a surgeon; the question was how long I could delay before getting him there. Calling for a casualty evacuation of our wounded could take the medical birds offline for over an hour. Normally this wouldn't be a concern, but with 10th Mountain and another special operations team conducting missions northeast of our location as part of a larger operation, I considered the consequences for my fellow Americans. With limited air-medical evacuation assets in the region, our request for an EVAC could easily translate into a prolonged transit time for a wounded American, jeopardizing his life.

The wounded are surviving injuries that would have killed others in previous wars because of better personal protection and, more importantly, shorter transit times to advanced surgical care. This was undoubtedly the case in Iraq, where the vast majority of military hardware was located in support of that effort, including medical evacuation helicopters. There was also a disproportional amount of medical assets. In Iraq the number of Combat Surgical Hospitals in an area of operations often mimicked the number of Starbucks you'd find within a suburban mall, one every ten feet. Often surgeons would spend most of their time assisting locals, but in Afghanistan the medical support assets were considerably less, whittling away at the golden hour.

I wrestled with my thoughts for a minute as I continued dressing wounds and remembered having to choose between Chief and Ned only weeks earlier. Then it was clear, save my teammate, but now the situation was somewhat hypothetical; from the radio we knew 10th Mountain and marines operating north of our position hadn't reported any casualties, at least not yet. By the time I had assessed the last man, I had decided on my recommendation. Although the choice ultimately lay with Vic, I knew my thoughts would weigh heavily in his decision.

I would like to say there are no differences among allies, but truth be told there is always some friction between American soldiers and the ANA, including within myself. I had seen Afghanis join the national army only to defect once they received their weapons, at a rate that made it nearly impossible to grow the force, and there was no denying the ethnic frictions and brokering of influence and corruption among certain elements of the country's security forces. We might have removed the Taliban from power, but it was the Afghan security forces responsibility to carry the fight forward in order to establish a strong central government.

I couldn't risk it—the life of an American outweighed the need for an expedited transport to the CSH. The wounded would evacuate by ground with the rest of us. We needed to get moving soon. The sun was starting to set, and we had a long haul ahead of us through badlands.

I shared my thoughts with Vic, Tom, and Tom, and as I suspected they agreed with my recommendation. Tom kept a terp in his car and once again took the lead on our way to meet up with the 10th Mountain leadership. The target of our recon mission was either dead or long gone, so Vic made the decision to abort and head back to the Alamo. One of our vehicles was completely destroyed, and two more were banged up pretty badly. Our ammo was depleted, and night was setting in. The team leader for 10th Mountain offered to escort us part of the way back, and we gladly accepted. An hour later, we were on the road to Shkin, relieved the action was over. Or so we thought.

17

CRIMINAL ENCOUNTER

*Valor is a gift. Those having it never know for sure whether they
have it till the test comes. And those having it in one test never know for sure
if they will have it when the next test comes.*

—CARL SANDBURG

We traveled through the dark for another hour without a
hint of trouble. I was driving the command vehicle, with
Vic riding shotgun and our interpreter in the backseat
behind me. The mood was light, but the troops were ready to get back
to the firebase. Over the past seventy days the camp had lost five Americans and twice as many ANA commandos, and nerves were raw. As
we drove toward our haven in the middle of hell, I contemplated the
losses and engagements that had occurred since my arrival in Afghanistan. From the rocket attack to being trapped on the side of the mountain, it felt like a steady flow of death and destruction.

We reached a fork in the road, and 10th Mountain signaled us to
pull over. We could have said our good-byes over the radio, but after
everything we'd been through it just didn't feel appropriate. The patrol
leader dismounted and began walking toward our vehicle with his sergeant in tow. Vic, Muscle Tom, and Ranger Tom joined them while
I walked to the vehicle behind ours to reassess the casualties.

"Well, this where we U-turn. Are you good to go?" asked the patrol leader.

"We're good. Thanks for playing along. Keep your heads down and get home safe. Good hunting," said Vic.

"Will do. Give us a shout if you need anything, and we'll see you back at the firebase in a couple of days." Everyone shook hands before the 10th Mountain boys climbed into their armored Humvees and rolled off into the dark countryside to join up with the rest of their force.

Vic walked back toward our vehicle as Muscle Tom went to each ANA vehicle and informed them he'd be taking lead; more importantly, he reminded everyone to stay vigilant. Exfil is always one of the most dangerous components of any operation. The mental and physical drain placed on individuals as they execute the mission often fools soldiers into letting down their guard earlier than they should. Considering there was still plenty of Indian country to cover before we made it to friendly lines, we couldn't leave anything to chance.

The convoy saddled up and drove on for quite some time, the full moon and stars lighting our way like dim streetlights. We moved from flat desert terrain into rolling hills covered with scrub brush and clumps of trees, and every one of us became tuned in to our surroundings. It was getting close to midnight, and we'd just entered an area known for its criminal activity, which meant Taliban to me. I switched on my NVGs as the increased foliage disrupted the celestial light and peered out into the night, a greenish glow illuminating a country plagued by ancient and deadly customs.

When I first arrived in country, I was able to differentiate Taliban soldiers from the hordes of criminals that ruled the lawless land, but as the war went on they all seemed to blend into a single cesspool of opportunistic scum. In my mind every Taliban was a criminal, and at least half the criminals were Taliban. There was no governance under their years of control, only an agenda of intolerance and cruelty. I couldn't imagine my family growing up in a land where sons were often forced into servitude and wives and daughters were stripped of their fundamental human rights. The disregard for women shown by the majority of Afghani men disgusted me. I am who I am today because of my mother, but the Taliban would have prevented her from being the mom and woman she is. Rather than benefit from her strength, they would have destroyed it, along with her dignity, through public beatings and malicious acts intended to shame her into submission.

These were evil men, fearful of their own insecurities, which they hid behind their acts of brutality. What they couldn't accept they defied, and did so by establishing a rule based on ignorance and absolutism. If there has been one lesson I've learned over my years of service it's that intolerance feeds the fires of hate until prejudice becomes an accepted practice.

There were good men in Afghanistan, men like those who made up our Afghan force, but most were mired in ancient traditions and their deep-seated ambivalence toward women troubled me. If they didn't have the strength to stand up against the persecution of their own flesh and blood, then how could we expect them to have the strength to support a centralized government? We had already done the heavy lifting by freeing them from the oppression of the Taliban; it was their responsibility to move their country ahead and take advantage of the freedom. I could accept dying trying to free the oppressed of the world, but not one American life was worth sacrificing for people willing to accept tyranny.

"Vic, we've got a series of S-curves and hills up ahead." Muscle Tom's voice crackled over the radio and broke me from my trancelike state. "Slow it down while Tom and I take a look at what's ahead."

"Good copy. Go ahead, Tom," Vic responded.

The convoy slowed as the Toms drove forward to check the dark, winding road ahead. It was common for bandits to set up roadside "tolls" late at night at blind spots in the road to either shake down their countrymen for money and valuables or capture an allied vehicle that might have broken from a convoy. For reasons I never understood, the locals generally drove with the headlights turned off at night, allowing these thugs to establish roadblocks in positions that left a driver little reaction time. Our understanding of their tactics and ability to navigate the roads with our NVGs gave us a distinct advantage over the typical Afghani, and Tom wasn't about to throw that away.

He drove cautiously up and over the hill ahead of us, but as he breached the crest he spotted a group of men at the bottom of the grade pulling weapons from the back of a truck, roughly 50 yards ahead. Had he not decreased his speed they might have had him, but his instincts, along with Ranger Tom's assistance, once again saved us from falling into an irreparable predicament. Tom immediately punched the brakes and threw the truck into reverse just as one of the men at the "checkpoint" opened fire.

"Contact front, contact front," they called out over the radio as the sound of small-arms fire erupted from the enemy below.

Vic looked at me as if to say, "Really?" He then took charge and issued orders to our interpreter in the backseat. "Tell all the vehicles to follow us! Doc, lead them over to the rocky area just left of Tom's vehicle." Vic then keyed his radio and notified the rest of the world what we had stumbled upon.

"Roger that." I gunned the engine and pushed past the other vehicles and guided them to cover while Muscle Tom and Ranger Tom slugged it out with the enemy.

"Doc, be ready to rally up at the vehicles when I call, but right now I need you to take a fire team and cover our right flank. I'll set security to our left and rear," Vic said as he signaled a squad to reinforce Tom up front.

I nodded in response, double-checked my weapon, and grabbed four of the Afghan commandos and headed for the right flank. We ran thirty yards perpendicular to the road into a sparsely wooded area and then circled back toward the bottom of the hill. We patrolled quickly and kept careful watch on the only avenue of approach the landscape allowed. As we reached a clump of trees, I held up my fist, signaling the men to freeze. Although the thin foliage afforded us little protection, it prevented us from silhouetting ourselves from maneuvering enemy.

The NVGs definitely gave us the advantage. I spotted about half a dozen armed men leaving their ambush point and moving toward our position. Three of the men moved slowly forward while the others remained near their vehicles at the bottom of the hill. I pulled the commandos close and signaled for them to lie low and hold their fire unless I said so; otherwise their muzzle flash would give us away. Unlike our ANA counterparts', our weapons were outfitted with equipment that could project a pinpoint beam indicating exactly where our rounds would impact, and it was only visible to our NVGs. We had the upper hand, so it was paramount the ANA didn't give our advantage away.

I whispered into the radio mic, "Vic, I have what appears to be four men at the base of the hill moving toward your position and a few others possibly looking to fishhook around on us."

"Good copy, Doc. Tom is tracking the others. Birds are inbound, Five Mike." Air support was five minutes out. They had to be close. Later I discovered 10th Mountain had seen their fair share of fighting since we left them, and the birds had just returned from a refuel and reload stop.

I kept a close eye on four men as they continued toward the crest of the hill, until a series of explosions stopped them in their tracks. Ranger Tom was gifted with the M-203 grenade launcher mounted under his weapon and had put it to good use. He had an uncanny ability to put the rounds right on target every time, and tonight was no different. I couldn't tell if any of the men were killed or wounded, but they certainly weren't moving forward any longer.

The remaining four realized a frontal assault would be futile and began sweeping around toward our position. Their uncoordinated movement confirmed my earlier suspicions; they were fleeing Taliban turned opportunistic vandals out to rob their neighbors. Rather than act as a unified fighting force, they moved as individuals out for their own interests, a mistake that left them vulnerable to counterattack. As I drew a bead on the one closest to me, I saw a distinctive laser light up two of the men on the end of the line, closest to the crest. Tom's team was about to do some damage.

Three seconds later, those two men were dropping in their tracks while the other two shot wildly into the dark. I opened up immediately with two controlled bursts, and they joined their friends on the ground.

"Rally up. I want everyone back at the vehicles," Vic's voice commanded over the radio.

I signaled the commandos to follow, then patrolled back to the formation. Vic was speaking to the birds when we arrived, and Ranger Tom was near the crest of the hill on overwatch, guarding against a second wave of bandits should they be dumb enough to move toward our position.

"Let's roll," said Muscle Tom. He didn't have to say it twice.

We mounted up and watched as the helos approached, their guns locked on the vehicles at the bottom of the hill. Ranger Tom low-ran from his position, and Vic called out "Cleared hot" as we pulled out heading back in the direction we came. I heard the birds open up with their cannons, then circle for one more pass before peeling off and leading us back to the base.

We doubled back and found an alternate route that took us around the ambush area and off the main roads. It added an hour to the trip, but even with the helo escort Vic felt it was better safe than sorry. The remainder of the voyage home was uneventful. We were tired and hungry but otherwise very lucky to have survived two engagements in one twenty-four-hour period. We continued on to the Alamo and, as on so many missions before, rolled into the gates just as the sun started to rise in the east.

18

RETURNING HOME

*On the mountains of truth you can never climb in vain: either you will reach
a point higher up today, or you will be training your powers so that
you will be able to climb higher tomorrow.*

—Friedrich Nietzsche

In mid-December, Wil, Vic, and I gathered for a quick meeting in
the main hooch. After months of intense combat, it was time to
turn over Firebase Shkin to our replacements. By the end of the
month the next crew would be in place and we'd be back at home with
our families. I missed my fiancée Korrina, and wanted nothing more
than to spend time with her and my little girl, especially knowing how
she worried about Daddy being injured. She needed to see that I was
OK, not just hear me tell her over a satellite phone. Yet for some reason
I didn't want to leave.

"Doc, looks like some of us will be heading back separately. After
talking it over among the group, we felt you should be the first one out
in order to make it home for Christmas." I knew what it meant; I'd be
leaving real soon. I had a genuine look of surprise on my face but had
to act as if I was pleased to hear the news.

"Doc, we've got you scheduled on a rotator bird for tomorrow morning. You've done a hell of a job, but it's time for you to get to New Mexico to your mom and Tabetha," Vic chimed in.

Wow, these men cared more about getting me back for the holidays than I did. During off-duty hours, we'd gather for a movie and talk about our families, so Wil was very familiar with Korrina and Tabetha. He would also hear stories about Korrina and the family from JJ over our secure net. JJ worked at headquarters back in the States and looked in on Korrina and the kids when I was gone. Most of the time he'd stop by her clinic to say hi and scare her staff with his large frame, bald head, goatee, and naturally angry appearance. JJ would act as if he had a cold or joint ache, but he was really there to let her know the community hadn't forgotten about her. Korrina was incredibly thankful. She, too, trusted and cared for these men and would later spend countless hours of her off time tending to their wounds, but that's the type of people that make up the spec ops community.

I tried to get out of their plan to send me back first, but neither of them would let me off the hook. Since arriving, I'd been involved in nearly every one of the firefights, and the whole team felt I should be the first one out and home for the holidays. I finally realized I had no say in the matter and accepted it. Besides, Christmas was just over a week away, and even with JJ working his magic I didn't have much faith that he'd get me out on time. More than likely we'd all meet up in Kabul and head back on the same plane after the first of the year anyway.

"We've got the logistics covered. Go get yourself packed and say your good-byes. I'll see you in the morning." Wil looked and sounded tired. He'd been in Afghanistan longer than anyone else in the group. He had arrived in country soon after 9/11 and returned countless times through the years. He said it was because his wife was also constantly traveling for work, but that wasn't the real reason. Wil felt obligated to be there. He had seen his share of battles and shouldered the added responsibility of leadership with strength and dignity. I would miss him and the smoke-break conversations he made me take with him. Hell, I would miss all of the guys.

"Alright, sounds like everything is set." I smiled as I shook their hands. "See you tomorrow."

I walked through the cool night air, then ducked into the barracks and packed my gear. I really didn't have too much to pack; after all, it was an isolated base in a war zone, and personal effects were essentially a waste of space. I gathered up what geedunk (goodie items) I did have, such as candy bars, magazines, and the coveted flavored coffee creamer necessary to turn army coffee into a tolerable drink, and went out to a makeshift fire pit 10th Mountain had built near the entrance of their mud-hut barracks. A group of seven sat around the fire on ammo crates and Walmart folding stools, listening to a young soldier strum a guitar while another soldier, a wise-ass from the big city, cracked jokes about his "redneck buddies." It was a scene for the ages, men at war gathered for a moment of peace with their brothers. Except for the modern uniforms, they could have been Vietnam grunts or Colonial Minutemen.

The soldiers nodded and smiled as I approached but quickly returned to their thoughts as they watched orange embers fly into the night sky. I recognized some of the faces, while others were new to the base. The army also slowly rotated new guys in platoon by platoon to ensure the incoming company felt a sense of familiarity. One of the boys, who looked no more than nineteen years old, was reading a *Time* magazine article about Firebase Shkin entitled "Battle in the Evilest Place," written by a reporter who had visited months earlier and drove the spec ops team crazy as they hid out during his stay. It painted a grim picture of the outpost, and with good reason; Shkin was a hellhole on the edge of the earth, and everyone knew it. Even so, it served no good purpose to read a reporter's opinion of a very complex issue, especially when the "issue" is your day-to-day reality.

"You don't need to be reading this," I told him, "and your family or friends shouldn't be sending it to you. It really doesn't matter what's written in *Time* or *Stars and Stripes*. When bullets start flying, none of that is going to matter. All you'll think about is the guy next to you." The battle-experienced soldiers nodded in unison, and I realized how much older they looked than when we all first arrived.

"That's right, it's all about your bros. That magazine is elitist bullshit," said a thirtyish sergeant from the Southwest as he snatched the magazine from the kid's hands and acted as if he were throwing it into the fire. The young soldier began to protest but sensed the gravitas of the moment and wisely stood down.

"Doc, I heard you're leaving tomorrow," the guitarist said as he stoked the fire with his boot. "Any requests for a song?"

I handed out the geedunk to the soldiers, who gratefully accepted it.

"Know any U2?" I asked with great skepticism as I grabbed a crate from the burn pile for a stool.

"Let me think," he said as he shifted in his seat. He tuned for a few moments, then launched into "Where the Streets Have No Name," a favorite of mine I played many times in the camp medical clinic when I'd sit and have coffee with their medics. As he strummed and sang in a low, scratchy voice, we stared into the fire or off at distant stars, deliberately avoiding eye contact with the men around us. Eyes reveal uncertainty, pain, and homesickness, and every man had suffered doses of each.

I waited for the song to end, then rose and said my good-byes. Troops from all branches form unique bonds with their medics and corpsmen, and each man around the fire that night said farewell with a handshake or a quick bro hug, even if he'd never met me. I then crossed the compound, climbed the guard tower that faced out toward the main road, and gazed out at the medical clinic we'd worked so hard to build. I wondered if the clinic would stay open or end up an abandoned shell like I found it. I wasn't concerned about the money or the effort put into building it, but I damn well wanted to ensure the ANA and villagers had somewhere to go for treatment after I left. I'd spent months in one of the most dangerous places on earth, fought dozens of battles, and lost friends and colleagues. Yet it was the clinic that weighed heaviest on my heart as I prepared to leave, and as I turned to climb down from the tower I felt a sense of dread that stayed with me through the night.

The next morning, I rose early and met the team at the comms hooch. We traded contact information and said our see-ya-laters, knowing we'd probably run into each other somewhere down the road; another war, another base. Muscle Tom and I walked to the helo pad and traded small talk as the bird made its approach. As the bird touched down, I shook Tom's hand and shouted one final request.

"Keep an eye on the clinic for me!"

"They're shutting it down, Doc. No one wanted to tell you last night, but we got orders from the head shed. It's way above any of us. Be safe, brother!" Tom turned without further comment and low-ran back toward the Alamo. I suddenly felt a hairy arm reach down my throat and squeeze my heart. Was it all in vain? An aircrewman signaled from the bird and snapped me out of the shocked trance, then helped me onto the helo. I sat down and gave a weak thumbs-up to the crew chief, who then gave the pilot the word that we were cleared to lift off. My grip tightened around my weapon as we ascended above the arid desert floor, up and away from the Alamo, and I looked down at the clinic and saw an Afghan woman and small child walking toward it. I felt my heart seize as thoughts of Chief, Chris, and the others who died came rushing in. I questioned why the most powerful country on earth couldn't keep a clinic open for these villagers after we worked so hard to reach out to them. Then anger, contempt, and anxiety set in. Years later colleagues of mine would determine these missions as the root of my PTSD, but I choose to remember them as the days the enemy wounded my heart and my soul.

STATESIDE

Somehow JJ got me back in time to reunite with Korrina and the kids just before Christmas. I was grateful to be home and see the people I loved the most, especially after months of dealing with death in the primitive Afghan desert, but my feelings of elation were overwhelmed by anger and shame. I missed the burials of my friends, and it was eating at my heart, preventing me from finding the closure I needed. Chief had sacrificed his life for mine, and I watched Chris do the same for another. Yet somehow I was never able to say good-bye; there simply wasn't any time before they were flown off to Bagram Air Base, and for some reason I couldn't compel myself to visit their graves. I would tell myself they were buried too far away and the time it would take to travel to their hometowns would infringe on what little time I had with Korrina and the kids, but it was all lies. I felt their lives were in my hands, and the guilt of being home with my family when they were just a memory for theirs was too much for me to bear. I tried to reason with myself—they each had made their choice to be there, they received mortal wounds in battle and there's nothing anyone could have done, and so on and so on—but it was to no avail. Every night I would revisit the battlefield and wake full of fear and rage.

I'd walk the halls in our home and stare out the windows, careful to stay in the shadows, believing anyone who saw me would know what I was thinking. I wanted to speak to my teammates and the families of the fallen, but I was more worried about showing a weakness than I was about receiving help. Night after night I questioned every move that I made on that fateful day in Afghanistan. Why didn't I pop smoke earlier and go back for Chief after I made it to safety? Was I so concerned with being a warrior that I forgot my reason for being on the team? If so, what kind of warrior was I if I was willing to remove gear that I knew I needed? Not to mention forgetting what I was carrying on me, such as the grenades. Why didn't I try throwing the grenades when I had the chance? Why didn't I go forward with the Afghan troops? Tom made it clear my understanding of the enemy's position and the landscape was critical, but instead of going I let my teammate go in my place. Was I reaching out to a friend or was I subconsciously trying to protect myself at the risk of another? Why, why, why?

Even today I replay everything that transpired that day, disgusted with what I failed to do. Hell, the only ones who did their job were Vic and Tom, and I was hearing rumors that I was under consideration for an award. I didn't want a damn award! I just wanted my friends back and would gladly trade places with them if I could. I didn't know who I was anymore. I only knew I felt worthless and feared someone would pick up on it if I let people get too close, so I locked my feelings away during the day and sequestered myself alone at night. At work everything appeared fine; I smiled, laughed, and on a few occasions could even talk about what happened as long as it focused on the lessons learned or the heroic actions of others. At work I felt safe, maybe because it was in a secure compound, maybe because I was working among the best our country had to offer—maybe, but I doubt it. More than likely it was because once someone stepped through the gates it was all business. We'd still receive outside calls, and televisions would play CNN in the buildings, but everyone came to work for one purpose: to prepare for war or support those out there doing the job. Life was simple at work, but it wasn't that way at home.

At home I felt overburdened and insecure. The tidal wave of external input flooding my senses irritated me until I became furious with the world. At first I could control it by limiting the input to the absolute essentials. I would arrive home after work and retreat to an upstairs office I'd turned into my own personal prison cell. Hours upon hours I sat, stood, or paced, looking out a window that afforded me a clear view of anyone approaching our home. When I wasn't worried about someone invading my pseudo serenity, I would watch mindless television, benign programs that required little thought. I avoided infomercials or news updates, especially if they included a simulated ticker tape flowing on the bottom of the screen; there was just too much input, and I couldn't process it. I found an odd solace in war movies, especially those that showed realistic depictions of combat.

Somehow the chaos of battle seemed very black-and-white to me, while the world here at home was full color. In battle, I had clearly defined parameters in which to operate: Defeat the enemy. Stay alive. Treat the injured. Get back in the wire. Repeat. In the world back home there were hundreds of daily mundane stresses; the vivid colors of civilian life were greatly magnified. I found them frustrating and at times overwhelming. Opening mail and answering the phone could trigger an anxiety attack. Driving the kids to an unfamiliar school for day camp might result in a volcanic eruption of road rage. As odd as it sounds, the little things of home life were far more stressful than combat, and I began longing for the black-and-white world that awaited me outside the wire.

As the weeks went on, my symptoms worsened, at least in private. I was sleeping two hours a night and filled my time between naps by patrolling our home or watching countless hours of battle scenes or simply staring at a snowy, static television screen. I could equally identify with both, a clear-cut struggle between life and death or the constant fuzzy hum that equaled what I heard in my head when the world fell silent.

As medical officer, I had access to medications and fellow providers willing to write prescriptions for medications out of my purview, and I took advantage of it. I started with one sleeping pill a night and within a month was taking six just to squeeze out four to five hours of restless sleep, and when that failed, I'd supplement the meds with alcohol. Physically the pills had no control over me, but psychologically I felt as if they were my only method for any sleep whatsoever. On my days off

I'd sit in my prison cell, groggy from the medication, as I tried to find some peace.

I tried to revert to faith but couldn't make it line up internally. At first I would pray; then I began to slowly lose my faith. I applied logic to the spirituality of the church, and none of it made sense anymore.

Korrina tried to understand my internal battles and support me as I sorted things out, but I gave her nothing to work with. I would sit and stare out the window for hours on end and not say a word. She would rub my shoulder and I would get up and walk away. I needed her in my life; her affectionate touch deserved my reciprocation, but without any real happiness inside I had nothing to give. I didn't want the responsibility of a relationship or anything else in my life other than work. Yet I didn't want her to leave me alone; I needed her in the house so I knew I wasn't abandoned. I needed her to help me deal with all the colors that were flooding into my life, yet I pushed her away when she offered her love. I desperately wanted to turn it all around, and the only way I knew how to calm the inner chaos was to return to the battlefield. That may sound ridiculous, but the anxious feelings I was having disappeared when we ventured outside the wire heading into Mangritay and only returned when I started my trip home to the States.

In an effort to break out of what I was feeling, I decided to visit a friend who had recently taken a major position at the Bureau of Medicine and Surgery in Washington, D.C. What was supposed to be a pleasant visit only added stress to my reacclimation process.

Not wanting to deal with the traffic, I decided on trying the Metro, but if I'd known what it would entail I would have chosen differently. I parked at a mall in Pentagon City and jumped on the Metro, positioning myself in the end corner to prevent anyone from gathering behind me but still near the side door exits, and headed toward Foggy Bottom. The underground station at Pentagon City was cool, quiet, and fairly empty, but when the doors opened at the Pentagon people poured into the train like water from a spigot. The fact that the majority were in American uniforms and the ones that weren't were government employees gave comfort, but as the doors opened at Rosslyn and people were exchanged like cards on a poker table, my senses began to heighten. When the doors opened at my stop I quickly jumped out, trying to get ahead of the crowd that I knew would be rushing to exit the station. What was once routine to me had become overwhelming. People walked within inches of one another, bustling by at speeds reminiscent of someone either running into or away from a firefight. The tunnel atmosphere that was inconsequential to me before, suddenly made me feel trapped, and I quickly walked the long, steep escalator toward the top, trying to escape the walled environment that encompassed me. When I emerged from the Metro, things weren't any better. People were moving in all directions, some in pairs, others in groups, but mostly individually. The noise of their activity added to my confusion, and a couple of the homeless lying about brought back memories of corpses on the street after a suicide bomber attack. Knowing where I needed to go, I headed in the direction of the National Mall. I could see the State Department in the distance, giving me some indication of the distance I had to travel, and I felt at ease knowing I'd be right on time. That was the only comfort I'd experience as I walked past the university.

In combat people didn't approach you from behind; they walked on the other side of the street or at excessive distances. Only the children violated the unwritten rule of maintaining space as they often swarmed us for candy or other goodies we'd hand out, but even then I felt insecure. Who's to say they might not unknowingly be used to draw us into the crosshairs of a sniper or have a bomb strapped to their chest. Here people were swarming past me, five to ten of them every few seconds, none of them making eye contact, which made it difficult for me to tell their intent. In combat I would call out and have them stop their approach or move away, and if they didn't I'd raise my weapon to make sure to get my point across. I couldn't do any of that here. This was

America, where everyone is free to go as you please, but my mind was still tuned in to the militant environment of the battlefield. I did what I could to relieve the uneasiness of the environment. I varied my speed and moved to the outer/street side of the sidewalk and often walked in the gutter trying to keep the crowd from flooding over me, but just when I thought I'd found comfort a taxicab swooped in, nearly hitting me. If I'd had a weapon I would have drawn down on the occupants in a heartbeat; instead I had to remind myself that's how things are done back home. Although I was anxious, I wasn't paranoid, sweating bullets, or having a panic attack. Unless someone knew me well there was no outward sign of how uncomfortable I was. Everything seemed foreign to me now. I was accustomed to the feel and formalities of the battlefield, and now all I wanted was to get back to where I was comfortable, to where all this would stop. Rather than seek help, I did what I thought was rational at the time. I found my way back to combat.

19

FINDING PEACE

I have never advocated war except as a means of peace.

—Ulysses S. Grant

I joined a new team near Khowst, an ancient, dusty city near the Pakistan border 225 kilometers south of Kabul. To the north of the city was the rapidly expanding Forward Operating Base Salerno, which held the 352nd Combat Support Hospital, a multifunctional aviation task force, and some of my old friends from the 10th Mountain Division. The group I was assigned to primarily operated out of Forward Operating Base Chapman, a smaller, moderately fortified compound three miles southeast of the city. The team was tasked with a number of missions, but the only thing that mattered to me was the peace that had come over me once I touched down in Afghanistan. All the noise from the outside world quieted as my mind focused on the black-and-white elements of the battlefield. I wasn't sure if it was the combat environment or being surrounded by my teammates, some of whom I felt were experiencing similar difficulties, that calmed my nerves, but it really didn't matter to me. I was back, this time to help build the infrastructure the country needed to sustain its newly formed government.

I looked forward to training Afghanistan's security forces, working with the local leaders to strengthen ties with their national government, and reaching out to the native people in surrounding areas in hopes of increasing the cooperation necessary to quash the al Qaeda insurgency. It was textbook asymmetric warfare that Army Special Forces Operational Detachment Alpha teams had been working for nearly a year. However, operational commitments had grown at a steady rate, requiring specialized personnel, and I would be one of them.

As the helicopter approached the firebase, I could see the remnants of the Soviet aircraft lining each side of the airstrip. As we touched down, I saw a vehicle rolling toward the helo pad and assumed it was my ride. I grabbed my bags and low-ran toward the truck, to be greeted by an old friend and mentor.

"Great to see you, Maark," Doc C said in his New York accent.

"Good to be here, Doc," I replied as I shook his hand and jumped into the truck. Doc C was a Special Forces medic who somehow managed to spend the majority of his time assigned to the Ranger Battalion. He, too, had moved up from the enlisted medical ranks to become a physician assistant, just as I had done. Only Doc C had done it years earlier, setting the example for special operations medics from all the services, including myself. He was getting closer to retirement but was as hard as ever, and I felt better knowing I would once again be working side by side with my mentor and friend.

"I'm sorry about the loss. I knew Chief from Ranger Bat, and he was a hell of an operator," he said, pulling into the gate.

"Thanks, Doc, but right now I just want to get back to work."

"I know you do," he replied in a voice echoing years of experience. I could tell he knew what I was feeling. Doc C had more combat time than any other PA I knew and performed exemplarily every time, earning him the prestige of being one of the few men to make the Ranger Hall of Fame—but also validating my theory that the stressors of combat may affect someone at home but dissipate in war.

"Did they tell you they shut down the clinic at Shkin?" he asked.

"I found out the day I departed. It crushed me. After all the work we put into it, they didn't send my replacement." Doc C was the man who started the campaign to build the clinic, and I was sent in to finish what he'd started.

"No worries, I've got a plan." He went on to explain how he was able to recruit two Afghani doctors willing to work in Khowst and Shkin, a monumental task considering how dangerous the border areas were. One of the men was already seeing patients at the medical clinic the Special Forces team had built just outside the compound walls. "All I need now is approval," he said with a smile. A classic special operations maneuver: Get it done first, then ask for permission or forgiveness later. Still, reviving a program that was shut down was a little much for any operator. If he hadn't been such a well-renowned medic with an impeccable war record he'd never get away with pulling shit like that, but he was and he did.

We arrived at the medical hooch, our living quarters for the foreseeable future. "It's just the two of us in here," he said as we walked into the living quarters.

I spotted a small folding board game sitting on the rickety table he used as a desk. "I see you brought your Scrabble game. Are we going to have time to play?" I asked.

"Plenty" was all he said as we started bringing my gear in. Once everything was stowed he turned to me and said, "You doing alright?"

"I'm fine," I answered. "Hell, Doc. We actually have a real building to live in this time, and this one even comes with a mattress," I said jokingly as I lifted up the two-inch Afghan sleeping pad that lay on top of the wooden bed frame.

"You know what I mean," he said, walking over to me. He looked me in the eyes, sighed, and said, "It'll get better."

"Thanks, Doc, but does it ever end?" I asked as we walked over to the comms hooch to get me read in.

"No" was all he said.

It didn't take long for me to adapt to the familiar routine of war. I was once again living in the monochrome parameters of combat, and the demons that haunted my sleep retreated into the darkness of my psyche. The missions at Khowst were not as intense as at Shkin, but they were just as dangerous. After Mangritay, I never questioned myself again, but I also never felt the same about going into battle. I had proven to myself I could still perform under fire despite coming within inches of losing my life, and after experiencing the mental hell I went through in my office back home, I wasn't afraid to die; in many ways, I welcomed it. I lived through ambushes that no one should have survived, so I resigned myself to the notion that if I were to end up on the *X* again I probably wouldn't be coming home. It wasn't that I doubted my abilities or those of my teammates; it was simply a matter of statistics. No longer would the apprehension about an ambush dominate my mind as we moved toward our target. Here my nemesis would be the enemy's rockets, mortars, and improvised explosive devices.

IEDs were the poor man's artillery, and the Taliban was quickly mastering the nuances of remotely denoted bombs. The mission tempo was high, and so was the stress. The bombs were nearly impossible to detect from a moving convoy, and no area was safe. IED attacks were just as common on deserted highways as they were in the streets we traveled around the city. Firebase Chapman was well fortified but still within striking range of enemy rocket fire from a nearby mountain, or mortars from within the city of Khowst.

Over the next couple of months I felt the need to go on every mission. It may seem odd, but I was far more comfortable engaging in a direct firefight or even an ambush than dealing with indirect fire or an IED. As a SEAL, I was trained to react and counterattack and had a modicum of control over the situation. However, the random nature of rockets, mortars, and IEDs never took into account the skill set and experience of the warrior. It was simply a game of chance, adding new demons to my psyche that I wouldn't find out about until my next trip home.

HOME AGAIN

My time at Khowst eventually came to an end, and I once again returned home for rest and relaxation and quality time with the family. The first few days were filled with enthusiasm, and I was effectively managing all the colorful input that irritated me before I left, but there were changes going on that even I couldn't deny.

Ever since I could remember I'd had a persistent, mild headache. At first I thought it was because I was dehydrated, so I began carrying a water bottle with me wherever I went, but time and constant infusion of water proved that wasn't the cause. More concerning to me, I began noticing trouble focusing on what I was reading, hearing, or even watching on TV. I would often find myself confused to the point of reaching for words, despite knowing what I wanted to say. Over time my problems would fade, but they never seemed to disappear. They'd sometimes reappear at the most inopportune times, and I felt like my intellectual capabilities were riding a yo-yo of clarity, but it definitely wasn't a showstopper. I learned how to work with it.

The constant time apart was taking its toll on Korrina, so I decided a weekend getaway might be just what we needed to get reacquainted. I wanted to make it a special occasion, so I rented a convertible and drove home to pick her up, proud of myself for the big surprise. However, it didn't take long before a dark storm started brewing inside of me.

Traffic had always annoyed me, but after repeated overseas tours I found the anxiety caused by bumper-to-bumper traffic to be nearly unbearable. To counter the maddening nervousness I experienced during a traffic jam, I'd started leaving for work extremely early and staying late, but this only added to my difficulties at home. Debris in the road or the homeless walking up to the car panhandling for money would raise my heart rate because it reminded me of the modus operandi of suicide bombers and how bad guys planted IEDs.

I pulled up to the house and honked the horn. Korrina loved the car and was looking forward to the trip to wine country. We packed a couple of light bags, jumped in, and headed west, with no particular agenda other than to relax and enjoy each other's company.

We drove for two hours with no problems and caught up on conversations that had been neglected for months. Korrina seemed very happy for the first time in ages and was finally beginning to unwind when suddenly, *pop!* A rock flew out from underneath the driver's-side front tire and crashed into the bottom of the car. The sound was reminiscent of an AK-47, which immediately took me back to being on the *X*. I downshifted and floored the gas pedal, yelling, "Move, move, move." I maneuvered past two cars, then braked hard and turned quickly onto a side road. I then whipped the car around to ensure I was able to escape farther down the road if I needed to. My heart was racing, and once again anger consumed my body. As I brought the car to a sudden stop I flung the door open, jumped out and peered down the road, trying to assess the trapped vehicles that didn't exist. Realizing what had just happened, I walked back to the car and sat down in the driver's seat and grabbed the steering wheel.

"What the hell is wrong with you?" Korrina yelled.

"I don't know," I yelled back at her, eyes red and watery with shame.

"OK, I understand that you don't want to see anyone because you're afraid it will damage your career."

"I'm not afraid!" I yelled, cutting her off.

"That's exactly what I'm talking about," she yelled back.

I gripped the steering wheel as if I were trying to choke the car to death. She waited a few moments to allow the situation to cool down, then continued in a much lower tone.

"Mark, I can't help you if you won't let me in."

"Well, I'm home now, so if you want to talk we can talk," I answered sarcastically.

"Don't lie to me. More importantly, stop lying to yourself. We both know you're going to lock yourself up in that damn room like you always do. When you do come out, the rest of us walk around the house on pins and needles, careful not to say or do anything that will set you off or send you back upstairs into your damn isolation chamber."

"What am I supposed to do?" I answered in a tone that didn't welcome an answer. "I'm the medic, I'm the guy everyone is supposed to come to. What kind of doc would I be if I were the one with the disorder? Would you rather have me drink it away with the boys? I can take care of this myself."

"That's just it, Mark, you're not supposed to treat yourself. You know that." She spoke in a voice on the verge of yelling and crying. "You need to talk to someone. If not me, then find someone, because what you've been doing hasn't been working."

I knew she was right but just couldn't admit it to myself. I'm a SEAL, damn it! I had been given the tools to handle anything life throws at me. Besides, if she really knew what I'd gone through she'd realize this wasn't a manifestation of mental weakness but a display of mental tenacity. Not everyone can box things up and store them away. Sure, I was taking excessive amounts of medications, but that was only for my sleep, and the only alcohol I was consuming was to supplement what the drugs could no longer do on their own. I wasn't some basket case. I remembered what I learned in my early years watching the older veterans turn to the bottle at the local watering hole, each one of them in his own way telling me not to use drugs or alcohol as an escape. This wasn't a weakness that needed counseling; this was a display of strength! I just needed more time.

"Mark." Hearing her voice snapped me back into reality. "This is only stressing the rest of us out. You're making life much harder on everyone."

"How, by coming home and telling everyone how much I love them?" I immediately fired back, adamant that I wasn't the problem.

"Yes! Yes." The car fell quiet as her answer set in. "Mark, I love you and I'm not going to leave you," she said in a soft, sincere tone, "but you come in for a few weeks, maybe a month if we're lucky, then zip back out again. No one knows where you're going, and that's fine. I serve in the same navy as you and understand the need for operational security, but half the time we never know when you're coming home. A week turns into a month, and a month into who knows when. How can I, how can *we* prepare for that?"

"So why does it matter when I come home? It's not like I'm out gallivanting around," I said.

"If you can't see it in me—" She paused, then fired back, "Think about what you're doing to the kids!" The car got deathly quiet. We both sat and stared straight ahead for what felt like eternity. "Summer is right around the corner, and both of the kids will be here. You need to think about being home for part of it, and not coming and going through the revolving door you constantly use. It only disrupts our routine; they need stability, not uncertainty, in their lives." She lowered her voice even further and softly said in a tone that echoed the sadness in her heart, "It's almost better if you just stay gone."

I continued staring straight ahead, not wanting to accept any of it. I just couldn't believe what I was hearing.

"Mark, if you think Tabetha is isolated from all of this by living in New Mexico, you're wrong. It's great that you visit her every time you go back home, but you're still missing all of her major events in life."

"I call," I said with a tired voice. "I call all of you as much as I can."

"Honey, it doesn't help when the call is interrupted by a *boom* and the sound of gunfire in the background."

I angrily interrupted her, feeling she was covering the same ground she walked moments before. "No one knows when the firebase is going to be attacked! It wasn't like I said, 'Hey, it looks like we're going to be rocketed. I think I'll go outside and place a call home with the satellite phone.'"

"But I don't want to hear that!" she cried back at me. I took a deep breath and closed my eyes, remembering the distinctive sound of incoming rocket fire and how vulnerable I felt each time it happened, and realized I felt the same way now. Korrina reached over to pull my face toward hers and said, "I don't need to hear that. I just want you home." I knew she was right. I was making things worse for the people I loved. I knew I had to do something, but I wasn't ready to talk, so I did the same thing at home that I was doing everywhere else. I boxed it up and locked it away, figuring the colors would either fade to black and white or I'd deal with it later, but now wasn't the time.

I spent the next month with the family, even taking everyone on a vacation for a couple of weeks. It was the first time since I could remember that I felt truly happy, but I knew once we returned home it probably wouldn't stay that way for long. I needed to get back to the uncomplicated world of black and white, so once again I jumped on the next trip that would take me back to the simpler world of life and death.

20

ADRIFT

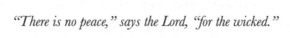

"There is no peace," says the Lord, "for the wicked."

—Isaiah 48:22

I kept my sanity by bouncing back and forth to Central Command. At first it was my only means of finding peace, but later it satisfied a different need. The whirlwind of adrenaline, anger, and fear related to combat had become a drug, and I was addicted. As a SEAL medic in combat, I was required to control my emotions during periods of extreme danger and immediately assess the situation and react within my limitations in the face of death. To me it was the greatest test of strength and fortitude for the noblest of causes, protecting the lives of others, and the operational tempo was more than accommodating. There were never enough men to cover all the missions and even fewer special operations medics. On occasion, I would come across a savvy officer who could keep his eyes on both the battlefield requirements and the mental health of his medic. They'd do what they thought necessary to ensure I was fine and send me to the psychiatrist for an evaluation, but the psych department never had a chance.

The pre- and postdeployment questionnaires were all based on the member's own desire to open up to the provider about the symptoms he or she was having. It was a good step in the right direction, but the small series of questions wasn't nearly enough to expose anyone's difficulties, especially if the person's intent was to hide them. Then came the battery of written tests. *Come on now*, I'd think, laughing to myself. *Like I haven't seen these before.* I was a medical provider, too, so I was familiar with the many psychological testing procedures being utilized at the time, especially the particular one they used. On a few occasions we'd have an interview session, but that wasn't anything new either. I knew exactly how everything operated. Hell, I was the guy that sent his patients to the experts for evaluation when the care fell outside of my expertise, and when they'd return from their appointment I'd get a call from the doc to discuss their treatment plans. I certainly didn't have the knowledge they had on the diagnosis and treatment of mental conditions, but none of them had ever been under fire. That made it easy for me. Each time I'd walk in for an evaluation, I felt as if I were about to be taught how operate a semi truck by someone who didn't even have a driver's license. It didn't matter if he had built the truck from the ground up and knew every part of it like the back of his hand. The fact was he'd never driven it, and the only way he could experience what it was like to slide sideways on an icy road was to either drive the damn thing or jump into the passenger seat, and I wasn't about to unlock the door.

As a young man in New Mexico, I watched recovering addicts receive treatment by other addicts because they were the only ones who could spot their bullshit and call them out on it. It took "street cred" to reach them; even then it was dependent on whether they were willing to receive the message being sent by the counselor. However, the one thing they had to do whether they believed in treatment or not was to come off the drugs—but how was the military going to manage that? We were fighting a two-front war, and there was no way to slow things down even if that's what the commander wanted. The die was cast; we were in it for the long haul, and that meant my need to be in the action and my ability to find relief were safe. At least I thought they were.

"Doc," TJ said as he walked into my office.

"TJ, what are you doing here?" I politely asked. TJ was an old friend that I'd first met years earlier when my SEAL platoon landed on the USS *Saratoga* in the middle of the Red Sea. The aircraft carrier was our home for a few months while we readied ourselves for the First Gulf War. TJ was a small-boat captain who had seen combat a few years earlier when Special Operations Command was tasked with protecting U.S. oil tankers against Iranian mine and gunboat attacks. His experiences in Special Warfare as a Mark III boat captain and later as an intelligence officer eventually led to a position managing security issues at the Pentagon, so it wasn't a real surprise to see him walking through the door.

"You have a minute? Can we talk privately?" His voice sounded serious.

"Sure. Let's use the boss's office," I said as I stood and walked him to the empty office.

"Whatcha got, TJ?" I asked as we both sat.

"Doc, turns out that some equipment is missing. No one suspects you or any members of the team, but there's going to be an investigation, which means you're going to have to stay put for a while."

I couldn't believe what I was hearing. I sat and thought for several seconds. "Is there anything I can do to speed things along? How long should this take?" I asked.

"Just answer any questions by the investigator when he gets to you, and in the meantime just stay put." He went on to explain that it might take months and that he'd already spoken to my superiors and explained why I needed to stay put.

I thought about what he said, and the idea of being trapped made me feel apprehensive, angry, and jealous of everyone around me. I couldn't believe it; even the yeoman who checked people into the command could go downrange. The one thing I wanted to do the most, deploy to the battlefield, was stripped away from me. On the outside I nodded, smiled, and carried on smartly, but on the inside my anger was building, and I wasn't sure if I would be able to control it. I was unsure what the future held, so I went home and spoke with the one person in my life that mattered the most.

"I've got great news," Korrina said with an ear-to-ear smile and an aura of happiness I hadn't seen in years.

"Well, tell me, I could use some good news right now," I replied as a smile erupted on my face, her joy contagious.

"I got offered the job as the PA at BUD/S!" she said, almost jumping out of her skin. "At first I wasn't going to take it, but then I thought about all the time you spend away and I thought it might work out better for us. At least for now, right?" She watched as I absorbed the news.

I was devastated but managed to muster up a smile. I had put her through hell over the last few years, and now was my time to put her first. "Derrick and Sara are out there, you know," I said stumbling to find something to say.

"Yep, we've got a lot of friends there," she answered, slightly confused.

"That is good news." I paused, trying to think what to say next. "When do you ship out?"

"I'd leave in a couple of months for a school, then check in at Coronado after that."

"How many years are your orders going to be for?" I asked, trying to calm my voice as my heart thumped in my throat.

"The navy says three years, but I can leave at two if you can't get orders out there. If you *do* get orders there, I can extend," she said calmly. She could read me like a book and was trying to keep the anxiety at a minimum.

"Wow, you've thought of everything," I said as I rubbed my eyes, still absorbing the news.

It was obvious she'd given this some serious thought and planned out how to make it work. Korrina loved the warm San Diego sun; it invigorated her, and the opportunity to return filled her with joy. Plus, in California she'd be back with some of our closest friends, whose support she could really use right now, and the kids would be much happier spending their summers on the warm beaches of California than in the humid climate of Virginia. The only thing she didn't account for was the news I'd heard earlier that day, and I wasn't going to tell her, at least not yet. For years she'd put her life on the back burner for mine, and the shoe was now on the other foot. I had no choice but to support her, so I packed my emotions into another box, and we planned how we'd both make it work.

SAN DIEGO

Several weeks later Korrina left for California. Departures are common for a military family, but they never come easy and this one was particularly hard on me. Korrina was more than my fiancée. She was my best friend and confidant and the one person who brought organization to the chaos of the colors encircling me. Years earlier we had our first good-bye. She was leaving for officer indoctrination, and I was heading off to the war. The night before was one of the hardest experiences in our lives. We both lay awake in bed trying to console one another with promises of commitment, but deep down each of us wondered if the relationship would endure the distance or if that night was the beginning to our end. As difficult as that night was, it felt like a parting of sweet sorrow compared to what I was going through, but I wasn't about to let her experience that anguish again. She was happy, and I wanted her to stay that way, so I did what I could to relieve any worries she might have about how I'd fare without her.

We'd had more than our fair share of depressing "last nights" together, so I took her for a relaxing dinner at one of her favorite restaurants and joked about all the things we'd be able to do with the time away from each other. I told her I planned to watch every single basketball game during March Madness, and she told me her TV would never leave the Lifetime Channel. Her excitement about what lay ahead made me feel alive, but more importantly it kept her unaware of what was actually brewing inside of me. The next day we laughed as I wrestled with her oversized suitcase and placed it in the backseat of her Jeep, but as she drove away I felt a dark emptiness well up. I knew the separation would be good for her, and good for our relationship. The distance and time apart didn't concern either of us. We'd already proven we could weather those storms. The question was, could I stay afloat long enough to enjoy our next reunion?

Work was becoming increasingly more difficult. Or perhaps it's more accurate to say I was becoming increasingly more difficult at work. I still hadn't received approval to deploy, and without Korrina to help alleviate my frustration I began to feel I was more of a hindrance than a help to the community. Being stuck in the stateside garrison opened me up to a whole world I never knew before. I went from working with hardened and experienced warriors to being around a mixture of sailors and highly skilled specialists who instead worked in support of the operators overseas. All of them were extremely competent, and the majority were humble professionals who accepted their position as backside support but relished any opportunity to deploy forward supporting men who wore a Trident or Beret. Many of them had experienced the intensity of a firefight or understood the extremes of sustained combat, and those who had never discussed it, but there were always the vocal few, the men who had never been on the receiving end of a rifle but chattered as if they'd stormed the beaches at Normandy. At first I ignored their stories of glory, but they eventually crawled under my skin. I wondered if they understood how ridiculous they sounded, but then again maybe it was just me. I had changed, and there was no use denying it. Despite witnessing great acts of valor on the battlefield, I found no glory in war. I relived the battles over and over again, and all I remembered was fighting for my teammates. No longer did I view fighting terrorism as some philosophical doctrine. It was simply a dirty job that needed to get done, at least until we brought those responsible to justice. I wasn't comfortable in my role at the garrison, and it was apparent that it was time for me to leave the fast-paced world of special operations and return to medicine.

Korrina was settled in out west, and I hoped to join her there. The navy kept me in Virginia for the short term, though, so instead of moving across country I transferred across town. I received orders to Naval Medical Center Portsmouth and transferred with little fanfare, making it easier on me, as I was still having difficulty dealing with tumultuous situations outside of combat. I remembered being an extremely gregarious individual but had become far more reserved due to constant exposure to battle. The quietness of an empty home made me much more withdrawn. I tried throwing myself into my new job but found the relatively calm tempo of the medical clinic monotonous. However, the simplistic routine was helping me deal with my memory and concentration problems, as did working with a smaller crew. At the clinic I found enjoyment by working with young doctors and with corpsmen who'd returned from their time with the marines. I befriended a former corpsman turned nurse who was married to one of the most dedicated corpsman chiefs in the navy, and she and I swapped sea stories between work assignments. At home it was a different story. Once again I started to self-medicate with sleep medications and alcohol, trying to find ways to sleep past the ghosts that visited me throughout the night. Luckily I was able to change my work shift to the afternoon versus the early morning, which happened to be the only time I was able to sleep.

———

The days were manageable, but the nights would tear at my soul, especially on major holidays or the anniversaries of battles. Nothing compared to the agony I'd feel on the eve of a child's birthday—the child of a fallen teammate. On those days misery would rush over me like a raging river, nearly drowning me in guilt. I knew the difficulties Chief's wife faced rearing their youngest son without his father, but knowing Chief had sacrificed his life with his children so I could be with mine made those birthdays almost too much to bear. I wished I could ignore them or pretend the whole thing never happened, but the kids deserved more, and so did I. Those moments were the only way to keep their memories alive.

"Hello." Brooke's distinctive voice came through the receiver.

Despite caller ID she always seemed a bit surprised to hear my voice, probably because many months would often pass between calls.

Children of military parents sometimes struggle with adjustment issues, especially when Mom or Dad deploys frequently. Even short trips can lead to an uncomfortable period of reacclimation as the parent tries to adjust to the family's schedule. The parent has to relearn bedtime routines and catch up with housekeeping needs and financial matters, and just when things start to get into a groove, off they go again.

"Hi, Brooke, how are the boys doing?" I asked, worried about what I might hear about her sons.

"Things are well, but could certainly be better. Then again I guess I could say that with just about everything," Brooke said with a slight laugh in her voice as she tried to keep a positive attitude about it all. She was a special woman who had endured decades of a lifestyle that could have easily bred bitter feelings, but instead she dedicated herself to Chief's kids and thought about the day when she'd be able to retire.

"That's good to hear. Things are going fairly well over here, too."

Brooke and I always started our conversations by telling one another about all the good things going on in our lives, then after a few minutes, we'd begin to open up to one another.

"Mark, I can't help it, I'm still angry over the whole thing. It's not fair! I did everything I was supposed to do, believing one day Chief and I would have our time together, but that never happened. I know eventually it will get better, but when is that day coming?"

"I'm not sure, Brooke, but it will get better."

"For some reason, I'm stuck in the past and just can't break free," she said, her voice full of tears.

I felt ashamed for being alive as I listened to her talk. Her anger wasn't directed at me; it was a venting of cumulative frustration felt by a grieving military widow, and her words nearly echoed words that had been said in my home. So many times I told Korrina and the kids I was only going to be gone for a little while, but the little whiles kept running into one another. Brooke had heard that from Chief for years, and it still haunted her.

"I know what you mean. I've been trying to get past this, too," I said, thinking about how every wounding or death seemed to stir up anger and disappointment about the wars. "When I close my eyes, I imagine Chief is just off somewhere on a mission and one day he'll come walking through the door." I didn't know what to say beyond that, so I just listened. I didn't want to risk making it worse. She told me about her dreams, and they were anything but crazy. They merely reflected the military lifestyle she had known for most of her adult life.

Chief was 100 percent warrior, spending nearly every moment of his career *operating*, a term we use to describe life on a spec ops team. Although operating is what every SEAL, Green Beret, Ranger, etc., lives for, the time away from the family can be extensive. Whether it's deploying into combat, training stateside, or training foreign troops thousands of miles away, it's always the same for the family back at home. Everyone from the parents to the wife and, of course, the children copes with the operator's absence. For Brooke, the absence was permanent, and the struggle was exacerbated by raising a teenage boy transitioning to manhood with no father at home.

"Mark, you know how proud we are of Chief, but he chose to be a full-time warrior and part-time father. Now that he's gone his sons don't even have that anymore."

"Brooke, if I had the opportunity to trade places with him, trust me, I—" I tried to finish the sentence, but she cut me off before I could.

"Don't say that, Mark."

I tried to continue but could only stumble over words as I attempted to justify how it would have been better if I had been the one who died that day.

"Enough!" she yelled.

The phone went quiet, and I once again wondered what things would be like had he turned the vehicle in the other direction.

"Brooke, I am so sorry for what everyone is having to go through," I said, trying to make us both feel better.

"Mark, it's not your fault. I know what you're thinking; I can hear it in your voice. We love you, and you know there's nothing more that you or anyone else could've done." Brooke never once faulted me for Chief's death, but the conversations about the boys were always a bit awkward.

"I can't help it," I said. "You know I never wanted it this way."

"None of us wanted it this way, Mark. All we can do now is try to make the most of our lives. It's what all of them would have wanted us to do."

"I'm trying, Brooke, but it's hard. I'm learning to become a dad again and not just be a biological father."

We spoke for several more minutes, then said our farewells, both of us missing Chief in a bad way.

I then took a deep breath and began dialing Chris's father.

A few weeks later, I took leave and flew out to San Diego, hoping the warm California sun and quality time with the family would calm the turmoil I was feeling. Korrina had settled into her job at Coronado, and by the time I arrived Tabetha had already joined Korrina and her stepbrother, Cody. Our first forty-eight hours together were fantastic and full of laughter and happiness in the home. On the third day, however, the train flew off the track when an inattentive driver nearly ran me over as I took the dogs for their morning walk. I would've been fine had he not cursed me as the car screeched to a halt. I stood there confused for a second or two, but when I saw his face full of anger I was suddenly consumed by an aggressive rage, and he saw every bit of it. He sped off quickly, and I watched as he pulled in in front of the corner coffee shop. I quickened my pace to confront him. My heart was racing and my throat was dry as anger and angst flowed through every inch of my body. Thankfully, by the time I got there he was on his way out of the shop.

"You almost ran me over and you're cursing at *me*? You stupid f***ing imbecile, if you can't say 'I'm sorry' then you keep your damn mouth shut!" I yelled at him as my mind focused on one thing: battle. His surprise turned to fear, very quickly and with good reason. In my mind I went from walking the sunny streets of San Diego to patrolling the back roads of Iraq or Afghanistan. I dropped the dual leash and stared him in the eyes for less than a second before scanning his hands for a weapon and his torso for a possible explosive vest. Even as my eyes kept close watch over him and I moved myself into a position that would prevent anyone approaching me from behind, I started to examine every object on the outdoor tables that I could use to defend myself or as a weapon.

"Look, I didn't see you and—" he yelled back with an attitude.

"Shut the f*** up! And get over there!" I yelled, interrupting him midsentence. Pointing toward the street, I continued to maneuver him into a position that would allow me time to react. He walked backward into the street, and as my eyes swept the area I felt like a part of me had stepped outside of myself and was watching everything that was occurring. I tried speaking to myself, "Let it go, you're wrong, you need to just let it go," but I wasn't listening.

"Hey, I'm sorry," he said trying to defuse the situation.

I snapped out of the combat trance, and my rational inner voice told me to let it go.

"Go! Get out of here! Now!"

He jumped into his car and drove away. My hands started to shake, and a thousand pounds of weight fell upon my shoulders, forcing me into a patio chair. *I'm so f***ed up*, I said to myself. Or maybe I said it out loud; at that point it was impossible to separate reality from delusion. *I can't go home this way; maybe I shouldn't go home at all?* As I contemplated the irrationality of my behavior, my dogs came to my side, each leaning on the chair as if to say, *We're here, too*.

I found out at an early age that nothing is more dangerous than a cornered beast. Size and strength are indifferent when humans or animals are trapped. They'll fight with extreme violence to the very end because they have nothing to lose but their lives. I used to think of this only in the literal sense, but now I realize it's far more dangerous when a man is so mentally or emotionally wounded that he feels his life has become meaningless. I first witnessed this in my father's eyes and later reconfirmed it on the battlefield as I stared into the faces of enemy fighters who absorbed round after round, yet still kept coming. Men in this state of mind neither understand nor accept the threat of physical violence or pain being used against them; it only strengthens their resolve.

I sat for two hours before returning home to ensure I left any residual anger in the street and out of the home. I couldn't let the rest of them know that I was still locking myself in the upstairs office, yet trying to figure a way out.

the next I might be broodingly angrily or locking myself away. I allowed the deployments and isolation to separate me from my family, and I didn't know how to get back.

Work had become a way to pass the time until I made it home to a bottle of vodka and anything in the medicine cabinet that would help me to sleep through the night. When not at work, I'd sit on the couch shifting my eyes from the scenes outside the window to pictures of Korrina and the kids I hung on the wall for inspiration, but it wasn't working. I found myself constantly thinking about how the slow decline of my father nearly destroyed our family, and how the pattern was repeating in my own. His battles may not have been as up close and personal as mine, but it looked like the end result might be the same. I wondered how much longer it would be before I couldn't walk away from a confrontation and my anger would turn to violence. I had already begun to experience explosive episodes of rage, and despite my best efforts I couldn't stop myself from self-medicating with alcohol. I was lying to the folks I loved the most, and with Korrina thousands of miles away there was no way for her to know any different. Every few days a friend would stop by or invite me to dinner, concerned for my well-being, but I deflected their concerns and locked myself away. I was self-destructing and I knew it; I just wondered if I would end up wrecking my family in the process.

I felt alone and scared of what I might do. I wanted to call Korrina but knew it would only increase her stress and in turn increase my feelings of despair. I turned the television on, but the snowy screen and constant sound of the static failed to provide their normal relief, so I drank until the bottle was nearly empty. I remember getting up and walking into the bedroom, thinking I would finally be able to close my eyes. I spotted my weapon case peeking out from under the bed. I'm still not sure what I was thinking, if anything at all, but for some reason I carried it back to the living room. I placed it on the coffee table in front of me and unlocked it. Next thing I knew, I had the pistol in my

21

DARKNESS AND LIGHT

It is a brave act of valor to condemn death, but where life is more terrible than death, it is then the truest valor to dare to live.

—Sir Thomas Browne

I returned to Virginia and managed to keep it together at work, but each week I'd receive disheartening news about another friend being wounded or killed. As I struggled to put it all together I reached out to an old mentor, only to receive word that the son of another close friend, who was killed the year before Chief and Chris lost their lives, was continuing to have difficulties adjusting to the loss of his father. His family was still having trouble, too; it was demoralizing. I began to realize how truly ignorant I was about the total effects of war. The more I thought about it, the more depressed I became, until irrational thoughts of responsibility started to fill my mind. I remembered the day he was buried, and how I felt the war was finally over for them when in reality their battles were just beginning. Hearing the sons and daughters of close friends and teammates were suffering made me feel as if I had somehow abandoned them—but what could I do? I was still trying to deal with keeping my Jekyll and Hyde temperament hidden from my own family. One moment I'm loving and joking, and hand and had pushed a magazine through its handle, loading the gun. Like so many times before, I felt as if I were watching myself from across the room. I remember thinking I wasn't angry, I wasn't sad; in fact, I had no emotion whatsoever. I was indifferent to everything around me; all I knew was I needed help before I hurt someone. I gripped the pistol and went back to staring out the window. The phone rang, and I felt that instead of ignoring it, I had to answer.

"Marky, this is your mother. Something told me to call you," Mom's voice said over the receiver.

"Something or someone, Mom?"

"Oh, you know, it was either God or one of the invisible men your sister talks to when she's here with me, but at my age I can never tell which is which," she said, laughing. "Besides, I know they're just messengers from God. Now if I can just get them to tell her to remember to take her medication it would be much easier for both of us." I couldn't believe she was able to laugh in spite of all the difficulties she'd encountered as a parent of a schizophrenic daughter, a husband suffering from dementia, and a house full of youth trying to reform their lives.

"Mom, how do you do it?"

"Do what, mijo?"

"How do you keep going? Life's been hell, but it always seems like it doesn't matter to you." My voice was starting to crack as I tried to hold back the tears.

"Mijo, I don't do anything. When things get too much, like they are for you now, I ask for help. You know, people want to help. You just have to let them know how."

"I need help, Mom."

"I know you do, mijo, that's why I was told to call you."

We talked for hours, and I listened to stories about my father and how he always let his pride get in the way. She mentioned how he gambled the car away when I was much younger, something I never knew about. We talked about the drunken fits, which nearly put her in the hospital, and the other problems she still encountered as she balanced time between Dad and my sister. It tore me up to hear about it, but Mom talked as if she were telling a story about work or the meaning of the priest's homily.

"Mom, why do you talk about Dad that way?" I asked. "You speak about him as if he's a saint, even when you're talking about how much of a devil he's become."

"Marky, that's the only way your father knows how to let me know he needs help, and I'm just trying to be there when he calls." She paused for a few seconds to let the frustration she heard in my voice settle. "In his spirit your father is still a good man, and that's all that matters, at least to me. Now promise me you won't ask of Korrina what your father asks of me. It's time to swallow your pride, mijo, and accept some help."

"I promise, Mom. I promise." Just as I hung up the phone, the sun started to break over the horizon. I went up to the third floor and watched it cast its light across the ocean, thinking about what I had promised.

JOURNAL THERAPY

During the years that I served, the military was accustomed to utilizing two components in the treatment of PTSD (post-traumatic stress disorder), pharmacotherapy and psychotherapy. Being a medical provider, I knew that most of the psychiatrists utilized pharmaceuticals as an adjunct to alleviate some of the more disruptive manifestations of combat stress while concentrating their time with the patient on treating the underlying condition. Although I knew I might benefit from the use of meds, I wasn't willing to consider taking any type of psychiatric medicine, at least not initially.

Early on I had been given various sedatives in the treatment of my insomnia. Initially the drugs provided some relief, but it didn't take long before they'd lose their effect, leaving me mentally and physically groggy. I blamed the failure of the sleeping aids as my primary reason for adding alcohol to my nightly routine, so I was uncomfortable with the idea of having another class of drugs enter the mix. If the mainstay of treatment was psychotherapy, why cloud the issue with meds? It might not have been the best approach but it was the only one I was willing to accept. Despite realizing I needed help, I wasn't willing to *completely* trust my care to another provider or admit to friends and colleagues what I was going through. My mind was made up: no medications, and any care I received was going to be a clandestine operation.

I had heard that one of the psychologists who came to the clinic a couple of days a week wasn't the typical touchy-feely psych provider, which is exactly what I needed. After casually bumping into him in the hallway, I briefly explained my situation and the embarrassment and shame that accompanied it. He was obviously familiar with requests for anonymity and agreed to meet me in his office under the guise of sharing a lunch break.

Much to my surprise, he never asked me how I felt, which was a huge step toward earning my trust. Instead he concentrated on taking a history of all the events that had happened to me over the last decade—the blasts from RPGs, all the hits I had taken over the years in everything from from parachuting to hand-to-hand combat training—and, of course, an overview of my physical health. It was a comfortable blend of clinical evaluation and informal therapy. We were just starting down the road, but I knew it was time to unlock the passenger door and let someone join me on a hellish ride inside my mind; he would be the first.

My therapy included a series of written homework assignments, which at times added to my anxiety as I concentrated my writing on specific events. The goal was to modify my pattern of thought in order to deal with the shame and guilt I was feeling, yet I was finding it extremely hard to place some of it down on paper. It was easier for me to talk about it in his office than write it down in a journal. Somehow my writing not only made me acknowledge everything I was feeling but also confronted me with the totality of my symptoms, making it impossible for me to deny or diminish them any longer.

When I was able to write, I couldn't stop until I began to feel paranoid or ashamed. My reactions, thoughts, and feelings were all tied to circumstances related to the special operations community and classified operations. More often than not I'd find myself shredding what I had written. Although I never wrote anything that was the least bit compromising to national security, I felt as if I were being disloyal to the country and community I loved. Just thinking about the situations that drove my actions made me feel as if I were betraying an unspoken code of sacrifice.

One of the things we don't do in special operations is discuss our work or publicly give an opinion that might stain the community. Sure, there was storytelling, but nothing of importance or remotely detrimental to the history and image of the SEAL Teams. Yet here I was journaling about what some might perceive as a weakness smattered with personal perspectives on everything in the community that caused me consternation. Although we operated as a team, I had been trained to be self-reliant as both a SEAL and a medical provider. I was given the tools to deal with stress, compartmentalizing the pain so I could continue on, but for some reason I couldn't do it any longer. Writing it all down demonstrated my shortfalls, making me feel inadequate and as if I didn't belong in the first place.

Maybe that was it; maybe I was great at being neither a SEAL nor a medical provider. Maybe my attempt at balancing two obligations diametrically opposed to one another and never fully committing to either produced inadequacy in the world of the elite. As my writings transcended my assignments, I realized I wasn't some prodigy. In fact, I was never the best at much of anything. I was just someone who had

a strong work ethic and was able to endure times of personal degrada-
tion and humiliation to accomplish a goal. It wasn't talent or aptitude
that got me there. It was because I was either too stubborn, foolish, or
determined not to give up, and more importantly because someone was
always there to help me through it.

The more I wrote, the more I realized everything I achieved was
due to the support of others. My mother and brother helped me escape
the problems I faced as a young kid. The marines at the battalion helped
me make it through the Reconnaissance pipeline. Hell, I never would
have stood a chance in BUD/S if it hadn't been for the support of my
boat crew and class, and the SEAL Teams were no different. Each of
my teammates always kept me sharp, and when it came time to move
on they made sure my transition was a success. Medicine was much the
same; half the class studied with me my first year, while four friends
kept me from falling apart the second. I had accomplished a lot of
things in my life, but none of it was on my own. It was finally starting
to register; I wasn't Superman or the messiah, and there was nothing I
could have done differently that would have saved my teammates' lives.
However, just as I was finally learning how to accept it, the past would
add a whole new layer of guilt.

PENDING TRANSFER

I was standing at the doctors' station writing a set of patient orders
when my phone began to vibrate with an incoming call. Mark Denny,
who I might have only known for a short time, and I had become
good friends, so despite having a full waiting room I decided to take
the call.

"Hey, Doc, I got a good deal that you might be interested in." His
voice was fragmented from the poor reception I always seemed to have
on base.

"I have you broken and unreadable, over," I answered jokingly as I walked outside, trying to get a better signal.

"No, I'm serious this time," he answered with his typical laugh.

Although Mark worked at the Pentagon, his position kept him in contact with the navy surgeon general, so I knew whatever he was calling about was either important or an epic practical joke. "I know you've been living alone since Korrina moved to San Diego. Some of the programs are starting to grow, so we were wondering if you'd be interested in moving to the Beltway."

"Who's *we*, and what kind of programs are *we* talking about?" I asked, suspicious about how much of a good deal this might not be.

"Spec ops programs," he said before his voice was drowned out by a pair of F-18s flying overhead.

I couldn't make out everything he said, but what I did hear sounded interesting. In spite of the progress I'd been making with my psych appointments I'd wanted a change in scenery, and there was more than enough support at NNMC, the National Naval Medical Center, to handle anything a sailor might need.

"Mark," I yelled into the phone, "I'd like to hear more. How about I call you later tonight. I can't hear a damn thing you're saying, and I've got patients stacking up."

"Sure, call my cell."

I called Mark on my drive home, and he told me they were looking for someone who would be able to provide both medical and administrative support to a gamut of programs supporting the special operations community. Over a series of conversations my name kept coming up, and after speaking to the DSG (deputy surgeon general), he agreed that I'd be a perfect fit. Normally the navy doesn't allow someone to transfer with less than two years on station, but since the detailing shop would be receiving the request from the DSG's office, exceptions could always be made. I told Mark to pencil me in, but there was still one more person I had to speak with before they could cut me orders.

The time difference made it ideal for calling the West Coast. Korrina would be ending her workday and on her way home for the weekend. She'd just come off a hard week treating a flood of illnesses and injuries related to Hell Week, but Mark needed an answer by Monday. I thought about waiting a couple of days before bringing this up, but with Korrina the only thing worse than bad news is bad news delivered late. After everything we'd been through, she wasn't going to be happy to hear that I was considering returning to SOF no matter how long I waited. We talked for over an hour, and after I explained to her that this position was more of a desk job managing operational functions than a deploying billet, she reluctantly agreed. I'd begin planning my move to D.C. in the coming month.

22

A CROSS TO BEAR

★ ★ ★

The truth of the matter is that you always know the right thing to do.
The hard part is doing it.

—Norman Schwarzkopf

I sat down behind my desk and listened to the voice messages while the computer came to life. I was off to a late start after working the evening shift the night before and had a flood of e-mail and voice messages to sort through before I could grab a patient chart and get to work. The messages were pretty standard: routine updates from the nursing staff, corpsmen, and other departments and, of course, one hypochondriacal patient asking about his test results. The final message was from TJ, my old friend and colleague. He and Mark Denny were in town and wanted to pay me a visit. Great news, but a little surprising; I had just seen them both of them a couple of months earlier when I was at the Pentagon for a conference.

As I wrote down the details about the meeting, I received a phone call from a medical administrator I knew from my early days as an officer. We caught up briefly, and he jumped right in.

"Mark, I thought I'd give you a heads-up about a meeting later today in Admiral Cullison's office about you. Do you know anything about it?" I let him know I had a good idea what was going on, and it wasn't anything to worry about. I also thanked him for the call.

"Well," I told myself out loud as I put down the receiver, "it seems TJ and Mark aren't just stopping by while they're in town for business." Turns out *I* was the business they were in town for, and our meeting was just a courtesy call. I was certain they wanted to talk to my chain of command about a particular battle that happened a few years earlier outside of Firebase Shkin. When we returned home from the deployment, I'd received word that some of the senior brass were looking into awards packages, meaning medals for the troops. Like anyone else in the special operations community I welcomed the idea of the group being recognized, but the idea of receiving personal acknowledgment when others made the ultimate sacrifice didn't feel right to me.

TJ and Mark and I had agreed to meet at a corner coffee shop in Old Towne Portsmouth later that day. We ordered coffee and set up camp at a table in the corner of the room. TJ's big frame barely fit into the small chair that seemed to be intended more for décor than utility, making him look like a dad trying to have tea with his five-year-old daughter. We jabbed back and forth with a few wisecracks about our idiosyncrasies, and it felt like old times. There was no use avoiding the reason for the meeting, though, so when the opportunity presented itself Mark began.

"Doc, I know how sensitive this subject is with you, but we need to let you know you're in for an award," he said, then paused long enough that TJ finished his thought.

"Mark, you're going to receive the Navy Cross."

Suddenly I felt as if I'd been punched in the gut. I guess I always knew there was a possibility of receiving an award for Khand Pass, but I never imagined it'd be the nation's second-highest award. I took a moment to gather my composure and carefully craft my words.

"You're two of very few that actually know what happened out there." I paused for a deep breath before going on. "I treated a lot of men, and lost some close friends and allies. Not a day goes by that I don't think about them . . . they're the heroes, not me."

"I understand what you're feeling, Mark, but—" TJ politely tried to interject, but I kept on talking.

"I didn't do anything that anyone else on the team wouldn't have done if they were in my shoes, and to be honest I couldn't have done it without them. I just don't see how I can accept that award."

Both men fell silent and looked at one another before TJ answered. "Doc, we thought you might feel this way, so we'd like for you to talk with a friend who understands how you're feeling."

I liked TJ and Mark, but their proposal didn't sit well with me. Would I have to go in front of some admiral and explain myself? Well, if that's what it took, then so be it. Besides, I shouldn't be asking someone else to carry the water for me.

"Doc," Mark said in his naturally friendly voice, "come on up for the day and share a drink at Kitty's with some of the boys."

Their plan was starting to unfold. They'd probably asked some of my old teammates pulling the mandatory administrative tour in the Beltway to speak to me. Instead of looking forward to seeing them, though, I began to dread the idea. We'd each had a lot to deal with since then, and I certainly didn't want to put any more weight on any of their shoulders. I sat quietly thinking about it as TJ explained how they were to meet with my admiral because, despite it being a medical command, he was still my commanding officer and needed to know about this.

Admiral Cullison might have been a doctor, but like me he hadn't started out as one. Tom had been awarded a Bronze Star for Valor for actions in Vietnam as a diving officer, not a physician. His time as an orthopedic surgeon didn't start until after the war, which gave him a unique perspective on the warfighter. I knew he'd be supportive of my decision, but only after I met with folks TJ wanted me to see. Which meant, like it or not, I was going to D.C.

By the time I made it back to the clinic, the department's leading petty officer, HM3 Pines, was waiting for me.

"Sir, the command suite called and said you'll be going TAD [temporary assigned duty]. Is there anything you need before you go?"

I looked at him and smiled, not answering right away. I still had a lot on my mind and hadn't even started to think about getting orders cut, but it really didn't matter anyway.

"HM3," I said as I sat down in my chair, "we both know you have already taken care of everything, so how about you tell me, is there anything I need to sign?" Pines was one of the best corpsmen in the navy, efficient, well read, and professional. Aaron had administrative and leadership skills far beyond his rank, and like many of his cohorts he had proven himself under fire caring for his marines.

"Aaron?"

"Sir?" he responded curiously, with a look on his face as if I were speaking in tongues.

"Relax, this is a Mark and Aaron conversation, not an LT and HM3 conversation."

"OK, sir, what is it that I can help you with?" he asked, looking confused as he closed the door behind him.

"Aaron, what did you feel when the marines put you in for a medal of valor?" He looked taken aback and took a few seconds to reply.

"Uncomfortable, sir," he answered, looking away. He clearly didn't care to discuss it.

"Why? What made you feel uncomfortable?" I asked.

"I didn't want it . . . I didn't think I deserved a medal for doing my job," he said, looking me in the eye, two battle-tested medics who *got it.*

"Did you ever think of turning it down?"

"You were a marine, sir," he answered in a witty tone. "Can you think of a time when a third-class petty officer could tell a marine commander no?"

"No. No, I guess not," I said with a grin, realizing how ridiculous that sounded. "But if you could have turned it down, would you?"

"Yes!" he answered back without any hesitation and with firmness in his voice only heard while on an ambulance call or in the field with the marines.

"Thanks, Aaron. You're a man of many words," I said with a chuckle.

"Yes, sir," he said as he opened the door and began to exit.

"Wait," I said, catching him before the door shut.

"Sir?" He turned back to me.

"There is one more thing you can help me with," I said, trying to hide a sinister smile that was forming on my face.

"What's that, sir?" he cautiously asked.

"Do you have the clinic keys for the—"

He held up a hand, stopping me midsentence. "No, sir. I'm not going to get caught up in another one of your practical jokes on Nurse Raniowski or anyone else, so don't bother." He started to pull the door shut and then, with only his head visible between the door and the frame, he said with a laugh, "You know everyone gets in trouble for your antics except you."

I headed home and began to prepare for my trip, dreading the D.C. traffic. I departed early the next morning and hit the first traffic jam somewhere near Fredericksburg. I gutted through, reached the Pentagon with an hour to spare, and through the grace of God found an open visitor slot in the parking lot. I grabbed my cover (hat), locked the car, and started the long walk toward the navy's south entrance, wondering what I'd gotten myself into. I was in my khaki uniform, but I wore the Ike jacket to cover my Trident. The SEAL device always draws attention, and with fifteen thousand military personnel hustling through the halls on government business I wanted to be as inconspicuous as possible. The sick feeling I had from the other day was still haunting me, and my stomach began to grumble, reminding me I hadn't eaten anything since early that morning, so I decided to walk into the cafeteria and grab some fruit and a bagel.

"You still trying to eat healthy, Doc?" came a voice from behind.

I recognized the voice and smiled as I turned to address him. "Colonel, are you still eating everything you shouldn't?" I asked even before looking down at the heap of bacon on his plate.

"Wouldn't have it any other way," he replied with a laugh.

"Dave, I heard you're still working with TJ?" Dave might have been a Marine Corps colonel, but he had a special operations background, so anytime we were away from the rest of the military we'd revert back to the relaxed atmosphere of a platoon hut.

"I thought I'd stick around awhile and keep ol' TJ honest," he said. "I heard you were coming up. I've been looking forward to speaking with you." We continued the small talk as we paid for our meals and carried the plates to their work space. I explained how I'd ended up in the Pentagon for the day, and he informed me that he was the "friend" TJ had recommended I meet with.

We walked into the space, and I spent a few minutes saying hello to old friends before joining Dave in TJ's office. TJ sat behind his desk, while Dave was at a large wooden conference table devouring his fried pork and eggs. I went to my usual spot, a chair under a framed poster illustrating the sinking of *Llandovery Castle*, a World War I Canadian hospital ship that had been torpedoed by a German U-boat. It sank in flames, and as the survivors struggled to survive in the treacherous seas the U-boat surfaced and fired upon them. The story struck a chord with TJ, so he searched high and low for a poster and had it framed, then prominently displayed it in his office as a daily reminder of the atrocities man was capable of. I considered the chair under the poster "mine"; it was one of the few places I felt I was understood as both medic and warrior.

We made small talk and enjoyed our breakfast, feeling no urgency to jump into business. A half hour passed, and TJ changed tack and went ahead full speed into the issues at hand.

"Doc, this is a different kind of war. We're uncertain how the enemy will react if we publicly recognize certain troops with awards and medals." I had heard the Pentagon was concerned about the possibility of terrorist retribution against special operations and their families should their names be tied to missions, but I never thought it would affect me. Suddenly the administrative differences between fighting a sovereign nation and a network of rogue terrorists became apparent.

"Doc, it's going to be the office's recommendation that you have a closed ceremony," TJ said. The colonel nodded in agreement.

The wheels were in motion, and I hadn't yet bought a ticket. "Gentlemen, this has been a fascinating conversation, and I must say I thoroughly enjoyed it, but like I said in Portsmouth: I'm not interested in having any ceremony at all, private or otherwise." TJ looked at Dave and looked at me.

"Come on, Doc, let's go next door. We'll have a quiet place to talk," Dave said. I knew better than to argue with him. He was in his colonel mode again and it wouldn't have done any good to push back.

We entered an office that was obviously under construction, a random mess of half-built desks, missing ceiling tiles with wires hanging down, and cheap government furniture still in its plastic wrapping. Dave dusted off a couple of chairs and set them in the middle of the room. We sat and faced each other, our knees nearly touching.

"Doc, I want to tell you something an old gunny sergeant from Vietnam told me a few years ago. Back when I felt exactly the way you do now." Dave was a Silver Star recipient for his actions in Desert Storm. "Like most lessons in the military, it probably didn't originate with Gunny, but he was the torchbearer then and passed the torch to me, and now I'm giving it you." The mood in the room had definitely changed. We'd switched from friends to mentor and student.

"Hell, maybe Chesty Puller said it first, to one of his men." I kept listening and noticed my throat was starting to dry up. Conjuring Chesty's name was heavy business between marines.

"Doc, there are two types of awards in the American military, those given for meritorious service and those given for valor. Meritorious awards recognize an individual for his or her achievements. They earned it, it's theirs, and they should wear it proudly for a job well done." He took a deep breath as if he were bracing himself for what he was about to say next. "Then there are awards that are given for acts of valor. Courageous deeds performed solely in sacrifice for another. For his brothers." The emotion in his voice made it obvious that what he was saying was coming from something far more meaningful than a military instruction or regulation. "Valor awards don't belong to the recipient. They belong to everyone but the recipient." My heart began to pound as the gravitas of his words set in.

"Doc, awards for valor represent the appreciation of every citizen and member of the armed forces for sacrifices that were made at that exact moment in time." His voice became a bit sterner as he continued. "The medal they want to present to you isn't about you. It's about all the soldiers, sailors, airmen, and marines that were there with you. You may be the recipient of the award, but it will never be yours. Medals of valor belong to America . . . and that's why they're so damn hard to wear." His eyes had teared up, and I empathized with his sense of burden.

I looked down at my knees, trying desperately to contain emotions that were overtaking me. My thoughts were consumed by the faces of my fallen teammates. The room was deathly quiet, and neither of us said a word for quite some time. We finally looked at one another, and I tried to speak, but the words were stuck in my throat. The colonel continued.

"Mark, the navy can't force you to accept the award, but you and I know folks are eventually going to hear about what happened, and if those actions go unrecognized, the public may question our country's commitment toward honoring the sacrifices of those who protect her. Are you going to tell everyone it was your decision to decline the medal?"

I knew he was right, but I still hadn't come to grips with it. Then he hammered me. "Doc, it's not your medal to turn down." Silence followed for a few seconds as we sat and reflected on battles past. "Your job is to wear it for your team and country, and that means accepting the burdens that come with it." Dave was speaking to me like an older brother to a stubborn younger brother. He was right, and I knew what I had to do.

We sat and talked for over an hour, and I listened as he recounted the weather, the sounds, the smells, every detail fighting men absorb in the heat of combat. He told me about the men he lost, and I began to understand the pain and guilt military leaders experience watching their men die in front of them. I'd lost friends; the colonel had lost men he'd led into harm's way. I think Dave knew what I was going through, or wanted to confirm his suspicions, but the clock saved me before we got there.

"Colonel, Doc," said Marc, an officer from TJ's office, as he entered the room. There had been three Toms at Shkin, but there were three Marks in TJ's office, and they were all brothers to me. "I know there's a lot of bonding going on here, and I'd hate to break you girls up, but we need you next door." Like the others, Marc and I had a close relationship and he obviously felt comfortable taking full advantage of it.

"No problem, Marc, I was just leaving anyway."

As I got up and headed for the door Dave called out, "One last thing, Doc."

"Yes, Colonel?" I asked, expecting another witty remark.

"You can be pretty emotional at times, and Lord knows we all love you for that. It's probably why you do what you do."

"Damn right. He's all kind of weepy," Marc quipped. I shot him a look, which, of course, gave him satisfaction.

The colonel continued, "Do me a favor and try not to tear up at the ceremony."

"After everything we just talked about you're telling me not to get emotional?" I asked, looking at him as if he were nuts.

"Yes, and I'd make it an order, but you never listen to those anyway," he said with a wink.

"I'll try, but you stop eating so much damn fried food," I said, turning and heading toward the door.

As I walked out of the office, I could hear Marc say, "I got ten bucks that says I can get Doc to cry during the ceremony."

I smiled and thought, *No way I'm taking that bet.*

23

RETURN TO FAITH

Success is not final, failure is not fatal; it is the courage to continue that counts.

—ATTRIBUTED TO WINSTON CHURCHILL

Several months passed, and then the day finally arrived. The secretary of the navy graciously offered to host the ceremony in the navy's private conference room at the Pentagon, and after discussing it with my now wife, I accepted. Mom flew in from Albuquerque with my daughter, who was living with her mother at the time, and Korrina's mom, Judie, drove in from her home in Ohio. The guest list was strictly up to me, but I was still severely steeped in the turmoil from the battlefield and had returned to my reclusive retreat. Rather than deal with the decisions, I trusted TJ and his office to coordinate and invite the appropriate leadership and Mark to reach out to my teammates. Korrina sensed my anxiety about safety concerns and limited family and guests to our parents and children.

We met Mom and Tabetha at the airport, then checked in to a nearby hotel to rest and prepare for the next day. My wife helped assemble my dress blues while Mom and Judie took the kids to the pool.

"I know you wanted your father to be here, but traveling is hard enough on Mom as it is. Watching over your dad would drain her."

Neither of our fathers could make it to the ceremony due to health concerns. Dad's memory was so bad he probably wouldn't remember it anyway. Korrina's father, "Piv," was a Korean War veteran with the Marine Corps; his memory was sharp as a tack, but his physical health at the time was poor, and it hurt us both when he was unable to travel.

"From what Mom tells me, Tabetha watched after her more than she did Tabetha," I said as Korrina dusted off my shiny dress shoes. The rest of the night, the kids were kept occupied by their grandmothers, who spoiled them with attention while Korrina and I talked about the busy day ahead. We ran through the schedule and planned for every contingency, including morning bathroom usage. There were only two bathrooms between our adjoining suites, and no matter how hard we tried we'd probably be running late. So I picked up the phone and arranged for a driver to get us there on time, and Korrina wrote down the number of two backup car companies just in case, ever the efficient naval officer.

The car dropped us off at the Metro entrance, and we walked slowly toward the large ornate doors. In the distance I could see two escorts waiting for us to ensure we made it to Secretary Donald Winter's office on time. It was obvious Mom's dawdling with her cane was beginning to worry them, so the young sailor grabbed a wheelchair and hurried it out to her.

"Thank you, that's very nice, but why would I need that?" Mom asked in her naturally kind voice. "I still have two good legs to get me there. Let's save that for someone who needs it more than me."

He smiled and started to answer. "Ma'am, I can assure you we have plenty—"

"Petty Officer," I said quietly, interrupting him so he wouldn't waste any more time trying to coax Mom into the chair, "only the Lord our God and the pope have any powers of persuasion over her, and even the pope's is limited."

"I understand, sir," he said, sighing and looking at me as if he dealt with the same problem with his mother. Fortunately his counterpart was a savvy female marine who saw a solution to the problem.

"Ma'am," she whispered, bending down to mom's ear, "my feet are really tired, and I can take a motor cart, but only if you go with me."

"Oh, let's do that, we don't need you hurting," Mom said as she patted the gunny's hand, comforting her.

The cart dropped us off at the private corridor to the secretary's office. The hallway was pristine and lined with portraits of the past secretaries and other historic memorabilia. About halfway down the hall I saw Secretary Winter, Deputy Undersecretary Marshall Billingslea, and TJ waiting for us. Mom didn't know any of them, but it didn't matter, she jumped right in and told them how the navy needs to get more comfortable dress shoes for its troops. Her declaration confused the men, but you couldn't tell by looking at any of them. They smiled and promised to get right on it.

Secretary Winter walked everyone into his office and graciously spoke about the history of the position and the artifacts that filled the room. For nearly thirty minutes he sat with us and answered every question asked, from Mom's concerns about the war to my stepson's query about Theodore Roosevelt's standing desk. He then walked us across the hall to the conference room where the ceremony was going to take place.

We entered the room and found Mark, Marc, TJ, and the colonel, as well as a few members of my team, who were speaking quietly among themselves. Additionally, there were nearly two dozen senior military officers, including some of the navy's top admirals, all decked out in dress blues. I tried to distance myself mentally from the ceremony, but seeing everyone here, especially my teammates, brought it all back. I put on a smile but felt a profound sadness inside, brought on by the

memories of Chief and Chris and the others I was unable to save. To
the rest of the room, I seemed calm and at peace, yet my family could
sense the conflict raging inside me, especially Mom and Korrina. Mom
reached for my hand and patted it the same way as she did when I was
young. Only now my conscience was trying to rectify a burning self-
disappointment, and she could read it plain as day.

"It will be OK, mijo. Just remember God gives you the most strength
when you're at your weakest point." I had serious questions about my
faith and hadn't told Mom about them. Right then certainly wasn't the
time. Regardless of my belief or lack thereof, Mom's resilience and wisdom were unquestionable, so I concentrated on her words and not the
doubts I was feeling inside.

As the ceremony progressed, I was able to keep it together until the
citation for the Navy Cross was read and the medal was pinned to my
chest. It was then tears welled up in my eyes and a bitter, cold sorrow
gripped my heart. I tried focusing on a spot on the back wall while I
said a few words about the team and, most importantly, those who
made the ultimate sacrifice that day. I could feel the empathetic gazes
of my wife and mother as I stood there speaking to the crowd. Together they gave me the strength to get through the ceremony.

At the conclusion, Mom pulled me aside and looked at me the same
way she did staff Sergeant Sandoval nearly twenty years earlier. "Marky,
a few nights ago you explained to me what you feel these medals represent," she said as she pointed to the medals on my chest with her open
palm. "Now I'm going to tell you what they really mean." She paused just
long enough to grab my hand and raise it between us. "They mean when
you're in the public eye, your actions will mean more than ever before,
and if what you're doing doesn't make the mothers of America proud
you're doing it wrong."

Once again the honest simplicity of her words foretold what I had
to do. "I'll try, Mom, I'll try," I said as I hugged her, a few tears running down my face.

"I know you will, mijo. And when those who don't understand begin throwing stones, the Lord will be there to help you heal, even if
you turn away from him."

Following the awards ceremony, I took several days off to spend some
time with the family, most importantly Mom. Throughout my career, I
traveled to Albuquerque to visit my daughter and stayed with Mom
while there. I always kept our conversations limited to family and friends
and never discussed business. I also avoided talk of my visits to the
psych, or how I was questioning the idea of one omnipotent God having control over our world yet sitting idly as we tried to destroy ourselves. I held information back from her because she couldn't possibly
understand the horrors of battle, but in reality I was taking the easy
way out. Mom was, and still is, someone I dread to debate. She wasn't
a quick-witted intellectual or loudmouth know-it-all that steamrolled
the opposition in attempt to hide the truth, and she certainly wasn't
the cowardly type that went around spreading rumors, too timid to
face people with whom they disagreed. She was simply a tiny Mexican
mother filled with forgiveness and love, whose generosity rivaled Mother
Teresa's. I had nothing to fear and everything to gain by speaking with
her, but maybe that's why I avoided the conversation until now. Maybe
I was afraid of what I might hear, the brutal truth delivered with a
mother's love.

"Mom, I don't know how to tell you this, so I'll just say it right out in
the open. I believe I've lost my faith in God." I spoke in a tone reminiscent of my youth, hoping it would ease the blow for both of us.

"No, Marky, you're just questioning what you don't understand. All
of us do that at some point in our lives, but you haven't lost your faith,
mijo," she said with confidence.

"I don't know, Mom. I've been thinking a lot about God, religion,
the war, and none of it makes any sense to me anymore."

"Marky, not everything needs to make sense for you to believe it. It didn't make sense for me to stay with your father, but it was the right thing to do." I hung my head in shame, recalling how I pushed her toward a divorce when I was in high school and things were at their worst. Had she listened, Dad would have ended up living a lonely life as a forgotten man.

"Mijo, don't get caught up with what your mind tells you. It's what's in our hearts that drives us. Believe in good and good things will happen, that's all the Lord is saying. That's all faith is, mijo." She took my hand as she spoke, giving me a sense of comfort. Mom always had a way of making everything in life seem so simple. Perhaps that's why I had such anxiety about having the conversation with her. We sat quietly together, mother and son. She gave me the time to process her words.

I thought back on SEAL training. Certain trainees developed the mental tenacity required to weather life's storms, and it all came down to one word: faith. I remember listening to POWs recount the horrible conditions and torture they endured in the prison camps in Vietnam, and how they echoed the same words I heard from Holocaust survivors. Faith, they all had faith. I was beginning to realize my tower of strength was built on a foundation of faith in a higher power, and a belief in mankind wasn't strong enough to hold it together. I had seen too many atrocities in war to believe in the inherent goodness of man. There were certainly good men, but without a resilient foundation the bricks came tumbling down. How could faith in a benevolent God be any different, and why would a God encumber me with more responsibility instead of providing me with relief?

"Mom, 'faith' is much easier said than done," I said, trying to mentally shed the burden I carried inside the moment the secretary pinned the award to my chest.

"I know, mijo, but sometimes added burden is relief." I looked at her as if she were crazy. "You know, my father built our home with his hands, but it didn't start off so easy. The first time he tried, the foundation was weak, but he kept shoring it up. To the rest of us everything looked fine, but when he began to add more and more weight, it all came tumbling down. We all thought he'd be angry, but he just smiled and started all over again, and continued until he built the house that still stands today. Sometimes we have to lose everything in order to realize what we really have. It's time to rebuild, mijo. Just remember, if you do the right things for the right reasons, the right people will know it, and the people you try to reach will have better lives because of it. I have faith in you, and eventually you'll find your way. That's why God gave you that cross to bear, not the navy. His son bore a cross, too, you know." I sat there with a tear in my eye as she kissed me on the forehead, then stood and shuffled into the other room to check on her grandkids. I never had a chance to ask my grandmother about Mom's story before the Lord called her to his side, but it didn't matter. God was speaking through Mom, and I was listening.

24

TRIDENT

*In the end we are all separate: Our stories, no matter how similar,
come to a fork and diverge. We are drawn to each other because of
our similarities, but it is our differences we must learn to respect.*

—Johann Wolfgang von Goethe

Soon after I checked on board the Pentagon, Korrina was transferred from San Diego to a Naval Special Warfare billet on the East Coast. Pleased with the first-rate care she provided, the special warfare community tried to change the miles between us from a couple of thousand to only a couple of hundred. While she shared a large office with another PA, complete with its own refrigerator and coffee mess, I found myself sitting in one of the thousands of tiny cubicles that make up the Pentagon. There I addressed a litany of medical concerns that various support programs for spec ops were encountering. It didn't take long before establishing a few protocols, and placing the right medical providers at certain commands began to lighten my workload. Of course, just when everything seemed to be on course, I'd get a call with another fire to put out. This time it hit close to home.

It seems a navy chief at the Office of Naval Intelligence was having difficulty readjusting to home life after a yearlong deployment in Iraq. Mike Wade was part of a program called "Trident" that provided direct intel support to deployed SEAL Teams. While he wasn't a SEAL, he'd accompanied the assault team on numerous high-profile missions. After spending nearly an hour on the phone with his chain of command I learned Mike had worked as a firefighter and was one of the emergency responders at the Pentagon on 9/11. "That alone can carry a heavy burden," I said over the phone to John Jacobs, the programs operations officer. "But you're telling me he didn't have any problems prior to his going downrange?"

"No, he was good to go, a real workaholic. In fact, he was doing such a bang-up job they asked him to pull a back-to-back." That meant staying in country for an additional six-month tour in support of the incoming task force. "Doc, all I can say is when Mike returned from Ramadi he was a different man."

"In what way?" I asked, already knowing the answer but wanting to confirm my suspicions.

"Well, he'd only been back for a short period of time when we noticed everything seemed to irritate him and things weren't getting done. He'd always been a lead-by-example sort of guy, but now all the problems in his life were always someone else's fault. He just wasn't himself." John paused for a few seconds to answer someone who walked into the office. "After a night of heavy drinking and downing a crapload of sleep meds, he decided to place a few late-night threatening calls to the skipper. Thankfully, the police found him in one piece the next morning."

Since Trident didn't have a medical representative assigned to them, I agreed to act as their liaison until we had time to address it. "John, I'll get with the psych department at the hospital and get back with you, but I won't be able to tell you too much other than if he's okay. Patient confidentially limits medical information to only the commanding officer."

"Yeah I get it, but we're not wanting any more than that, Doc. We're just concerned about our shipmate."

"Thanks for understanding. You'll be hearing from me soon."

After a quick visit with Mike and his psychiatrist, I stopped by the radiology suite to get the MRI of my brain that Dr. Garsha had ordered, hoping to isolate my headaches. Turns out he'd been appointed head of Undersea Medicine right there in Washington, D.C., so I couldn't think of a better neurologist for me than my old mentor and friend. As I lay on the cold table, the technician placed the coil around my head and guided me into the tubelike tunnel. How ironic; here I was, helping Mike deal with his combat stress when I was under care for the same condition from another provider. My mind wandered between the similarities and differences between Mike and me as I tried to ignore both the ringing in my ears and the pounding of my heartbeat the earplugs accentuated during the procedure. By the time it was over I felt worse than when I started but hoped we'd have some answers. In the meantime I needed to get back to John and a man that most folks simply knew as the Bullfrog.

Captain Peter Wikul was Naval Special Warfare's "Bullfrog," a title reserved for the longest-serving Navy SEAL on active duty. He'd already served thirty-three years before receiving orders to ONI on what would turn out to be his last assignment. He arrived in Washington, D.C., soon after the war began with instructions to coordinate with naval intelligence for increased support to Naval Special Warfare. His plan was a simple concept: create a new multidisciplinary intelligence officer whose skill set mimicked the skill set of a SEAL, at least in principle. Instead of training up a sailor in diving, parachuting, weapons, demolitions, et cetera, he wanted to take a general intelligence officer and layer on discipline after discipline of intelligence analysis, outfit him or her with all the latest digital analytic tools, and then send that person forward to the battlefield. His rationale was "If I can only get one or two of my people on the battlefield, they damn well better be able to do it all." Mike was one of his best.

We met for coffee at a McDonald's not far from the Pentagon with a mutual friend and colleague. "Bullfrog, thanks for meeting with me. Even though I'll be visiting your office on Monday I thought it best to update you on how Chief's doing," I said as we walked to a table in the back corner.

"Thanks, Doc. Chief Wade is one of my top performers, with extensive experience assisting unconventional warriors in counterinsurgency operations. He may not be a SEAL, but he's certainly seen his fair share of battles."

Our conversation might have started out about Mike but quickly shifted to the effects multiple deployments were having on the force, then transitioned to how his concept for a new type of intelligence officer had proven so successful that it had been selected to become one of the four pillars of intelligence support ONI offered to the fleet. I was intrigued with what Bullfrog had been able to accomplish. They were in need of SEALs to assist in standing up the command, he said. I couldn't help but ask if he'd have room for a fellow frogman to join him at his new digs.

"Absolutely, I could definitely use you, but I don't want to steal you away from where you're at now. Those guys and I go back a ways."

"You go back a ways with half the navy, Bullfrog," I said with a wink.

He laughed, then said, "How about you let me speak to them first and see what I could do. As long as you think you'll be able to handle both jobs from my location, I don't see too much of a problem."

Captain Wikul pulled the necessary strings to transfer my desk from the basement of the Pentagon to the Office of Naval Intelligence to assist in the development of a fledgling navy command. The move into Bullfrog's Trident program was good for me both mentally and emotionally, and I definitely needed the support and flexibility the larger boat crew offered.

Not long after Korrina arrived on the East Coast she was told she'd be deploying to Iraq with the next task force. Although I knew her departure date months ahead of time, shamefully I didn't pay too much attention to it until it was only weeks away. Soon our roles would be reversed and I would be the one staying at home while she went off to war. Luckily the kids wouldn't be affected too much. Tabetha still lived with her mother in New Mexico, and with the travel my job entailed, we all felt better if Korrina's son, Cody, stayed with his father in Wisconsin.

We spent the last week together vacationing with the kids, preparing for the familiar separation we'd once again endure. Although Korrina had deployed in support of special operations in the past, this was the first time she'd be heading into a war zone. I knew she was an extremely competent naval officer able to take care of herself, her patients, and the corpsmen working under her, but the idea of her going into Iraq was still distressing for me. I had seen the effects of rocket and mortar fire firsthand, and lately I'd been reading intel reports about the increased use of vehicle-borne improvised explosive devices and suicide bombers inside the Green Zone. The only solace I had was that she'd be deploying with a SEAL Team, giving us direct communications over the secure net, and the knowledge that camp security would be wired tight.

Even so, she'd been my rock, faithfully staying by my side during the worst of times, and I couldn't imagine not having her in my future. In an effort to keep such thoughts off my mind I engrossed myself in work. As always, I would be wearing dual hats, but this time it was more SEAL than medic. My primary job would be as programs training officer, while my position as a medical officer slipped into a secondary role. Having recruited some top-notch corpsmen into a few programs that were in need of support freed up the time I needed for Trident.

As a young SEAL I served as an intel rep for my platoon when criminal and terrorist activity were among the nation's top priorities. Although intelligence work is more desk-intensive than SEALs prefer,

I found the time researching and reporting on the condition of the enemy intellectually stimulating.

Later, as I moved up the health care ladder, I noticed similarities between the sourcing of information for national security and patient care. Although there are times when the information gleaned from a military operation or clinical procedure is concrete, I was discovering that these instances were more the exception than the rule.

Intelligence analysts like medical providers pore over every piece of information with their colleagues, more often than not concluding they need more details before making any recommendation. Just as a patient is hauled back into the radiology suite for another look, SEALs are reinserted into the wild or a drone is launched, all three situations driven by experts trying to confirm or deny their hypothesis. It isn't as if they are intentionally trying to be difficult; it's simply the means to the end. Both the physician and intelligence officer understand that lives hang on their decisions, and neither wants to make a fatal error due to lack of information.

During my time on the wards I was reminded that medicine is not an exact science but rather a skillful art form based on knowledge, which is why it's called the *practice* of medicine. Likewise, good intelligence is also derived from the similar melding of information tempered by knowledge, logic, and experience. However, in both situations deduced theory can become eclipsed by passion unless every member of the team applies an honest evaluation of the circumstances, and of himself or herself, for that matter. Bullfrog knew this and demanded every one one of his crew take a brutally honest approach to everything. Intellectual honesty is the hallmark of the best officers and extremely difficult to maintain, so his expectation of brutal honesty resonated with me, in more ways than one.

For years I'd been mentally burying the effects of combat, for the sake of *driving on*. Deep down, I knew when I was brutally honest with myself it always had a positive net result, even though it could be painful getting there. As a teen, I had to face the cruel realities of home and accept the harsh realities of our family dynamic. The decision to enlist in the military took me away from friends and family but kept me off the streets. As a young marine, I lied to myself about my swimming ability, or lack thereof, and nearly died because of it. Admitting the weakness to myself led to swim lessons and countless hours of training to even become skilled enough to apply for special operations. Later, as a Recon Marine, I was drawn to medicine, and only when I was brutally honest about switching to the navy did I find my calling. The pattern continued as I entered the SEAL Teams; I fought like hell to make it through the toughest training on earth, yet my soul felt a calling to become a physician assistant. Acknowledging that internally, I went on to . . . Just then it struck me.

The captain was very clever when he delivered his rationale about brutal honesty when I checked on board. It emphasized the need for an objective approach regarding intelligence reporting, but it also accomplished so much more. It inspired me to confront my internal demons in an honest, check-your-pride-at-the-door way. I'd taken the first steps by meeting with psychologists at Portsmouth and later NNMC, and was strong enough to take a hard look at myself and see the ugly truth. I was slowly learning how to live with the stressors caused by combat and not suffer from them.

25

A COMMON BOND

$\overline{\qquad}$ ★ ★ ★ $\overline{\qquad}$

From day one, I've told [my troops] that killing is not wrong if it's for a purpose.
If it's to keep your nation free or protect your buddy.

—MAJ. DOUGLAS ALEXANDER ZEMBIEC, USMC

On most days I pulled double duty, first as training officer, where I'd write training plans, draft instructions, and horse-trade school billets for our guys. I'd then flip into medical officer mode and schedule appointments for the troops who needed specialty care such as orthopedics or mental health. Mike Wade was on my priority list for the latter. Mike was an extremely competent and respected intel specialist whose skills were needed for the protection of our country, but more importantly he was a teammate and my friend.

We could relate to one another in a number of ways, and I enjoyed his company while I waded through D.C. traffic. As the medical officer, I would often drive him to his appointments, and we'd take the time to catch up on much-needed conversation. Mike and I discussed everything from our family situations to combat stress. I started off with my plans for Korrina's return early next month and her new assignment as the command representative to a Special Operation Command initiative that provides advocacy to the wounded, ill, and injured of the community; he told me how comfortable he was working with his psychiatrist, which is always a very good thing considering there's little choice on which doctor you receive when you schedule your appointment.

The idea of being randomly assigned to a provider based on availability was always a bit unsettling when it came to something as personal as mental health, but it was the reality of military medicine and the main reason I sought out Doc Garsha. Unfortunately, with both of us traveling for work, our schedules rarely matched up. With the closest Special Warfare psychologist hours away, based on Mike's comments, I decided to book an appointment for myself.

Special Warfare's psychologists and Doc G had a direct, nonemotional approach to therapy, and I was comfortable with it. However, the mental health specialist I had been scheduled to meet with that day turned out to be the complete opposite: a hyperemotional provider who spoke in a soft voice and seemed to be constantly on the verge of tears. She was the epitome of a touchy-feely therapist, and the more I spoke with her, the more I resented being there. It wasn't because she was a woman; in fact, I specifically asked for a female provider, trying to avoid some egomaniac medical officer who would see the SEAL device on my chest and medical insignia on my collar and start telling blustery stories about all of the high-speed training he'd attended. It happens more than I'd like to admit. What I wanted was someone with a businesslike approach and a good-natured bedside manner.

I know she was well intentioned, but it was hard for me to discuss such personal experiences with someone who *I felt* reacted as if I'd been abused. Last time I checked, SEALs were an all-volunteer force drawn from an all-volunteer navy. No one forced me into those situations. I wanted to be there. I felt I had to be there. It was my calling! I tried to explain how the battles themselves weren't difficult for me; rather, my problem was the loss of close friends and teammates, heightened by the continual exposure of extreme levels of stress related to years of sustained combat. "It's not the killing, it's the death," I said, referring to the men who died as I was trying to save them. The taking of someone's life is not a natural impulse, but in combat it is an expected one. I have no regrets over killing men who were trying to kill my teammates or me. My actions were intended to be an instantaneous execution of violence, and when I was given the opportunity that's exactly what my enemy received. What haunted me then, and still does to some extent, was having to fight my way to a wounded man who'd entrusted his life to my hands only to have him die as I worked on him. Combat is a chaotic engine of death driven by a series of choices; I just wasn't sure if I'd made the right ones.

One of the pillars of the special operations community is an unwavering commitment toward one another, so the loss of any teammate weighs heavy on the heart of everyone in the community. Being the medic only deepened the pain. It was my job to preserve life and not let it slip away, but we were in combat and death happened. It wasn't about *what* I saw or heard, it was about *who* I lost, and as a medic there's no more painful memory.

I tried in vain to connect with her, and she with me, but we were clearly at an impasse, so I patiently waited until the end of the appointment. I reflected on how much progress I'd made since accepting I had a problem dealing with what I'd experienced, although I knew I wasn't anywhere near being done.

FOR WOUNDS RECEIVED IN ACTION

Mike's appointment ran much longer than mine, so I grabbed a coffee and set up camp in a coffee shop in the hospital lobby, my table facing out to the main atrium. As I sipped the joe and meditated on the meeting I'd just left, I caught sight of a large bronze sculpture of a corpsman pulling a marine to safety. It was a fitting tribute to the bravery of corpsmen and a nice touch in the hospital lobby. Having been both a marine and a corpsman, I was deeply moved by the artist's rendition of the bond between warrior and medic, and I wondered how many other war veterans felt the same when they looked upon this statue.

I then noticed an older couple clad in purple regalia, struggling to cart large boxes into the lobby. I walked over and offered a hand, and they gratefully accepted. When we were finished, the elderly man looked at me and offered a firm handshake.

"Thank you. Steve Cobb, Military Order of the Purple Heart," he said with a large smile on his face. "This is my wife Tatanya, but she goes by Tanya."

"How do you do," she said with a Russian accent.

"You're welcome, Steve. I'm Mark," I said as I reached over to shake Tanya's hand.

"So, Mark, you here for a medical appointment?" he asked as he spotted the Purple Heart on my ribbon rack.

"Well, yes, sort of. I brought one of my co-workers over for an appointment and thought about checking on a few things myself," I said, trying to be vague.

"You a doc?" He smiled, now looking at my collar.

"I'm a bunch of things, but yes, I was once a corpsman turned physician assistant, and yes, I'm a SEAL." I thought best to answer that one before he asked, since he was looking at the SEAL Trident.

"You're a long way from home, considering you're not an inpatient," he said with a laugh.

"You seem to know a lot more than the average retiree," I said with a large grin.

"That's because I'm an old army colonel with a little bit of experience about special operations. Right now I could use a rest. Let's sit." We continued talking as we moved to the coffee shop and grabbed a table. Tanya ordered coffee as Steve and I settled in. Apparently they were both old fixtures in the place, because everyone knew them by name and most would wave as they walked by.

"You a member of the Purple Heart?" Steve asked, referring to the Military Order of the Purple Heart, an organization I'd been invited to join but never really had much interest in.

"No, I'm never around, so I thought I'd wait until I had more time on my hands," I said quickly, making up a white lie so no feelings got hurt.

"Bull, it doesn't take any time unless you want it to. Now where are you stationed?"

"Right now I'm TAD to the area," I said, trying to be respectfully vague about where I worked.

Steve was an old pro and knew how to work me. We sat for half an hour discussing the Purple Heart, war, and what I needed to do before my first meeting the following month. There was no getting off the hook with the old colonel, so there was no use trying. He had magical powers of persuasion, and he used them for good.

A few weeks later I walked into an American Legion post to attend my first meeting and learned more about Steve. Much more. In addition to being the chapter adjunct, he was the recipient of multiple purple hearts and a Silver Star for action during Vietnam. He was also a former Hawaiian congressman and state senator. He welcomed me to the meeting and then introduced me to the esteemed members of the chapter.

The group of veterans in attendance had served in wars from World War II to the present day, and all of them talked openly about the same problems I struggled with. Several of the men pulled me aside and said most things got better but others never changed. They allowed themselves to be human and lean on one another in order to get past those dark days.

As the months went on, I spent more time with Steve and the others, and it hammered home the importance of finding someone to talk to. The meetings weren't all gloom, doom, and war stories. We simply didn't avoid the subjects if they came up in conversation. In the past I never spoke about them, afraid that emotion might overwhelm me. I was relieved of that burden when speaking with my fellow war veterans. The more I talked about experiences, the easier it was getting to accept them. Mike was learning this as well, as he met with fellow veterans at the VFW.

26

COMING HOME

You are today where your thoughts have brought you;
you will be tomorrow where your thoughts take you.

—James Allen

I drove down from D.C. to meet Korrina, arriving from her over-seas flight. She had spent her time downrange supporting the SEALs who were kicking doors and capturing and killing insur-gents while I supervised intelligence support stateside. This was the first time that our roles had been reversed, and the deployment helped me appreciate what families go through when their loved one goes off to war.

I missed her dearly, and because she was in a war zone, it made me realize how much I truly loved her. Despite all the chaos I had brought into our lives, she focused on the good in me. She spoke softly when I needed her support, reminding me how much my family loved and needed me, but she also called me out when I was coming up short and encouraged me to try harder. Korrina accepted my faults, and despite my resistance to her affection during my first year back she remained committed to loving me deeper than I ever had been loved before.

Sadly, it took the threat of losing her to the same enemy I had battled years earlier before I understood the enormous courage it took for her to be my wife. Now I just wanted her home!

After a wonderful but slightly awkward night getting reacquainted with one another, we woke with one agenda: planning a whole new future together. Our life had been one fragmented year after another, but instead of tearing us apart it strengthened our resolve. What we needed now was stability. We both had another two years on our current set of orders, but with her new position at her command I'd be the only one at risk of deploying.

Midway through the decade one of the Special Forces veterans from the Vietnam era came up with an idea to ensure the wounded and those who suffer from a severe illness or injury within the special operations community would never be left to their own devices. He pitched the idea to the leadership, many of whom he'd worked with or mentored along their way, and within a short time a coalition of support surfaced that advocated not only for the members but for their families and the families of the fallen.

Naval Special Warfare was a little hesitant at first, but once they realized the strength in having advocates and liaisons from within the community caring for their members, they wasted no time installing an official for the East Coast. Korrina was a wound care specialist and had treated more than a few wounds from training and war. This face time with leadership and understanding of the navy's procedures made her the perfect fit for the job.

With Korrina locked into a shore billet, all we needed to do was gather the kids and move into a home suitable until the time they'd move on to college or possibly military service.

EMERGENCE

At Trident I continued to work with the rest of the crew to build Bull-frog's program into one of four pillars of excellence within the Office of Naval Intelligence, and I greatly enjoyed the tempo and intellectual challenges that came with balancing responsibilities between intelligence, special operations, and medicine. Needless to say, Steve encouraged me to become more engaged with the local chapter of the Purple Heart. We visited Bethesda and Walter Reed and interfaced with wounded and severely injured troops, and it proved to be good medicine for me as well. On occasion Bullfrog would do the same when casualties from the special operations community came in from the regional medical center in Landstuhl, Germany. He, like all the other operators in the area, longed to spend more time with the wounded, but of course time was always limited, so visits were more of a monthly event. However, Bullfrog made a special point of visiting Jay Redman when he shipped home from Germany.

The last time I saw Jason "Jay" Redman was outside our living quarters in Panama. I was saying farewell to him and other members of the platoon before heading off to Howard Air Force Base to catch a military airlift back to the States. My orders to PA school had come in, and Commander Bosiljevac, my CO at the time, wanted to ensure I had enough time to get my personal affairs in order before making such a monumental move. Jay was serving in his first SEAL platoon, and the moment he walked into the team room the officers, Chief, and I knew we'd hit the jackpot with this FNG. Jay was a bright young SEAL with an intelligence background who was quickly moving through the enlisted ranks by utilizing both his intellect and sense of humor to their fullest potential. Jay was the type of team guy that could say something blatantly obvious but instead of sounding stupid or whiny he'd put you in tears laughing about it. Even when we were buried half frozen in a snowbank for days during a training exercise, he always found something humorous to say. He's the type of guy anyone would want as a brother, and the team was proud he was a part of our family, especially me. I guess that's why it hurt so much when we received word he had been seriously wounded in Iraq.

While I was studying medicine, Jay was picked up for a commissioning program and eventually graduated among the top of his class at Old Dominion University. He returned to the team as an officer just as the war was ramping up and led his men on mission after mission in very dangerous places. One fateful night, an enemy round nearly ripped his left arm off. As he feverishly applied the tourniquet to his arm and pulled the constricting band tight, another round entered his skull under his right ear. Although rocked by rounds and losing blood quickly, Jay continued to care for his wounds while directing his men to continue the fight. With the help of his medic, the combat surgeons, and hospital stops along the way, he made it to National Naval Medical Center Bethesda.

Bullfrog and I walked into the room unsure of what we'd see. We'd heard Jay was still breathing out of the tracheotomy tube protruding from his neck but was stable and able to communicate by pen and paper. We'd also heard the damage to his face was extensive. We washed our hands with the antiseptic and entered his room, only to see a smiling Jay giving us a thumbs-up as if he were able to defy death with a Harry and David gift basket. Bullfrog and I looked at one another and tried to keep ourselves from cracking up, unsure if it would be acceptable to laugh. Jay hadn't changed a bit, except he'd married a wonderful wife and started a family. I spoke with Jay as he scribbled his responses while Bullfrog spoke with his lovely wife, Erica.

"Wow, Jay. All things considered, you look great." I wasn't being sarcastic, either. Being a medical provider I'd seen and worked on plenty of wounded, and despite taking a few rounds to his upper body and face, he was much better than I expected. Cosmetically it did look bad, but his positive persona resonated through the room, making everyone feel brighter.

"You should have seen him when he first landed. He looked awful," said Erica, with a combination of humor and concern, but mostly out of love for her husband. I looked at Bullfrog, and we thought, *Where the hell do we find more of this?* They were the epitome of a grounded couple, focused on all the good that life had to offer.

As we thumbed through the photographs and listened to Erica describe the past few days, Jason flipped his notebook around and wrote that he was going to ask the plastic surgeon for a Brad Pitt nose.

"No, that's not what you want," Bullfrog said in a half-joking, half-salesman way as he pushed me aside to stand next to Jason. "You should ask for a big distinctive nose. A Wikul nose," he said as he turned his head upward to profile his nose. We all broke into laughter, but Pete stayed on point, very serious. "Big noses are legendary. Think of all the great men with a distinguished schnoz." He paused for effect as we tried to contain our laughter, "There was George Washington, Thomas Jefferson, Julius Caesar, Charles DeGaulle and . . ."

Jason turned his pad around. It said *No!* clearly underlined, yet Bullfrog continued to pontificate about the virtues of a prominent proboscis.

It was a shared moment of levity between friends and warriors who accept death and destruction as part of the job description. The laughter was a dramatic contrast to the gut-wrenching sorrow we felt each time a casualty report came across our secure network. Nose jokes were definitely fitting for Jay, who wasn't interested in pity parties. In fact, Jay fended off any visitors who dared enter with sorrow in their eyes and pity in their voices. He wrote a manifesto with a black marker on orange cardboard, informing the world that he received the wounds while defending the country he loved and that sorrow and sympathy were not in the recovery plan. Several days later, the poster was photographed and uploaded to the World Wide Web, and within a matter of days Jay went from being another patient at Bethesda to an Internet legend, encouraging optimism and speedy recovery for all wounded Americans.

Bullfrog returned to the office while I attended to a few hospital appointments of my own. I stopped by the coffee shop where Steve and I had first met, grabbed another coffee, and watched a group of visitors carry quilts, candies, and gifts through the doors as they headed up to the fifth floor to visit with the wounded troops. What a contrast to Steve's years of service. He and the other Vietnam vets told stories of the disrespect and downright hate they received when they returned home, mainly from a group of ignorant angry young Americans unsure where to focus their frustrations.

We certainly weren't suffering from that type of misdirected anger today. In fact, I can't remember a time when I wore the uniform in public and was treated poorly. It was quite the opposite. A walk through the airport always led to offers of coffee or beer, and handshakes were plentiful. Our wounded from Panama quietly received generous assistance from a handful of our country's millionaires, and our sailors and soldiers experienced warm welcomes home from the First Gulf War. Modern America loved her military, and we loved her back.

So what brought about the change, from anger to respect? It was the Vietnam veterans! The same men and women who served honorably and were spit upon for their service managed to hold their chin high and say, *"Not on my watch!"* They didn't do it for ticker-tape parades or public praise; instead they demanded respect for those that came after them. They simply refused to let another American service member experience the same hell they'd walked through a generation before. They served their country when their country called, and along with their fellow Korea and World War II veterans continue to serve America's service members today. Every time I'd hear "thank you for serving," I made it a point to say two "Thank you for supporting" back, one for the citizens of America and the other for the veterans of the past.

27

BRUTAL HONESTY

★ ★ ★

Honesty is the first chapter of the book of wisdom.
—THOMAS JEFFERSON

The next day I met up with Bullfrog's top intelligence officer to review the proposed training pipeline and discuss any significant events occurring on the battlefield that might require modifying our training regime. Bureaucracy didn't encumber the enemy; they were able to change tactics at a moment's notice, so to ensure our personnel were prepared, John Jacobs and I continually met with everyone returning from the front, including Dana, one of Bullfrog's top performers.

Dana was an intensely passionate and highly valued professional who had just completed a yearlong pump on the battlefield. She entered the navy as an enlisted intelligence specialist at an early age and worked her way up to the officer ranks; along the way, she developed proficiency in a number of disciplines. She spent the majority of her career supporting the SEAL Teams, serving as one of the first females utilized as forward support in combat operations. She opened doors and broke glass ceilings.

"Doc!" Dana said with a big smile as she gave me a quick hug. She'd been away on two weeks' leave.

"Welcome home, Dana. Did you actually *enjoy* your leave time, or was your mind still tracking terrorists?" Dana managed the collection and dissemination of information better than anyone else I knew. When a promising lead would come in she'd scour sources looking for corresponding leads. Inevitably she'd find the information and forward it to a spec ops team on the ground, and they would get their man. Her relentless attitude helped her find data on bad guys no one else could, earning her the respected title "Digger."

"No. Well, yes, but only a little," she said with her typical muffled laugh. "So let's see what you got." She reached out for a briefing package I'd prepared.

Over the next few hours we covered the work she'd done on the battlefield. Dana had sent a constant flow of reports, but there's nothing better for capturing every detail than getting it from the person's own mouth. The enemy's tactics had certainly changed, and increasing effectiveness of IEDs was taking a toll on our troops.

"I think if you implement these changes the next group will be as ready as they can be, but we're not going to be out of this anytime soon," she concluded.

"I know, and that's what's troubling me. I'm just not sure I believe in being there anymore," I replied.

"Where?"

"Afghanistan mostly, but I don't think we need to have troops on the ground trying to help countries that don't want our help. I just don't think it's worth it."

Dana and I finished our conversation over lunch and traded opinions based on war stories and personal experiences. When she left to head back to work, I stayed at the lunch table and stared at my coffee, lost in thought.

It isn't that I don't believe in fighting terrorism; that has to be done. I just question the need to have a large force on the ground to do it. I feel we can fight and contain terrorism without having American men and women doing a job the natives need to do themselves. As much as I like to believe our current strategy is going to work, I seriously doubt anything will change over there, and in the end all we'll have to show for it is war-damaged veterans and their families.

Bullfrog constantly reminds the crew of the need to be brutally honest with our assessments, because American lives are depending on it. Well, to be brutally honest, I'm not sure there's any winnable strategy for any invading force in Afghanistan, and only time will tell with Iraq.

Realizing how much time had gone by, I grabbed my tray and dropped it off at the scullery and returned to the office.

"Wow, you look like someone just told you you're on the way to the hoosegow," John said as I sat back down at my desk.

"Thanks, John, that makes me feel better," I said with a chuckle.

"Look, I've seen this before, you ain't feeling it. You're not going to be able to concentrate, so how about you just head home early today." John looked at me with concern, and I didn't bother arguing the point. I packed up and departed. As I walked from the exit to my car, my mind was still focused on the war.

During the drive home, I reflected on the conversation I'd had with Dana. I knew both political parties were comprised of patriotic citizens who passionately believed in our military leaders and our troops, as did I—but how could any strategy formulated in the depths of the Pentagon differ from those attempted in the past? The British had military officers living and interacting with villages throughout the Stans (Pakistan, Afghanistan, etc.) for decades, and the population ultimately viewed them as an occupying force, even though the British considered themselves merely advisers. The Russians had allied with the leaders of Afghanistan and helped build Kabul into a modern city, but when a segment of the country rebelled, the Russians invaded in an attempt to keep control and were eventually defeated. I wasn't interested in dissecting the politics or tactics of either the Brits or the Soviet Union. I'm positive they had political and military geniuses concocting a number of strategies that worked perfectly well on paper but failed miserably over and over again. What were we doing differently, and to what end?

I lived among the Afghani and Iraqi people. I fought *with* them and *against* them and treated their children and tribal elders with the best medical technology available. Yet they still viewed us as invaders. As I drove along, I caught a clear view of the Capitol Building, the Washington Monument, and eventually the Pentagon. My thoughts of war had changed since I put on the uniform for the first time. In Panama I wholeheartedly believed it to be a "Just Cause." America went in and did what needed to get done and got out. The pattern was repeated as we liberated Kuwait. What made the outcomes of those conflicts so different from what happened in Vietnam and what was occurring in Afghanistan today? I pulled into a local grocery store to pick up some supplies and saw a billboard for a nationally known retirement fund. Its message was prophetic: You can't plan a winning strategy if you can't define winning.

I was a Navy SEAL at an intelligence command deeply involved in warfighting, and I couldn't define what constituted winning in Afghanistan. From the Revolutionary War to World War II, we had a clear understanding of victory that could be conveyed to and understood by the American people. For me, winning a war meant defeating the enemy by destroying their ability to continue to wage war. This could be achieved by either physically removing them from the land as we did with the British or annihilating their armies and infrastructure as the Allies did with the Nazis. That definition of victory certainly didn't fit with Afghanistan. We destroyed the Taliban's hold on the country, but this was bigger than the Taliban or al Qaeda. The fight included terrorist organizations that most Americans never heard of, nebulous bands of loosely organized extremists and criminals that had no country, uniforms, or formal organization. Of course, maybe it's not a war at all. Maybe it's just a euphemism similar to "the War on Drugs," which definitely sounded better than saying "catching or killing criminals that kill others and need to be killed." If that's the case, why are we fighting it like a war? Why do we keep having American troops blown up by criminals that have no allegiance to their country, the Taliban, al Qaeda, or anything else?

In the First Gulf War we had clear objectives that everyone understood. Whether you believed the war was based on oil or liberating Kuwait was irrelevant to understanding the objectives: remove Suddam Hussein from Kuwait and prevent Iraq from having the power to invade its neighbors. When the goal was met we moved out. Maybe we had that opportunity in Afghanistan? Maybe after we ousted the Taliban we could have come home and begun hunting the masterminds as we are doing today? I don't know, and I am not claiming to be some philosophical genius with any of the answers. I'm a simple man who believes that before a free nation can fight a war, conflict, or battle, it needs three things: a military force capable of winning; political will, meaning elected officials who accept the consequences that may be related to a winning strategy, including the possible need for mass destruction; and most importantly the backing of the people, who like our military, were growing weary of continual battle.

It seemed to me America had a way to lose the war but no clear way to win it. However, if America's goal in the fight against terrorism is to keep our citizens safe, there are men and women who volunteered to carry that burden knowing damn good and well the risks they are taking. I was one of them, and now I worked inside one of the many buildings supporting them. In order to do so we have to be willing to take the gloves off and let special operations and the intelligence communities do what needs to be done to prevent another attack from happening.

I have fired a weapon in the heat of battle, and I have held my brothers as their lives slipped away. War is not an esoteric chess game; men die, and their wives and children suffer for a lifetime. I fully understand the consequences of war, and I pray that those who send our men and women downrange do so with victory clearly defined, and with the backbone to stand behind them long after the last troop comes home. I no longer believed the answer requires an army on foreign soil. It is time to bring our forces home and accept the fact that we cannot win "a war" against a nebulous group of criminals huddled away in countries that support them—but that doesn't mean we can't fight and defeat them.

28

THE DECISION

★ ★ ★

Be more concerned with your character than your reputation,
because your character is what you really are, while your reputation is merely
what others think you are.

—JOHN WOODEN

I had first thought about retiring when I took the kids to New
Mexico for Christmas with their grandmother while Korrina cel-
ebrated the holidays in Iraq supporting a SEAL Team. It was then
that I concluded my time in the military was coming to a close. However, rather than rush to judgment or try to discuss a life-changing
event over the phone, I decided on waiting a few months until Korrina
returned home from deployment so we could talk about it in person.

"Are you sure you want to do this?" Korrina asked as we sipped coffee and waited for our food at the only good breakfast shop in down-
town Norfolk.

"I've given this a lot of thought and prayer, and it's not what I want
to do, but rather it's something that I have to do," I said with a slight
sadness in my voice. Leaving the uniform was an uncomfortable idea,
but I certainly wasn't scared of change.

"What are you going to do, medicine? Intel? I hope it's not going
back to special operations. Even training comes with too many risks."

"I don't know, but I feel like I'm being pulled toward helping our wounded veterans," I said with a bit of uncertainty.

"Wounded veterans or wounded and veterans?" she asked, equally confused.

"I don't know that much yet, but I'll find out soon enough. There's a wounded conference where Carl Levin will be speaking that I'll be attending next week with Jay Redman, and I'm sure it will help shed some light on my decision."

"I don't know who that is," she said.

Realizing her allegiance to Ohio State I thought it best not to mention his being a Michigan senator.

"He's the chairman of the Senate Armed Services Committee, for Pete's sake," I said, trying to emphasize the importance of the event.

"Alright, but only because Jason is going with you."

EXPOSED

For nearly half a decade the navy helped keep my award private. I wore my uniform only on military installations; most of the time my work attire varied from camouflage utilities to civvies. When I did have to wear a uniform that brandished ribbons, I'd wear a jacket to cover my awards, weather permitting, of course. I wasn't trying to be secretive, although TJ's words about the navy's concerns for my family were always on my mind. I just felt awkward wearing awards I'd received for doing my job. Regardless of the reasons for my discomfort, I was about to learn how the press and public felt about keeping things from them.

I met Jay at the hotel, and we walked downstairs to the reception table to check in. I had business at the Pentagon earlier that morning that required a uniform, so I was still dressed in my khaki uniform with ribbons, while Jason was decked out in his dress blues. They escorted us in and placed us at one of the front tables, just off center and directly ahead of where most of the reporters were seated. I couldn't help but turn around to see how many people were attending, and I spotted "Sgt. Shaft," a military columnist for *The Washington Times*. His real name was John Fales, and he was a former Devil Dog (marine) who had served in Beirut before losing his sight in Vietnam. Sgt. Shaft's column provided advice to service members, veterans, and their families regarding some of their greatest concerns, so I had no choice but to go over and shake his hand.

"What was that all about?" Jay asked when I got back to the table.

"That's Sgt. Shaft. He's—"

"I got that. You told me before you went over. What's with the other guy asking so many questions?"

"I'm not sure. I think he just wanted to know how a medical officer had a Trident. Anyway, Sgt. Shaft gave me his business card and invited me to lunch at Ben's Chili Bowl," I said as I held up a red, white, and blue nail file with his contact information stamped into it.

"Interesting. You think he ever gets mixed up and hands out a regular nail file by mistake?" Jay asked in jest. We shared a laugh while I sat down to listen to our keynote speaker deliver his speech.

"Where the hell are you?" was all I heard John say when I answered my phone on my way into work.

"I'm in my car. It's only seven thirty. I'll be at the morning meeting on time. Why?"

"The SECNAV's office has left three messages for you, all saying to head straight to the deputy under's office."

"Well, I better turn around, because I just passed the five-sided genius factory a few minutes ago."

"Damn right, and when you get done, how about sharing the truth about what you did to get the SECNAV's office to call, Lieutenant? It's got to be a great story."

"I have no idea!"

"Yeah, right, that's what all you SEALs say."

I hung up the phone and thought over every piece of intel production, taskings, meetings, and general conversations I had been involved with over the last few months that could have warranted a summons to the secretary of the navy. "No use killing yourself over it, Mark. You'll find out soon enough," I said as I pulled into one of the many oversized parking lots servicing the building.

After checking in with the undersecretary's office, I learned an inquisitive journalist, perhaps the one at the table with Sgt. Shaft, had reported on a number of cases regarding stolen valor, including a naval medical officer who falsely claimed to have been awarded a Silver Star, a Special Forces Tab, and numerous other valorous awards and decorations five years earlier. So when he saw a SEAL Trident, Navy Cross, and Medical Service Corps device he immediately thought he was dealing with a similar situation. There was no name tag on my uniform, so he placed a call to the secretary of the navy's office. Much to his surprise the reporter was informed that I did indeed exist. The *Navy Times* ran an article titled "Lt. Earned a Navy Cross He Can't Wear," highlighting the peculiarity of the situation. Thankfully, the secretary's office was understanding about the comments that started flowing across the Internet following its release.

I was able to stay somewhat underground a little while longer, but they eventually discovered my name. Being the highest decorated Medical Service Corps officer in the history of the navy and the first medical officer of any corps (physicians, service corps, and nurses) to receive a Navy Cross since Vietnam, it was bound to come out. My first concern was for the safety of my family, which was the whole reason for keeping everything quiet, but after a conversation with Bullfrog I realized it was foolish to try to hide in the open, and it might be better to face this head-on. Whatever concerns we had years before had faded, and keeping things hidden inside was what caused my pain to escalate in the first place. This would be just another step in my lifelong therapy about my relationship with the real heroes of those battles. I just needed to find the right folks to talk to.

Nathaniel Helms had been an army door gunner in Vietnam and was an accomplished writer and reporter for *Newsmax* magazine. I was given his name by a lawyer of a friend of mine whom I met at the Army and Navy Club. I first met Nat over the phone, but it only took a few minutes before I could trust him enough to answer a few of his questions. I felt a little more comfortable with the situation after speaking with Nat and decided it was time to meet with *Navy Times* reporter Andrew Scutro, who wrote the first article, and put the rumors to rest.

29

TIME TO SAY GOOD-BYE

$$\bigstar\ \bigstar\ \bigstar$$

As we express our gratitude, we must never forget that the highest
appreciation is not to utter words, but to live by them.

—JOHN F. KENNEDY

C areer military men and women, those who serve for twenty
years or more, base their decisions to retire on several factors:
desire to move on, potential benefits on the outside, job satisfaction or lack thereof, and so forth. None of those influenced my decision. For me there was nothing more important than spending time
with my family. Arguably I could have done that by staying in the
navy, so I wasn't exactly sure why I felt I *had* to retire. I just knew it was
time to say good-bye, but apparently I seemed to be the only one. Despite dropping my retirement papers I was still selected for promotion,
something that almost never occurs. At first I thought I might be
making a big mistake and needed to reconsider, but there was no use
denying the voice inside of me telling me it was time to start over, the
same voice that took me away from home nearly a quarter century ago
and eventually guided me into medicine. Just as the Trident Program
would be commissioned as the Kennedy Irregular Warfare Center and
begin its naval "career," I would be retiring and ending mine.

I had thought about fading away quietly, but then I remembered how Dave educated me on how valor awards are more for those men and women who are still serving than for the recipient. It was the military's method of letting America know that no service member's willingness to sacrifice for others will be forgotten. The more I contemplated separating from service, the more I began to see the retirement ceremony in the same light. It would seem the ceremony would benefit the retiree, but actually it's the family who gets the most out of it. The ceremony validates the reasons they shared their husband, father, and child with the country. It acknowledges *their* sacrifice and offers an opportunity for friends and colleagues to thank them for *their* service. It is the closure that brings the family together by openly recognizing the end of the *family's* military service.

Once I understood the significance this would have for my family, I knew I had to have a ceremony. Now all I needed to do was identify a location that reflected the essence of my career, which turned out to be harder than I expected. I started as a marine and had served in a multitude of jobs in the navy, each one filled with friends and teammates who had helped me through the toughest times in my life, so it wasn't too surprising when each corps offered to host the ceremony. I contemplated the SEAL Teams, the Bureau of Medicine and Surgery, and the Office of Naval Intelligence, but I couldn't help feeling taking one over the other might diminish the impact the others had on my life. Rather than choosing a location myself, I turned to the ones the ceremony would benefit the most, my family.

CEREMONY

It was a beautiful fall day in the nation's capital, and I was blessed that I would be ending my career surrounded by so many family members and friends. The proceedings were held at the Navy Memorial in

Washington, D.C., neutral ground befitting the retirement of a Navy SEAL medical officer assigned to an intelligence command. Dina, the commanding officer's right hand, Dana, and a couple of lieutenants I'd grown close to planned the ceremony down to the last detail, but all of ONI and my friends at the Pentagon pitched in to make sure everything went off without a hitch.

Admiral Cullison, who'd been promoted from commander of all of navy medicine on the East Coast to deputy surgeon general of the navy, agreed to join the deputy chaplain of the Marine Corps and my close friend John, also a former Recon Marine turned Navy SEAL, to be part of the official party. Tim, Chris, and Dave, who made up half of the SEAL physician assistants in the navy, came in from across the country, as did Jim, one of the good Samaritans who worked so diligently with the other three to pull me through my tough times at PA school. Marshall Billingslea, who'd just finished his term as the Navy's deputy undersecretary, and some of his former staff joined Bullfrog, TJ, Dave, and the rest of their crew in the auditorium as well. Except for the skeleton crew needed for ongoing operations in Iraq and Afghanistan, the CO, Commander Whitworth, had all the officers and crew from Kennedy in attendance.

The auditorium was full, and I was moved by how many faces were there from the past. Some I'd lost touch with over the years; others sent their regards from the war zone, and I prayed for their safe return. TJ and Dave surprised me by presenting me with a paddle, a symbol of honor within the nautical arm of special operations, just before I moved to the podium to deliver my final words as a naval officer.

I started by letting everyone know the scars I received from service paled next to the gifts I'd been given from their friendship, and I tried to convey the feeling I had opening a letter from my daughter that explained an enclosed group of items she felt brought her luck and how she wanted me to carry them to keep me safe on the battlefield. I told how Cody's vigilance regarding his mother and sister gave me peace of mind while I was away. I thanked my mother for raising me and never giving up on my faith even when I had done so myself, and I praised my wife for loving me when I hated being alive.

I spoke about learning that even the worst of times are survivable if you reach for help and apologized for hiding my weaknesses for so long. I openly admitted that I was not without fear and only took the risks I did because I knew my friends and family were there to right the ship when I began to list. I spoke of a revelation I had a few days earlier that my career would not be judged by my achievements but by the accomplishments of those I mentored. I reminded my listeners they should not be fooled into thinking that a moment in time defines the essence of an operator or medical provider; instead it is the totality of our work. The medals I wear, I wear for others, but I was a good SEAL and medical provider; I might not have been great at either but never stopped trying to be the best. I wanted the navy to understand I was equally proud of serving in the special operations, medical, and intelligence communities, and deep down I knew all those I'd worked with had mastered each craft better than I ever did. "I'd like to believe part of it was because I gave every bit of knowledge I had to give, but for those who feel differently, I apologize and ask your forgiveness," I said. I closed with the message to avoid battle at all costs, but when you must fight, fight for others and not yourself—and as my good friend and mentor Pete Wikul always said, when called upon, fight to win.

At the end of the ceremony we moved outside, where my wife and kids joined me in the receiving line. It was a wonderful event, and seeing how much it touched my family I was thankful for having it.

"So what are you going to do now?" Chris asked as we shook hands.

"You'll find out soon, but it'll have to do with serving our veterans and their families while keeping me close to mine. I know people want to help; we just need to show them how."

30

THE ASSOCIATION

★ ★ ★

Help your brother's boat across, and your own will reach the shore.

—HINDU PROVERB

My time spent among combat veterans from the Purple Heart taught me that the mental wounds from battle are rarely cured. Rather it's a constant healing process, and emotional scars will reopen if circumstances allow. There are the obvious occasions when this might occur—anniversaries of battles, attending funerals of the fallen, and so forth—but there are also times when emotions can overtake a veteran for no apparent reason. The first few times this happened to me, I was able to handle things myself, having developed the skill set through training and later therapy to be self-sufficient. However, as life piled on one trouble after another in a condensed period of time, as it often does, circumstances started to overwhelm me once again. When I would feel this way in D.C., I would meet with fellow veterans whom I knew I could confide in, so rather than face it alone I met with a friend and fellow SEAL war veteran, Mike Day.

Mike had recently retired from the navy and begun work as a

wounded advocate for the SOF community under the same umbrella as Korrina. His time on the battlefield and ability to survive over two dozen enemy rounds gave him the credibility necessary to connect with even the most headstrong veterans, such as myself. In a series of early morning conversations, Mike was able to remind me how to get past the problems that ailed me. During our discussions I also realized that over time the emotional weight of any mental condition would increase as the mind and body weaken from age. It seemed to me the best way to keep such conditions in remission was to reach out to—or, as it was in my case, remain active with—organizations that provided the camaraderie and support necessary to tackle difficult times.

For SEALs it is our UDT-SEAL Association that facilitates that bond. Despite my disinterest in the association early in my career, as I matured as a frogman I began to realize its importance in preserving our heritage and friendships among those who served, as well as its ongoing efforts to support the SEAL community—but was it enough?

The public has rallied behind our troops, providing assistance to various foundations, including our own, supporting America's service members. However, "today's warfighter is tomorrow's veteran," and if we learned anything from the drawdown of previous conflicts it's that the needs of the American veteran won't fully be known until years after these men and women leave military service. Although the government is the mainstay of support, there is plenty that veterans, citizens, and businesses can do in partnership with one another to expand each of our capabilities and strengthen our country's commitment to the American veteran.

War, after all, is a societal decision. Regardless of how one may feel about politics, it is the vote of the people that decides who will represent our intentions; therefore war and its consequences are also a societal responsibility. Rather than sit and wonder about what needed to be done, I wanted to be a part of helping make things happen. Truth be told, these conversations actually started while I was still in the service when I met with my mentor and good friend Wade Ishimoto. "Ish" was one of the original members of the special operations community and had a storied past that most men could only dream of living. So when he asked me if I would be willing to consider helping a nonprofit that assists the veterans of the spec ops community, I couldn't refuse. Over coffee Ish told me that a group of former Special Forces veterans had formed an organization known as the OASIS Group, whose structure was specifically designed to work with each of the military services' fraternal associations in order to provide VA assistance for all spec ops veterans. It sounded like a great idea, utilizing existing infrastructure to reach those in need and then supplying the expertise to help them make it happen. Later, as I navigated through the retirement waters, I grew to understand the need, appreciated their guidance, and looked forward to bringing their assistance to the SEAL veteran community. However, as an association we were just beginning to understand that VA advocacy was only a small portion of the support our veterans might need.

Although we had an implicit veteran program based on the brotherhood of service, it primarily benefited those who lived near the SEAL community, most notably Virginia Beach and Coronado. Now we needed to formalize our intentions. The association had worked with other veteran organizations in the past, but in a closed community many of our members were still reluctant to ask outside organizations for help. What we needed was something from within, something that could team with existing programs to meet the needs of our members, a communication and coordination channel. This became more evident with the passing of one of my BUD/S instructors.

I walked into the office to meet with Jacky and hear more about a call she'd received. As the family support coordinator for the active-duty SEALs on the East Coast, it was her job to meet with the ombudsman from each team and spouses and family members to assist them with any problems they might be facing related to a husband's or father's service. The program, an extension of the ombudsman's outreach, had proven a striking success, but unfortunately her hands were tied when it came to veterans.

"Mark, I received a call from Lynn Bukowski. Her husband just passed away," she said as I pulled a chair closer to her desk.

I knew of Steve from my days at BUD/S, but I didn't really get to know him until we bumped into one another at the East Coast compound. Steve was a top-flight operator and leader, so the news of his passing was upsetting to everyone in the community.

"Hopefully it was painless," I said as I sat down while she continued.

"Lynn is having a terrible time trying to figure out what needs to get done, and there's only so much we can do."

Steve and Lynn had adopted a special-needs child years earlier and moved out to the country just prior to his retirement, which only complicated the sudden loss of her husband. She was left confused and feeling alone during an extremely trying time.

Jacky had a plethora of support options at her fingertips, but once Steve retired, programs previously available to his family were closed or at the very least extremely limited. Jacky and I had discussed this exact scenario with Jack Lynch, the president of the UDT-SEAL Association, and his executive director weeks earlier. All agreed that it was time to update the organization from a club to a service organization, but being in the initial stages we were still building our network of resources and establishing protocols.

"Well, I guess there's no better way to develop our process than the immediate needs of a member," said Jacky.

"I guess so," I said, as I started thinking about how to put new plans in motion. Having personally experienced the horrible effects of self-inflicted isolation, a common response by many veterans, I understood the importance of utilizing fraternal organizations to reach out to men and women and their families who might otherwise be missed. Likewise I had seen the positive effects of getting veterans and their surviving family members involved in activities affecting both their previous military profession and veteran community. No vet or family should ever feel that their alliance with the military ends when they separate from service. There are plenty of organizations from American Legion to VFW to join and I find spending a good amount of time helping fellow vets find support and camaraderie as they transition from active duty to the civilian world has helped me a great deal as well.

Needless to say, Jack's wife, Jeanette, and Heather, the spouse of an active-duty SEAL, immediately dove into Lynn's case. Working in conjunction with other organizations, they were able to help her. Unbeknownst to her, she became a catalyst for redirecting some of the organization's efforts from reacting to the passing of veterans to assisting them in life, and so started the consortium of support that continues to build today.

31

CLOSE

We are made wise not by the recollection of our past, but by the responsibility for our future.

—George Bernard Shaw

The invisible wounds of combat are difficult to treat, primarily due to each member's reluctance to reach for help. I feel a large part of their trepidation is because of society's misapprehensions about combat stress. Thankfully, the Veterans Administration, the Department of Defense, and our veterans from previous conflicts have been working to erase the stigma attached to post-traumatic stress. If we are going to reach these patriots and their family members, we must first recognize the problem for what it is, a condition and not a disorder.

The changes that combat causes in the mind and spirit are a result of exposing a normal mind to abnormal, horrific, terrifying, and continual stressful circumstances; it is a normal and expected reaction. In the world of special operations we learn to compartmentalize these stressors and moderate our emotions, thereby minimizing the ill effects while conducting operations. It is an inherent quality that is honed from the first day of training. However, it is important to understand

that although these stressors can be minimized, they are not eliminated, nor are the families of these brave heroes immune to them.

Anyone who experiences combat will be changed forever. The idea
that you can go into battle and not be affected by the death and destruction that accompanies it is ridiculous. If you were to visit the Louvre in
Paris for the first time, whether you found it an enjoyable or dreadful
experience it would be a life-changing event. The idea that somehow
going to a foreign land filled with hateful people trying to kill you or
experiencing the wounding or burial of your fellow soldiers isn't going to
alter your psyche is ludicrous. However, not all of those changes have to
result in harmful effects. Many of my friends and teammates have been
able to positively refocus their lives toward other endeavors, and I have
yet to come across one of our wounded who hasn't found some way to
benefit from his or her experience. I know I am a better husband, father,
and person for what I went through, but I also know that I will always
carry guilt and pain deep within me, requiring treatment.

As you can see, I am no hero. I, perhaps like many of you, boxed up
my emotions and locked them in a war chest deep inside my mind.
This allowed me to continue on with the mission, but only for the short
term. Over time my war chest became full and was unable to hold all
of my boxes. Yet I kept adding more until one day it exploded and sent
them crashing to the floor, releasing all of my demons at once.

It is impossible to know if or when this might happen to you, as
boxes come in all shapes and sizes. Some are large and completely fill a
war chest; others are small, allowing a much greater amount to be stored
away. The effects are still the same, a war chest full of heartache and
pain. Some of you may be able to keep the contents safely locked away,
but the majority won't. You might sustain a physical wound or injury,
and as your mind and body focus on healing, the lock weakens. Others
may overload the chest with new emotional experiences unrelated to
the war—the death of family member or a friend, or discovering that
the time to reconcile a relationship with a spouse or child may have

passed you by. It may be the fragility of age that loosens your lock, or any number of things that only you may know about, but eventually the chest will open. What happens when it does remains to be seen.

If exposing my vulnerabilities helps one of you, be it a soldier, spouse, or child, to realize it's better to seek help with unpacking your boxes before the inevitable bursting of the war chest, then all the criticism I will receive for writing this book will be worth it. It took years of heartache and pain that nearly destroyed my family and me and that deeply affected my friends, co-workers, and neighbors before I could admit to having this lifelong condition. I recognize that my anger only masked my fear and that much of my fear was derived from a stigma I chose to accept. My not wanting to be affiliated with what my colleagues branded a disorder only isolated me from the world, and the walls I built to protect myself from the indignity only perpetuated my condition. It wasn't until I started to speak to a trusted friend with similar experiences and my family convinced me to seek help that I began to recover. Don't let that happen to you! Combat stress is not a disorder. It is a circumstantial condition that affects everyone in the family, especially the kids. The only way to effectively deal with it is by continually emptying the boxes, and that takes talking to someone. It doesn't matter to whom you speak at first, but it is paramount that you talk. I intensified my problems with silence. Learn from my mistakes and be willing to listen to what is offered to you.

It took years before the services openly expressed a willingness to tackle these problems, but the programs are in place, and although there is room for improvement they are working. The number of medical providers permanently assigned to warfighting units has substantially increased, including psychologists and sociologists. Wounded advocates and family support programs once consolidated hundreds or thousands of miles away now reside at warfighting commands. The importance of this co-location cannot be stressed enough. Warriors and their spouses won't open up to individuals they don't know! It doesn't matter if they wear the same uniform, patch, or beret. If they are not working side by side with them every day, if they don't see them within their compound, they are viewed as outsiders. Trust is the most essential element for someone seeking assistance, and those military commands that have been willing to make these changes have the opportunity to address the problem before it starts. These are very personal issues that demand personal attention, based on a personal relationship.

Those of you who have never served or experienced combat may be asking, "What can I do to help these brave men and women?" The answer is simpler than you might think. First and foremost, assist in breaking the silence. As a society we must make it acceptable to speak openly about this condition, the same way you would about any other medical diagnosis. It should never be disastrous for a veteran, spouse, or child to be afflicted with any condition, especially when it is solely based on circumstances resulting from a service member's willingness to sacrifice for others. Educate yourself on this condition the same way you would on any lifelong ailment affecting a family member or close friend. Get familiar with and support veteran initiatives in your area and know where someone suffering from the condition can turn for help. Provide assistance whenever possible; most of the time all it will take is lending a nonjudgmental ear, but other times it may require much more as we try to prevent these patriots from becoming jobless or homeless or even taking their own lives. Hold America's feet to the fire when it comes to ensuring our service members, veterans, and their families receive the physical and mental care they deserve. If they can bear the cost of freedom, we can certainly manage the cost of their health care! Above all else, keep in mind that when you encounter a combat veteran there might be more going on inside than you know, and maybe, just maybe, you are the one person who will open the door to allow him or her to reach out for help.

ACKNOWLEDGMENTS

As I stated in the introduction, I never intended to write a book. Even after I began to transcribe my journals into a memoir I wasn't comfortable with the idea of publicizing my life. For nearly a year the partially completed manuscript sat on my dresser while I contemplated the impact this book might have on my family and me. It wasn't until my fellow service members began telling me how my admissions helped them deal with their own difficulties that I realized how important it was for me to finish the book. Therefore I would be remiss if I didn't start off by thanking those war veterans who rekindled my spirit.

If my comrades sparked the fire, Korrina certainly tended the flame. Thank you, my love, for believing in me and always finding a way to make things work. You cared for our kids when I needed to write and were my pillar of strength when my father passed away. You put love in my heart and fervor in my soul. I would be lost without you.

Tabetha and Cody, we will never get back the months I spent overseas, the days lost while I emotionally separated myself from the family, or the mornings I spent hitting the keyboard trying to express to the world what had gone on inside of me. I hope one day this book will tell you things that I never could. I love you both and wish I could have been more of a traditional father during your formative years.

Mom, words cannot express how thankful I am for having you as my mother. You've been my guiding light in a sea of darkness and my stalwart supporter when I was at my worst. All that I am is because of you. More importantly, the world is a better place with you in it.

Jedi and Ginger, my therapeutic canine companions, your gentle nature and unconditional love were monumental in helping me regain trust in my surroundings. Your ability to instantly omit my misgivings was a constant reminder to me how essential forgiveness is in order to find happiness. Korrina may have rescued you from the racetrack, but your company helped save me from myself.

I also owe an enormous debt of gratitude to following individuals who assisted me in writing this book. My coauthor, Scott Mactavish, understood how this was more about me saying what I needed to say than a historical listing of events. You're a great mentor and confidant. I couldn't have done it without you. Dwight Zimmerman introduced me to the literary world and educated me along the way. I wish circumstances had permitted us to write together; regardless, I never would have met Marc and the others without you or learned the intricacies of the industry, and for that I am truly grateful. Mike Atkinson was not only the catalyst that got me moving but also a friend willing to accept the nuances that are distinctively me. Mike, you are a great patriot and teammate for all SEALs; thank you. Dennis Kelly, your unwavering generosity with your time and energy is remarkable especially considering all the events going on in your life. You're a shining example of an officer and a gentleman. Jeanette Lynch, your sound advice and gentle feedback were essential in my sorting out a confusing time in my life. Doug and Pam Sterner, Violet and Mac Stroud, and Heather Connors, at various times each of you kept me energized and often unbeknownst to you reminded me of the reasons for my writing; thank you. Suzanne and Steve Vogel, I wish the world knew what dedicated and good-hearted people you are. When others criticized not only my efforts but also my intentions, your spirit helped remind me to focus on the good in them. You are truly compassionate professionals. Peter Wikul, at a time of war you still remained a big-hearted commanding officer, mentor, and close friend. You broke new ground and developed officers and sailors who continue to make a difference; thank you. To my team-mates, friends, and family not mentioned in the pages of this book, thank you for accepting me for who I am and guiding me along my ca-reer. I try just to remember the good times, unless the bad are required to prevent me from duplicating a monumental mistake or to impart a lesson from my life to others. I was told by an old gunnery sergeant when I first entered service that my appreciation for the military and those with whom I'd served would exponentially increase with age. He was definitely right! You are all such great individuals, and I am thankful for your being a part of my life.

To the families of the fallen, especially those mentioned or alluded to in my writings, you've overcome more adversity and heartache than the world will ever know, yet were still able to help me out along the way. I pray that one day your story will be able to be told; it is truly a remark-able one, but not as remarkable as each of you. From me, my family, and the team, thank you! I would like to close by giving my final thanks to the Lord for giving me the fortitude to bare my soul, the opportunity to reach out to others, and the strength to embrace change.

A PERSONAL APPEAL

There are a number of organizations assisting our service members that could use your support. If you are currently involved with one I encourage you to continue. However, the preponderance of those who serve will spend the majority of their lives as veterans. Therefore I have listed organizations that both impact the lives of the men and women in uniform as well as our veterans.

The UDT-SEAL Association *www.udtseal.org*
The association was founded in December 1969 by some of America's first Navy SEALs as a mechanism of support for its members and their families. However, due to the expansion of support to the community's active duty population by its sister organization, the Navy SEAL Foundation, the association has slowly segued its focus toward the community's veteran population. Working in partnership with other veteran service organizations, benevolent causes, and grants, the UDT-SEAL Association has been able to improve the quality of life of generations of

frogmen from World War II to our present day SEAL and SWCC
(Special Warfare Combat-craft Crewmen) warriors.

NSW Kids *www.nswkids.com*
Naval Special Warfare families experience hardships that can be extreme even when considered within the context of military life. Many of
these difficulties transcend their parent's military service. NSW Kids
works closely with established and proven organizations to provide educational, counseling, and other services that empower these children and
honor the fallen.

The OASIS Group *www.oasisgrp.org*
The OASIS Group provides veterans professional analysis and assistance
related to the Department of Veterans Affairs. Although the OASIS
Group primarily coordinates with the fraternal organizations within the
special operations community, it works with a multitude of veteran service organizations to ensure no veteran is left without the assistance they
deserve.

The Military Order of the Purple Heart *www.purpleheart.org*
Chartered by Congress in 1958, the Military Order of the Purple Heart
is composed of men and women who received the Purple Heart Medal
for wounds suffered in combat. Although membership is restricted to
the combat wounded, the MOPH supports all veterans and their families through a myriad of nationwide programs and their national service
officers.